CITIZENSHIP AND CRISIS

CITIZENSHIP AND CRISIS
Arab Detroit After 9/11

Detroit Arab American Study Team

Russell Sage Foundation • New York

The Russell Sage Foundation

The Russell Sage Foundation, one of the oldest of America's general purpose foundations, was established in 1907 by Mrs. Margaret Olivia Sage for "the improvement of social and living conditions in the United States." The Foundation seeks to fulfill this mandate by fostering the development and dissemination of knowledge about the country's political, social, and economic problems. While the Foundation endeavors to assure the accuracy and objectivity of each book it publishes, the conclusions and interpretations in Russell Sage Foundation publications are those of the authors and not of the Foundation, its Trustees, or its staff. Publication by Russell Sage, therefore, does not imply Foundation endorsement.

Library of Congress Cataloging-in-Publication Data

Detroit Arab American Study Team.
  Citizenship and crisis : Arab Detroit after 9/11 / Detroit Arab American Study Team.
    p. cm.
  Includes bibliographical references and index.
  ISBN 978-0-87154-052-2 (alk. paper)
  1. Arab Americans—Michigan—Detroit. 2. Muslims—Michigan—Detroit. 3. September 11 Terrorist Attacks, 2001. 4. Citizenship—Michigan—Detroit. 5. Detroit (Mich.)—Ethnic relations. I. Title.
  F574.D49A6538 2009
  305.892'7073077434—dc22
                    2009003527

The paper used in this publication meets the minimum requirements of American National Standard for Information Sciences—Permanence of Paper for Printed Library Materials. ANSI Z39.48-1992.

Designed by Genna Patacsil.

RUSSELL SAGE FOUNDATION
112 East 64th Street, New York, New York 10065
10 9 8 7 6 5 4 3 2 1

CONTENTS

About the Authors   vii

Acknowledgments   ix

INTRODUCTION   1

Chapter 1   Citizenship and Crisis   3
Wayne Baker and Andrew Shryock

PART I   COMMUNITY IN CRISIS   33

Chapter 2   Arab American Identities in Question   35
Andrew Shryock and Ann Chih Lin

Chapter 3   The Aftermath of the 9/11 Attacks   69
Sally Howell and Amaney Jamal

PART II   BELIEFS AND BONDS   101

Chapter 4   Belief and Belonging   103
Sally Howell and Amaney Jamal

Chapter 5   Values and Cultural Membership   135
Wayne Baker and Amaney Jamal

Chapter 6   Local and Global Social Capital   165
              Wayne Baker, Amaney Jamal, and Mark Tessler

PART III   POLITICAL IDEOLOGY   191

Chapter 7   Civil Liberties   193
              Ronald R. Stockton

Chapter 8   Foreign Policy   227
              Ronald R. Stockton

              CONCLUSION   263

Chapter 9   The Limits of Citizenship   265
              Andrew Shryock and Ann Chih Lin

              Index   287

ABOUT THE AUTHORS

Wayne Baker is professor of management and organizations and professor of sociology at the University of Michigan. He is also a faculty associate at the Institute for Social Research and holds the Jack D. Sparks Whirlpool Corporation Research Professorship.

Sally Howell is assistant professor of history at the University of Michigan–Dearborn.

Amaney Jamal is assistant professor of politics at Princeton University.

Ann Chih Lin is associate professor of public policy and political science at the University of Michigan.

Andrew Shryock is Arthur F. Thurnau Professor of Anthropology at the University of Michigan.

Ronald R. Stockton is professor of political science at the University of Michigan–Dearborn and was formerly head of the Center for Arab American Studies.

Mark Tessler is Samuel J. Eldersveld Collegiate Professor of Political Science, vice provost for International Affairs, and director of the International Institute at the University of Michigan.

ACKNOWLEDGMENTS

We would first like to thank the Russell Sage Foundation for its generous support of the Detroit Arab American Study (DAAS) and the allied Detroit Area Study (DAS). We are grateful to administrators and staff at the Foundation for their patient cultivation of this project, especially Eric Wanner, Suzanne Nichols, and Stephanie Platz. We thank Helen Glenn Court for expert copyediting, and we benefited greatly from the constructive criticism we received from the two anonymous reviewers of our manuscript.

We appreciate the additional funding provided by the Andrew W. Mellon Foundation, as well as the institutional and financial support provided by the University of Michigan–Dearborn and several units within the University of Michigan–Ann Arbor: the Institute for Social Research; the Provost's Office and Office of the Vice President for Research; the Center for Local, State, and Urban Policy (CLOSUP); the Stephen M. Ross School of Business School; and the Gerald R. Ford School of Public Policy.

The DAAS was produced through an intensive collaboration of the University of Michigan Institute for Social Research and the Center for Arab American Studies at the University of Michigan–Dearborn. We are grateful to Daniel Little, then-Chancellor of the University of Michigan–Dearborn, and David Featherman, then-Director of the Institute for Social Research, for their leadership, steadfast support, and guidance from the beginning of the project through completion.

Thanks go also to Hassan Jaber of the Arab Community Center for Economic and Social Services (ACCESS), who was a friend of the project from the beginning, and to Radwan Khoury of the Arab American and Chaldean Council (ACC), who was a strong advocate of the study. Renee Ahee, who organized our media relations campaigns, deserves a special measure of gratitude. Ishmael Ahmed, Warren David, Siham Jaafer, and William Salaita aided the project in many ways.

The DAAS would not have been possible without the contacts, direction, and good advice made available to us by members of our formal advisory panel, a consulting body of more than twenty secular, religious, and social service organizations. These include the American Arab Chamber of Commerce, the American Muslim Center, the American-Arab Anti-Discrimination Committee, the American Syrian Arab Cultural Association, the Arab American and Chaldean Council, the *Arab American News,* the Arab American Political Action Committee, the Arab Community Center for Economic and Social Services, the Chaldean American Ladies of Charity, the Chaldean Federation of America, the Congress of Arab American Organizations, the Islamic Institute of Knowledge, the Islamic Center of America, the New Generation Club, Our Lady of Redemption Melkite Catholic Church, the Ramallah Club, St. George's Antiochian Orthodox Church, St. Mary's Antiochian Orthodox Church, the United American Lebanese Federation, and the Yemeni American Benevolent Association.

We are grateful to Nabeel Abraham, Kristine Ajrouch, and Michael Suleiman for insightful advice and consultation on the questionnaires, and Khaled Al-Masri for translation services.

Scores of professionals at the Institute for Social Research helped us carry out this project. We are grateful to them all, and we offer special thanks to Steve Heeringa, Diane Swanbrow, Patrick Shields, Barbara Ward, Susan Clemmer, Terry Adams, Jenny Bandyk, Yvonne Ragland, Lillian Berlin, Elfriede Georgal, Alisa McWilliams, Kat Donahue, Stefani Salazar, Jamie LeBoeuf, Ashanti Harris, Ken Szmigiel, Jody Lamkin, Turknur Hamsici, Masahiko Aida, and the team of interviewers. We also thank Jonathan Fazzola, Jennifer Huntington, and Ifie Okwuje.

Likewise, we appreciate the many professionals and students who carried out the DAS: Martha S. Hill, Judi Clemens, Kathy Powers, Jeffrey Shook, Stefani Salazar, Erica Ryu, Loni Benkert, Anna Camacho, Sawsan Abdulrahim, Sarah Brauner, Kenneth Coleman, Geoff Goodman, Meadow Linder, Emily McFarlane, Beatricia Noguira, Andy Peytchev, Lai Sze Tso, Paolo von Nuremberg, and James Wagner.

Finally, we extend our heartfelt thanks to the members of the Arab American community who, during a time of crisis and intense suspicion, welcomed us into their homes and participated in the study.

INTRODUCTION

CHAPTER 1

Citizenship and Crisis

Wayne Baker and Andrew Shryock

The terror attacks of September 11, 2001 have led to radical changes in American society, new laws and governmental agencies, new wars, and new ways of seeing the world. The U.S. military has invaded and now occupies two (formerly) sovereign nation-states; a war on terror is being waged around the world, with covert operations, secret prison facilities, and detention camps in which those designated enemy combatants have languished for years in defiance of international law; the U.S. Department of Homeland Security, formed in response to the 9/11 attacks, has grown into a massive bureaucracy whose authority reaches from immigration and naturalization policies to border patrol, customs regulation, and airport security; and the USA PATRIOT Act has given the U.S. government immense leeway to infringe on civil liberties of American citizens in its fight against terrorism. Many of these developments are now taken for granted, have become part of history, and have even become part of our daily lives, shedding in the process much of the ominous novelty that once characterized them.

This book intervenes in the post-9/11 process of normalization, slowing it down to enable careful analysis and clear understanding. We create this effect by taking a close look at the lives of Arab Americans, a population whose post-9/11 experiences have been especially traumatic. Our focus is greater Detroit, home to some of the oldest, largest, and politically most prominent Arab and Arabic-speaking communities in North America. Through a careful analysis of systematic data collected on these communities and on the general population in the same region, we hope to make two contributions. First, we aim to insert accurate, objective information into the vigorous and often misinformed public discourse about Arab Americans. Our topics include basic demographic patterns, the 9/11 backlash, attitudes about civil liberties, social identities, religion and religious practices, values, social capital, political beliefs, and attitudes about U.S. foreign policy. Second, we intend to contribute to contemporary debates about citizenship. Citizenship has become an increasingly prominent theme in the social sciences, legal studies, and the humanities, as well as politically contested terrain in the lives of ordinary and influential people alike. We will argue that political crisis intensifies citizenship debates, making them a focus of public concern and political action, all the while revealing deep-seated contradictions in American society. By analyzing this dynamic against the backdrop of 9/11 and its effects on Arab Americans in Detroit, our goal is to make sense of the new regimes of citizenship and security that are reshaping American society.

In this chapter, we introduce our conceptual framework. We consider two key themes in the discourse about citizenship: citizenship as rights and citizenship as multiculturalism. We argue that, for Arab and Muslim Americans, citizenship has been shaped by crisis in historically specific ways, most of which predate the so-named war on terror. After explaining how this particular history can help us think about citizenship in more critical and comparative ways, we provide an overview of our chief sources of data—the Detroit Arab American Study (DAAS) and the Detroit Area Study (DAS). We then preview the chapters in the book, describing how each contributes to our understanding of citizenship as rights and as multiculturalism in an age of crisis. A brief account of Arab Detroit and some of its distinguishing features puts the context in which this study was undertaken into perspective.

ARAB DETROIT: AN INITIAL PORTRAIT

Detroit and its suburbs are home to a large, diverse population of Arab immigrants and their descendants.[1] Population estimates vary widely— from 125,000 to 475,000—but even the most sober calculations suggest a population that, by 2010, will approach 200,000. Arabs in greater Detroit tend to settle in the city's inner and outer suburbs. The most visible concentration is in Dearborn, where Lebanese, Yemenis, Iraqis, and Palestinians, most of them Muslim, have built a vibrant array of mosques, ethnic business districts, social service agencies, political action committees, village clubs, Islamic schools, and neighborhood associations. A more modest concentration of Yemenis is in Hamtramck, a working-class municipality surrounded by the City of Detroit. Another enclave, located along Seven Mile Road in Detroit, is home to Iraqi immigrants, almost all of them Chaldean Catholics, a Syriac and Arabic-speaking minority from northern Iraq. The Seven Mile neighborhood is small, and its population has shrunk radically over the last decade. Few new immigrants settle there, and most of the area's Chaldean families have moved to the northern and eastern suburbs, where they and other Arabic-speaking immigrants are widely recognized as an influential business and professional community. Detroit's grocery and liquor store trade is dominated by Iraqis. Lebanese, meanwhile, have specialized in gas stations and convenience stores. According to figures generated by the American Arab Chamber of Commerce, there are more than 5,000 Arab and Chaldean-owned businesses in greater Detroit. Despite obvious success in the small business sector, most Arabs in greater Detroit are not entrepreneurs; they can be found in all sectors of the local economy and at all income levels.

In addition to new immigrants, whose numbers have increased steadily since the 1970s, many well-established first- and second- (and even third- and fourth-) generation Arab Americans also live in metropolitan Detroit. Immigrants from Ottoman Syria had established small enclaves in the city by the 1890s. Mostly Christians from what is today Lebanon, these early arrivals worked as peddlers and shopkeepers. Detroit became a magnet for other Syrians in 1914, when Henry Ford began paying his factory workers five dollars a day. Restrictive immigration laws reduced the number of new arrivals from the Arab world between 1925 and 1965, but political turmoil in the Middle East and economic opportunity in the United States continued to draw new immigrants to Detroit for much of the twentieth century. The most significant recent wave of immigration was precipitated by the Lebanese civil war, which began in 1975. Between 1983 and 1990, just after the war's peak, more than 30,000 immigrants came to the United States from Lebanon, and nearly 4,000 of them settled immediately in greater Detroit (Schopmeyer 2000). The relationship between instability in Arab homelands and migration to Michigan holds for each of the nationalities that make up Arab Detroit.

Although Lebanese are the largest and most visible, the city also hosts the largest Iraqi and Yemeni communities in the United States, as well as sizable populations from Palestine, Egypt, Jordan, and Syria. As we discuss in subsequent chapters of this book, the factors that bring immigrants from the Arab world to the United States often result directly from political and economic policies pursued by the U.S. government and its allies in the Middle East.

The Arab national groups that predominate in Detroit represent odd inversions of the demographics of their home countries, giving some indication of the forces that have made migration possible and necessary. For example, Christians make up less than 5 percent of the Arab world, but in Detroit more than half the community. Detroit's Iraqi population is predominantly Catholic, yet Catholics are a small minority in Iraq. Detroit's Palestinians, too, are disproportionately Christian. Detroit's Lebanese, once overwhelmingly Christian, are increasingly Muslim, but Shi'a, a minority in Lebanon, greatly outnumber Detroit's Lebanese Sunnis. If Arab Detroit appears culturally distinctive to members of the larger American society, it seems even more peculiar in comparison to the Arab world. The broad range of lifestyles, national backgrounds, and levels of assimilation found among Detroit's Arab and Arabic-speaking population make it a difficult community to represent, both intellectually and politically. It is not simply an American ethnic constituency. Parts of this community make sense only in relation to economic development in the Yemeni highlands, conflict along the Lebanese-Israeli border, U.S. military interventions in Iraq, or the expansion of Jewish settlements in the West Bank. Yet Arab Detroit is hardly an integral part of the Arab world. The city is home to thousands of Arabs who cannot speak Arabic and have never traveled to the Middle East.

Given Arab Detroit's historical complexity and its diversity in the present, we cannot assume that its inhabitants experience American citizenship in similar ways, that the 9/11 backlash has affected them all alike, or that Arab Americans, in general, understand terms like *citizenship* and *crisis* in roughly the way other Americans do. Indeed, the meaning of these terms is constantly changing. Before we can arrive at a more precise sense of what they might signify in Detroit, we need to examine claims now being made, about citizenship in particular, among political theorists and social critics who, in discussing problems of inequality and cultural difference in contemporary society, depend increasingly on this term.

TWO THEMES OF CITIZENSHIP: RIGHTS AND MULTICULTURALISM

Like so many useful political ideas, "the concept of citizenship has become less clear as its relevance and prominence have increased" (Heisler 2005, 667). This trend reflects the growing range of problems citizenship is expected to solve, the divergent perspectives of those who invoke the term, and the changing political and economic conditions in which the meanings of this concept evolve. If citizenship is relevant to so many people, in so many ways, it is perhaps because the concept rests on a tension inherent to political life in contemporary nation-states. In theory, citizens of a state are—or ought to be—equal with respect to certain laws and official definitions of membership. In reality, this legal equivalence is difficult to attain and often considered undesirable. Nations are not as culturally uniform or politically unified as nationalists once thought they should be, and states cannot (and often do not wish to) devise legal systems that protect the rights and privileges of all citizens equally. Still, ideals of human equality and national community are firmly entrenched in modern political thought, and discourses about citizenship, failed or potentially put right, are now a popular medium in which to hash out inconsistencies in democratic governance.

To give our discussion of citizenship a sharper focus, we highlight two themes that pervade both popular and scholarly approaches to the subject. What we call the rights theme considers the shift from narrow, territorially defined citizenship to broad human rights models. The multiculturalism theme explores how diversity and value differences are reconciled with the need for national unity and shared conceptions of belonging. These themes overlap in theory and practice, but separating them analytically help us understand the situation of Arab Americans as both a problem of rights and a problem of identity, recognition, and belonging.

The Rights Theme

Modern theories of citizenship began with Thomas Marshall's ([1950]1964) expanded definition of the term. Arguing that the traditional view of citizenship as a set of civil rights and obligations was too narrow, he defined it to include civil, political, and social rights. Civil rights include rights to speech, thought, religion, private property, contracts, and justice. Political rights include the right to participate as a member or voter in the governing political body.

And social rights cover a broad spectrum of guarantees, ranging from "a modicum of economic welfare and security to the right to share to the full in the social heritage and to live the life of a civilized being according to the standards prevailing in the society" (Marshall 1964, 94). Marshall's definition extends the array of rights inherent in citizenship, but assumes that citizenship is coterminous with a territorially bounded nation-state. Globalization and transnational migration make this assumption problematic; each process has contributed to a crisis of the Westphalian model of state sovereignty, disrupting traditional notions of citizenship (Benhabib 2001, 2004). Economic globalization erodes national sovereignty (Sassen 1996), and migration disturbs "the sense of boundedness" (Heisler 2001) felt by people who live in countries with growing immigrant populations. For an increasing number of migrants, permanent residence in a single national homeland is becoming less the norm. "In many ways," John Solomos wrote, "the idea of diaspora as an unending sojourn across different lands better captures the reality of transnational networks and communities than the language of immigration and assimilation. Multiple, circular and return migrations, rather than a single great journey from one sedentary space to another, have helped transform transnational spaces" (2001, 209). Dual citizenship, a legal innovation developed to address these conditions, makes it even harder to define rights of citizenship in ways that privilege a single nationality (Carens 2000).

Rights-based responses to the challenges of citizenship are in abundant supply. Tomas Hammar, for example, argued that long-term immigrants in Europe who are not citizens are denizens with rights based on residency, not nationality (1989). Ranier Bauböck suggested that citizenship rights should be based on municipal residence instead of nationality because many immigrants have multiple countries of residence (2003). T. Alexander Aleinikoff and Douglas Klusmeyer recommended giving voting rights to long-settled immigrants who are not formal citizens to promote civic engagement and naturalization (2002). Yasemin Soysal proposed a "postnational" model of citizenship in which territorial boundaries are fluid (1994). Citizens of one nation may live and work in another, enjoying certain rights and privileges in the host nation. This model permits multiple statuses; for example, some migrant groups and citizens would receive more rights than others. Generally, the main task for policymakers and theorists who focus on the rights theme, Martin Heisler argued, is the "extension of at least large portions of, if not all, rights enjoyed by citizens to those who enter the domain of a democratic state. These are immigrants, transnational migrants, asylum seekers, and refugees" (2005, 669).

The basic assumption driving these recommendations is that rights are the essence of citizenship. The rights of citizenship, however, are differentiated both within a nation-state and internationally. At the international level, there is a hierarchical system of nation-states. The United States is the sole occupant of the top tier, "globally dominant in military, economic, and political and cultural affairs" (Castles 2005, 690); at the bottom are states like Sudan and Iraq, which cannot provide security for their citizens, cannot prevent the encroachment of other states, and cannot supply basic economic and social services to their populations. On a world scale, U.S. citizens enjoy a wide array of formal rights, along with stable democratic structures and a strong legal system to ensure them. Within the United States, however, ethnoracial and religious minorities and women routinely experience exclusion and discrimination (Castles 2005, 691). Clearly citizenship, defined as a legal status with attendant rights and obligations, has dimensions that function apart from the strict legality of this status, and these dimensions produce systematic and pervasive inequalities. That one is a citizen of the United States, or Nigeria, or France, does not guarantee that one belongs to those national communities. The lived reality of citizenship, the everyday experience of belonging (or being excluded), is diversely conditioned by political, economic, and social factors that make individuals, and entire populations, distinctive. Whether citizenship can—ideally or in practice—be framed without an explicit recognition of these cultural differences and geopolitical hierarchies of power is now a matter of intense debate.

The Multiculturalism Theme

Societies have always used difference—birthplace, parentage, class, ethnicity, race, gender, religion, and so on—to draw symbolic boundaries around their members. These boundaries define insiders and outsiders, their rights and obligations, and the process (if any) by which outsiders may become insiders. Assimilationism, "the traditional American response to difference" (Hartmann and Gerteis 2005, 218), is a mode of incorporation in which the pressure to conform is intense and immigrants are converted to American values in a "rigid and uncompromising way" (Taylor 2001, 185). For example, in the early twentieth century, Chicago School scholars assumed immigrants would eventually lose their distinct cultures, blend into mainstream society, and become American (Park and Miller 1921; Park 1950), though they disagreed to some extent about how this assimilation would occur (Warner and Srole 1945). The melting pot is the well-known metaphor for the process by which difference is dissolved into the social whole.

Multiculturalism and assimilationism are often thought of as opposite ends of the same spectrum. This unidimensional image creates theoretical confusion and makes the value of diversity in modern societies difficult to appreciate. Analysts who see multiculturalism as the opposite of assimilation consider diversity a threat to their conception of the ideal society, which is culturally homogeneous and unified. Arthur Schlesinger, for example, portrayed multiculturalism as the "disuniting of America" (1991). In this perspective, multicultural society is a "collection of discrete and presumably divided ethnic and racial communities" (Hartmann and Gerteis 2005, 220). These communities, Samuel Huntington argued, either resist assimilation or are considered "indigestible" by mainstream society, tendencies he considered exemplified in Mexican immigrants in America and Muslim minorities in predominately non-Muslim societies (2004, 187–89). Others have argued that the United States "has thrived not because of its efforts at cultural homogenization, but despite them" (Flores and Benmayor 1997, 5). Worries about immigration as a threat to national unity or stability are overblown, according to Will Kymlicka, because most immigrants want to integrate and participate (1995). Polyethnic demands for group representation, for example, are evidence that minority groups want to be included in mainstream society, not separated from it. Likewise, rising religious diversity is not necessarily a harbinger of conflict, because Americans exhibit rising tolerance (and even a preference) for religious difference, and the religious beliefs and practices of immigrants have tended, over time, to become homogenized in the American context (Fischer, Hout, and Stiles 2006).

As we have already noted, globalization and transnational migration are rendering monocultural visions of society obsolete and steadily replacing them with new political understandings of human diversity. David Jacobson described how these changes are causing people to think of nationality and group membership in ways that contradict Benedict Anderson's 1991 model of national community, which now seems overly contained: "The 'imagined community' of the nation-state was bounded, finite, and internally characterized by a deep, uniform, and horizontal comradeship. Other nations, beyond its borders, belong to the 'foreign' or the 'alien.' In the emerging order, we still have imagined communities—be they ethnic, religious, or in other forms—but instead of being horizontal, territorial, and boundary oriented, they are transterritorial and centripetal. Boundaries are culturally (rather than politically or physically) meaningful" (Jacobson 1996, 133).

Some scholars have proposed the concept of cultural citizenship to accommodate expanded, multicultural conceptions of political belonging (see, for example, Ong 1996; Pakulski 1997; Turner 2001). Cultural citizenship allows minority groups to establish special communities in which they feel safe and at home, "while still situating themselves in the broad context of continental American society" (Flores and Benmayor 1997, 13). Cultural citizenship produces cultural rights, freedom from marginalization, and acceptance of difference (Pakulski 1997). Blanca Silvestrini separated cultural citizenship from legal citizenship, the former representing unity and connectedness whereas the latter represents homogeneity and the absence of culture in the public sphere (1997). Renato Rosaldo and others have noted an emerging cultural citizenship among previously marginalized groups who express their agency, and their alternative sense of belonging, by demanding rights to their own social space from the larger society (1997). Citizenship, from this vantage, is about who "needs to be visible, to be heard, and to belong" (Rosaldo 1997, 37).

Kymlicka suggested that shared identity must be formed in the post–nation-state period through accommodation of diverse national identities rather than suppression of them (1995). Calling on Charles Taylor's notion of "deep diversity" (1991), Kymlicka argued that societies must accept that citizens of different ethnoracial, religious, and national backgrounds will not always understand their membership in the larger polity in the same way. The result is a national identity that, though overarching, cannot be portrayed as uniform, a predicament that explains the appeal and political necessity of multiculturalism in the United States and other countries where diversity is favored in public discourse and social policy (Baumann 1999; Maddox 2004).

Soysal, in her research on Islam in Europe, suggested that "the universal right to 'one's own culture' has gained political legitimacy, and collective identity has been redefined as a category of human rights" (1997, 513). However, as Joseph Carens noted, these cultural rights are often harshly questioned when they are asserted by less powerful and stigmatized cultural groups, such as Muslims in France during repeated debates over the foulard, the Muslim headscarf (2000). The extent to which members of minority populations can, in fact, maintain their own culture apart from that of the larger society is limited, and the value of cultural distinctiveness—of wearing a headscarf in

France or speaking Spanish in the United States—is determined in contrast to dominant cultural patterns that cannot be ignored and are not uniformly rejected by members of minority communities.

Debates about multiculturalism reflect the changing social landscape, conflicting political agendas and ideologies, and international political events. It is apparent, however, that these debates center on a basic contrast between citizenship understood as a legal status, a bundle of rights, and as a sense of belonging that is felt, or should be felt, in relation to a larger national community marked by sociocultural diversity. It is also clear that both understandings are fundamentally concerned with the problem of membership, with the placing and crossing of group boundaries. For this reason, citizenship is a concept indispensable to national security. It is extremely sensitive to crisis situations in which the moral and political boundaries of the national community are perceived to be threatened.

CRISIS

The September 11 attacks on the World Trade Center and the Pentagon were traumatic for all Americans, but those of Middle Eastern descent suffered the "tribal stigma of race, nation, and religion" (Goffman 1963, 3). The subsequent war on terror has raised questions about the values, sympathies, and loyalties of Arab and Muslim Americans, subjecting them to intense public scrutiny, backlash, and government surveillance. After 9/11, fewer than half of all Americans (46 percent) evaluated Arab Americans positively, versus 70 percent giving positive evaluations of African Americans and 79 percent of white Americans (Traugott, Groves, and Kennedy 2002). Whites and blacks alike in the Detroit region prefer more social distance from Arab Americans than from any other group (Farley, Krysan, and Couper 2006).[2]

September 11 was not the first event to focus attention on Arab and Muslim Americans. The 1967 Arab-Israeli War, the 1973 oil embargo, the Iranian hostage crisis (1979 through 1981), U.S. intervention in Lebanon (1982 through 1984), and the 1991 Gulf War also subjected members of these groups to scrutiny and backlash. But September 11 and the so-named war on terrorism elevated to a peak hate crimes, discriminatory immigration policies, racial profiling, domestic spying, defamation by public figures and the media, and other acts of discrimination and harassment (Cainkar 2002; Ibish and Stewart 2003; Cesari 2004; Naber 2006). September 11 and its aftermath also prompted the U.S. military invasions of Afghanistan and Iraq and gave rise to the USA PATRIOT Act, which greatly expanded the government's authority to spy on U.S. citizens as it reduced checks and balances on these powers (Cole 2003; Hagopian 2004).

A study of Arab Detroit conducted in the aftermath of the 9/11 attacks will strike most readers as the perfect setting in which to explore how the interaction of citizenship and crisis is unfolding at ground level. Justifying a study of this kind is not difficult, largely because the link between Arab Detroit, as a place, and the 9/11 attacks, as historical events, seems so consequential, so unavoidable. Yet this impression is itself symptomatic of deeply entrenched ways of thinking about Arabs and Muslims in America. The links between Arab Detroit and the 9/11 attacks are many, but seldom those that flourish in the popular imagination. The 9/11 attackers were not from Arab Detroit and none had personal ties to Detroit—indeed, most were Saudi nationals, and very few Saudis live in greater Detroit. The 9/11 attackers were not U.S. citizens and most Arabs who live in greater Detroit are. Finally, the 9/11 attackers were Sunni Muslims and most Arab Muslims in Detroit are Shi'a. Despite these and many other distinguishing factors, the post-9/11 backlash was immediately and dramatically felt in Detroit. Some of the first arrests were made there, and men accused of belonging to an al-Qaida operational combat sleeper cell were tried and convicted in Detroit (though their convictions were soon overturned). Detroit was drawn into the war on terror almost by political reflex, and this outcome seemed as inevitable to Arab Americans as it did to most other Americans.

As we show throughout this book, the links taken for granted between Arab Detroit and crisis events in the Middle East—as well as crisis events inside the United States that involve Arabs or Muslims—are part of geopolitical and historical patterns that have shaped, and continue to shape, popular notions of citizenship and belonging in the United States. This larger context is the setting in which, to paraphrase Aihwa Ong, Arabs are made, and make themselves, American (2003). It is a social space shared by many American immigrant and ethnic groups, but it also has highly distinctive features. Arabs are set apart from other hyphenated American populations by aspects of U.S. foreign policy that drive a sharp ideological wedge between Arab and American identities. Specifically, Arabs and Muslims living in the United States repeatedly face situations in which their countries of origin, or Arabs and Muslims generally, are cast as enemies of the United States and its allies in the Middle East. As a result, Arab American identity is seen, by Arabs and non-Arabs alike, as an identity in question, as an identity that must continually prove itself. As a practical condition of citizenship, Arab Americans are expected to assure their fellow nationals that they belong, that they are loyal, that they are not a threat to national security, and so on.

Public demand for these proofs of citizenship has intensified greatly in the wake of the 9/11 attacks. Once again, Arabs and Muslims are associated with danger, and their hold on U.S. citizenship and its legal protections is jeopardized. Likewise, their normative status as Americans is vulnerable to critique. It is no coincidence, given current trends in the theory and practice of citizenship, that Arab American identity formation has produced a "structure of feeling" in which the rewards of legal citizenship, economic success, and other forms of integration cannot overcome—but can in fact accentuate—a lingering, politicized estrangement from the cultural mainstream. In a real sense, Arab Americans are experiencing a concentrated version of the anxieties about identity and boundary maintenance that are now endemic to the contemporary nation-state. Their community, like the larger American society, is increasingly vulnerable to global political and economic forces beyond its control. For this reason, a careful analysis of Arab Detroit can provide important insights about national belonging and the crisis moments in which it is tested and transformed.

In the chapters to follow, we argue that Arab and Muslim Americans live in a contested zone of overlap between forms of otherness that, for much of American history, have been considered especially problematic and, at times, threatening. These markers are variable, and they intersect in complicated ways, but the most important ones, for our study, can be sorted into three categories: ethnic and racial differences, religious and value differences, and differences in basic political ideology. Attempts to include and exclude Arab Americans along these familiar dimensions produce odd outcomes, and these peculiarities reflect the marginal location Arabs now occupy in the politics of American citizenship. As a result, comparing Arab and Muslim Americans to other minority communities in the United States is both difficult and necessary.

In matters racial and ethnic, for instance, Arabs in Detroit do not identify consistently as white or nonwhite, nor do all Arabic-speakers and their descendants call themselves Arab American. Advances made in the study of Asian and Latino panethnicities (Espiritu 1992; Takaki 1989; Garcia 2000; Davila 2001; Suarez-Orozco and Paez 2002), advances in our understanding of how groups are racialized in the United States (Omi and Winant 1994; Lowe 1995; Waters

1999; Wu 2003; Rodriguez 2003), and the political gains that have accompanied these new understandings cannot be carried neatly into the study of Arab and Muslim Americans (see Jamal and Naber 2008). Likewise, although Arab Americans are commonly thought to be Muslims, most are Christian, a fact that complicates attempts to root Arab cultural difference in Islam, even as it makes Arab Muslim identity highly sensitive for people who are Muslim but not Arab, Arab but not Muslim, or simply Muslim first (Naber 2005; Modood 2005; Read 2007; Jackson 2005). On the political front, Arabs are often associated with radical, anti-American politics, yet most Arab Americans are socially conservative, have highly positive views of American society, and are eager to enter the political mainstream. Analysts and commentators of diverse sorts have noted that Arab Americans are linked to a generic cultural enemy defined as Muslim, racially non-European, and averse to democracy and human rights (Joseph 1999; McAlister 2001; Salaita 2006). In greater Detroit, however, this linkage consistently breaks down at the empirical level. We consider how Arab and Muslim Americans deal with this misfit, how it is used to create an alternative local politics, how it affects the experience of citizenship, and how the political crises that drive these processes have actually been built into Arab and Muslim identities in assertive, defensive, and highly adaptive ways.

It is important to better understand these processes, not only because they affect a vulnerable American population, but also because they highlight contradictions in the multicultural ethos that currently dominates the theory and practice of U.S. citizenship. Arab and Muslim Americans are widely associated with enemies in a society that loudly proclaims its belief in pluralism, diversity, and tolerance. In earlier periods of U.S. history, links to enemies were handled in ways that, by today's standards, would seem extreme. During World War I, laws were passed in the United States making it illegal to speak German in public, or to teach it in schools, or even to use it in church services (Higham 2002; Reimers 1998). During World War II, 110,000 Japanese living in the United States, 70,000 of whom were U.S. citizens, were imprisoned in concentration camps run by the U.S. military (Weglyn 1976; Irons 1983; Saito 2001). In the wake of the 9/11 attacks, no laws have been passed against speaking Arabic in public, or teaching it in schools, or using it in mosques. Similarly, internment camps built specifically for the detention of Arab and Muslim U.S. citizens have not materialized, although they loom as a threat, despite the logistical difficulties entailed in incarcerating even a small percentage of the roughly 6 million Arabs and Muslims now living in the United States.

It is obvious, nonetheless, that Arab and Muslim Americans have been singled out for intense discipline and scrutiny. In Detroit, this treatment includes selective programs of surveillance, deportation, and detention without due process, presumptive freezing of financial assets, vandalism, and personal insult. We catalog these practices, building on the growing number of studies that have chronicled the post-9/11 backlash in the United States (Cole 2003; Dudziak 2003; Ewing 2008). At the same time, however, and in direct response to the post-9/11 crackdown, great efforts have been made in Detroit to include, protect, and accept Arabs and Muslims as full members of American society, and much of this activity has proceeded along lines laid down for recognizing and incorporating other minority communities in the United States (Howell and Shryock 2003; Shryock 2004). This politics of inclusion receives little attention from scholars, but is a powerful force with profound effects on the development of Arab American identities. Since the 9/11 attacks, Detroit has seen the establishment of the Arab American National Museum; the expansion of Arab American community organizations; the election and appointment of Arab and Muslim citizens to political office; new partnerships between Arab American civil rights organizations, the Federal Bureau of Investigation (FBI), and the U.S. Department of Homeland Security; the creation of Arab American and Islamic studies programs in area universities; and the founding and expansion of at least a dozen new mosques.

This blend of pervasive stigma and urgent attempts at social integration produces a distinctive process of citizenship and identity formation we call disciplinary inclusion. Ideally suited to multicultural politics, this mode of citizenship is not new to Arab Detroit, nor are Arabs and Muslims uniquely subject to it. Instead, it is a highly generalized process, experienced differently by different groups and persons in American society, but with effects that inevitably bring Arabs and Muslims into larger, public discourses about American identity. By exploring how disciplinary inclusion works in Detroit, our goal is to enhance the critical potential of a literature on citizenship that has proved indispensable to understanding how power and identity interact in contemporary political systems.

THE DETROIT ARAB AMERICAN STUDY AND DETROIT AREA STUDY

Our analyses are based on a unique combination of data: the Detroit Arab American Study, an intensive survey of the Arab communities in the Michigan counties of Wayne, Oakland, and Macomb, and the Detroit Area Study, a survey of the general population living in the same counties during the same period. Figure 1.1 presents the geographic coverage of these surveys by county and local area, and the location of the three counties in the state of Michigan. Both the DAAS and DAS were designed and conducted using scientific survey methods and procedures. An overview of our samples and research methodology follows (for a more detailed technical account, see www.detroitarabamericanstudy.org).

Today, Michigan has the highest concentration of Arabs of any state in the union (1.2 percent of the total state population), growing by 51 percent in the 1990s (de la Cruz and Brittingham 2003).[3] About 2.7 percent of the population in Wayne County reports Arab ancestry, with 1.2 percent in Macomb County and Oakland County (de la Cruz and Brittingham 2003).[4] The cities of Dearborn and Dearborn Heights, which border Detroit to the southwest, are a well-known area of Arab concentration (this area is labeled Near SW Detroit in figure 1.1). For example, about 35 percent of Dearborn's residents are of Arab origin, and more than 60 percent of students in Dearborn's public schools are Arab American. Although no other enclave rivals Dearborn in size or political prominence, the majority of greater Detroit's Arab and Arabic-speaking populations live elsewhere, and most live in neighborhoods that cannot be characterized as enclaves.

The DAAS was designed to be a representative survey of all adults of Arab or Chaldean descent living in the three-county region, meaning that we can generalize from our sample to the Arab American population at large in the Detroit region (for technical details on sampling methods, see www.detroitarabamericanstudy.org). We worked closely with representatives of local Arab American communities. Our DAAS Advisory Panel included individuals from more than twenty of Arab Detroit's secular, religious, civil rights, and social service organizations. During several long planning sessions, our advisors suggested themes to pursue and warned of pitfalls to avoid. They gave input on the questionnaire, provided feedback on its translation into Arabic, publicized the project in their communities, and offered interpretations of our preliminary findings. Given the intense scrutiny Detroit's Arab communities were already experiencing—in the media and under the close watch of several U.S. government agencies—our sustained collaboration with community leaders and key organizations built trust and enabled us to create a survey instrument that addressed not only

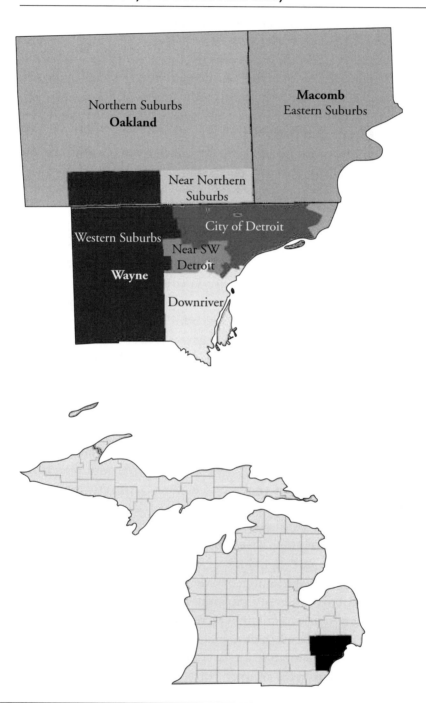

important scholarly issues but also matters of direct concern to people we interviewed.

To be eligible for our survey, respondents had to be at least eighteen years old, live in households in the three-county Detroit region during the survey period, July to December 2003, and self-identify as Arab or Chaldean (Chaldeans are mostly Iraqi Catholics).[5] Arriving at these criteria for inclusion was not simple. Ideas about who is Arab and how that identity should be defined are highly variable, even controversial. Language is frequently mentioned, yet many Arab Americans do not speak Arabic well, or at all, and some people who reject Arab identity speak only Arabic. Generally, descent from parents who consider themselves Arab is important, as is coming from, or having an ancestor who came from, an Arab-majority country. Still, a person might not identify as Arab because she would rather be called American; this same person might watch Arabic satellite television and attend a church where most people speak Arabic. Some people prefer a more precise national label, such as Lebanese, Palestinian, or Iraqi. Others know they have a parent or grandparent of, say, Syrian descent, and are proud of this heritage, but seldom identify as Arab in their everyday lives. Finally, in greater Detroit, there are many people (notably Iraqi Chaldeans) who come from Arab countries, speak Arabic, and share many cultural traits with Arabs, but who do not identify consistently as Arab.

Instead of trying to streamline these alternative forms of identification, all of which are common in greater Detroit, we opted for a flexible, inclusive approach. Our interviewers asked people if there were anyone in their household of Arab or Chaldean descent; in other words, was there anyone in the household who had "parents, grandparents, or ancestors" who were Arab or Chaldean. If people were not sure, they were shown a list of Arab-majority countries and, if further clarification were needed, a map of the Arab world. Using this approach to eligibility, our goal was to conduct 1,000 face-to-face interviews. We obtained 1,016. The American Association for Public Opinion Research (AAPOR) response rate was 73.7 percent, meaning that about three of four people asked to participate in the survey agreed to do so. Face-to-face interviews were conducted in the language of the respondent's choice, English or Arabic. Of the fifty-two interviewers who administered the survey, forty-seven were of Arab or Chaldean ancestry, and thirty-four were bilingual in Arabic and English. The English-language version of the questionnaire is provided on the DAAS website.

The DAS, our companion study, was designed to be a representative sample of the general population living in the counties of Wayne, Oakland, and

Macomb (figure 1.1). The DAS survey population included only eligible adults (age eighteen or older) living in households. Our goal was 500 face-to-face interviews of members of the general population. We obtained 508, bringing the total sample for the combined surveys to 1,524. The AAPOR response rate for the DAS was 56.6 percent, which is about the same as the average response rate for the annual Detroit Area Studies conducted since 1997 (Clemens, Couper, and Powers 2002). The DAS and DAAS were explicitly designed to compare Arab Americans and members of the general population. About 85 percent of the questions were identical in the two questionnaires, permitting comparisons of these two populations over a wide range of topics.

OVERVIEW OF BOOK

The chapters that follow, though varied in analytical focus and perspective, all address the intertwined ideas of citizenship and political crisis in Arab Detroit. Our chapters are in conversation with each other, and central arguments build progressively throughout the book. Still, each chapter can be read as a freestanding analysis, with interpretations and conclusions unique to it. The chapters are organized in three parts. Part I, Community in Crisis, explores the logic and history of Arab American identity formation, laying essential groundwork for our examination of how the 9/11 backlash affected different sectors of greater Detroit's Arab American community. Part II, Beliefs and Bonds, examines two aspects of community—shared values and social capital. These are essential elements of belonging and inclusion, and each has been questioned in the aftermath of 9/11. Part III, Political Ideology, engages the political and legal dimensions of citizenship, exploring political attitudes among Arab Americans and about them, with special emphasis on civil liberties and U.S. foreign policy, two domains that generate serious contradictions in the way citizenship is extended or denied to Arab Americans. In our conclusion to the book, we build a synthetic model of Arab American citizenship that acknowledges the vital role political crisis has played in shaping Arab American identities over time, giving them distinctive characteristics that are well suited to their location on the margins of multicultural pluralism in the United States today.

Part I. Community in Crisis

In chapter 2, "Arab American Identities in Question," Andrew Shryock and Ann Chih Lin examine the internal composition of greater Detroit's Arab populations—their religious, national, and socioeconomic diversity—to determine how larger, more inclusive Arab American identities are made. Working with data that are both detailed and general, Shryock and Lin show how Arab American identities are shaped by characteristics people bring to the United States from their countries of origin, by the extent to which immigrants and the American-born are incorporated into the larger society, and by the ethnic and racial categories people embrace (and reject) as markers of their personal status and collective identities. Across Arab Detroit, these factors interact to produce a wide range of communities, each with a distinct understanding of what it means to be Arab, American, or Arab American. This process of identity formation is situated within larger political and historical contexts that operate as constraints on the expression and recognition of Arab American citizenship. The authors conclude by discussing the historical emergence of these constraints and how they are visible in the DAAS findings and in the spatial organization of Arab Detroit itself.

In chapter 3, "The Aftermath of the 9/11 Attacks," Sally Howell and Amaney Jamal chronicle the post-9/11 backlash in greater Detroit, focusing on local responses and the role played by the federal government. Because the Arab communities of Detroit are long established and well incorporated, public officials, community activists, and regional media were able to protect local Arab Americans from the more severe forms of public backlash experienced elsewhere in the United States, especially among low-income and recently arrived Arab immigrants. At the same time, however, Detroit's prominence as a center of Arab immigration and cultural activity attracted the attention of multiple federal agencies interested in locating threats to national security and creating tactical relationships with Arab and Muslim allies in the U.S. war on terror. Howell and Jamal provide a rich portrait of the demographic, social, and historical patterns that make Detroit exceptional, in systematic and telling ways, to Arab Americans in other cities and in the national context. By closely analyzing Detroit's experience of the backlash, the authors sort out the complex mix of opportunity and insecurity that animates Arab American efforts to engage in public discourse as citizens. They also explore how feelings of coercion and empowerment overlap in attempts to define Arab Detroit as a national resource (a hub of foreign trade and investment, of cultural and linguistic expertise) and a national risk (home to concentrated populations of Arabs and Muslims whose loyalties are endlessly cast in doubt).

Part II. Beliefs and Bonds

In chapter 4, "Belief and Belonging," Sally Howell and Amaney Jamal consider how participation in churches and mosques shapes ethnic and religious identities, political involvement, and perceptions of discrimination or estrangement from the larger society. Historically, Arab houses of worship have played a central role in the incorporation of immigrants as citizens, but in recent decades, as Islam has taken on a more problematic status in American political culture, this process have begun to work differently for Muslim and Christian Arabs. Howell and Jamal find that Christians are well along the path to full American citizenship. For Orthodox Christians and those who are moderately pious, church attendance leads to greater identification with Arab American ethnicity and greater concern about stereotyping and discrimination. Similar effects are not found among Chaldeans, however, or among those strongly committed to Christianity. Among Muslims, those highly committed to the practice of Islam feel a greater sense of discrimination than other Muslims do. Local mosques do not necessarily foster this sense of stigma, but mosque participation does encourage some Muslims to express their dissatisfaction through the political process. Higher incomes, more education, and increased time in America actually contribute to a sense of marginalization among Muslims (and among some Christians as well). Religious piety and attendance at Friday prayers or Sunday services play a less important role. As Arab Muslims become more American culturally, their awareness of not being accepted as Americans by their fellow citizens grows more acute. These findings suggest that the war on terror, by singling out Muslims and Muslim institutions as potential threats to national security, has denied Muslims the same access to the benefits of citizenship as other Americans.

In chapter 5, "Values and Cultural Membership," Wayne Baker and Amaney Jamal compare the values of Arab Americans in the Detroit region with members of the general population living in the same area, with Americans nationwide, with the peoples of several Arab nations, and with a large number of other societies around the globe. They use two dimensions of values: a continuum of traditional versus secular values and another of survival versus self-expression values. The first taps a constellation of values about God, country, and family; the second focuses on values about security, trust, tolerance, and well-being. The assimilationist view of citizenship assumes that immigrants attain cultural membership by adopting mainstream values. Baker and Jamal find that, on average, the values of Arab Americans are closer to those of the Arab world—strong traditional values coupled with strong survival values—than they are to the values of the general population in the Detroit area or nationwide. The strong traditional values of Arab Americans do not vary by legal citizenship, place of birth, language, religion, or residence. Education is one of the few factors that secularizes values. More self-expressive Arab Americans are closer to mainstream American society: they tend to be U.S. citizens, be born in the United States, speak English, and be Christian. Arab Americans who had a bad experience after 9/11 are more survival oriented, and those who received expressions of support and solidarity are less so. Baker and Jamal conclude that how one interprets differences in the values of Arab Americans and other Americans depends on one's theory of citizenship (assimilationist versus cultural) and one's frame of reference (local, national, or global).

In chapter 6, "Local and Global Social Capital," Wayne Baker, Amaney Jamal, and Mark Tessler assess the state of local social capital (that bound to the Detroit region) and global social capital for Arab Americans and for the general population. They use the short form of the Social Capital Benchmark Survey that was included in the DAAS and DAS, as well as questions about transnational ties. Social capital and civic engagement are mutually reinforcing, and each fosters a perception of common bonds with fellow citizens. The authors find that, like other largely immigrant groups in America, Arab Americans have less local social capital than the general population. For example, Arab Americans are less trusting, less involved civically, less involved in voluntary organizations, and less likely to socialize with people from other neighborhoods or other races. Arab Americans do have more global social capital than the general population, however. Once the authors control for immigrant status, as well as immigrant markers such as Arabic language use and enclave residence, the differences shrink between the two populations. The factors that elevate local social capital and depress global social capital are those related to assimilation success: higher education and income. Thus, one way to enhance the social capital of local immigrant communities is to ensure that avenues to economic and educational achievement remain open.

Part III. Political Ideology

In chapter 7, "Civil Liberties," Ronald Stockton explores the dilemmas of citizenship created by the attacks of September 11, giving primary attention to the problem of equal protection under the law. Although Arab Americans and the general public are similar in their distress over the 9/11 attacks and in their willingness to support restrictions on civil liberties, large gaps open up between the two populations when restrictions are targeted at Arab Americans. Most members of the general public are resistant to ethnic or religious targeting, but among Arab Americans resistance soars (especially among those at special risk, such as Muslims and noncitizens). Stockton finds that, consistent with national studies, the willingness to restrict rights increases, among the general population, with fear. For Arab Americans, however, the pattern is reversed: those who are afraid and those who had a bad experience after September 11 are more likely to resist limitations on rights. Arab Americans who perceive the media to be hostile to them are also exceptionally resistant, this being an aspect of fear often overlooked. Identity also plays a role. Those proud of their American identity are more accepting of restrictions, whereas those who identify with the term Arab American are more resistant. Finally, some Arab Americans are afraid that extremists of Middle Eastern origin could compromise their position in the United States, and are therefore willing to support limitations on civil liberties to protect the country against those who would do it harm. Stockton argues that Arab Americans are clearly torn between a desire to protect society from future attacks and a fear that their own communities will be targeted.

In chapter 8, "Foreign Policy," Stockton examines the foreign policy attitudes of Arab Americans. Like members of the general population, Arab Americans form their political attitudes according to ideological, religious, cultural, and informational patterns. Arab Americans are distinctive, however, because they retain ties of affection and concern for homelands that are (or are perceived to be) in conflict with the United States. Whereas some American ethnic groups with homeland ties—Irish, Jews, Vietnamese, Cubans—are seen as supporting policies consistent with American domestic and foreign interests, Arab Americans are associated with foreign regimes and movements that confront U.S. policy. Arab Americans, Stockton argues, are allowed to function as citizens with the right to petition, protest, and object, but only as long as their behavior is not seen as the expression of a collective Arab or Muslim identity hostile to the United States. Four key patterns emerge from Stockton's analysis. First, there is a consensus among Arab Americans in favor of a Palestinian state. Second, on U.S. policies in the Middle East, most Arab Americans have doubts, but Iraqis, Christians, Republicans, and those proudest to be American were more supportive. Third, on the causes of the September 11 attacks, Arab Americans agree with the general public that U.S. policies toward the Arab

Gulf states and Israel may have been a factor, but few feel that there is a funda-mental clash of civilizations. Finally, Stockton argues that some Arab Americans hold back their opinions on the causes of the September 11 attacks. Those with a heightened sense of insecurity, and those who perceive a hostile media, often declined to answer questions about the attacks. In this regard, concerns about the loss of civil liberties combine with foreign policy attitudes to act as a constraint on freedom of expression among Arab Americans.

Conclusion

In chapter 9, "The Limits of Citizenship," Andrew Shryock and Ann Chih Lin provide an integrative conclusion to the book. Using patterns discussed in pre-vious chapters, the authors reassess key assumptions about national belonging. These assumptions affect the way non-Arabs see Arabs, but also influence the way Arab Americans represent themselves to mainstream society. This reciprocal influence is both a practical constraint on the public acceptance of Arab American citizenship and a powerful motivation (for Arab Americans) to express national belonging in broadly intelligible ways. Focusing on pop-ular notions of otherness, loyalty, and political opposition, Shryock and Lin scrutinize widespread beliefs that Arab Americans are not like most Americans and do not really support the U.S. government or feel solidarity with other American citizens. They show how these beliefs distort a more complex real-ity, foster misconceptions about the relationship between cultural diversity and citizenship, and lead to faulty conclusions about how, and to what extent, Arab Americans identify as U.S. citizens. The authors argue that rethinking the relationship between citizenship and crisis might enable a better understanding of why Detroit's Arab and Chaldean communities have adapted to the pressures of the war on terror with a resilience many observers find surprising.

THE DAAS: AN EXPERIMENT IN CITIZENSHIP

Unlike Arab populations in many other American cities, Arabs and Muslims are not an oddity in greater Detroit. They are a prominent community, with ample representation in mainstream institutions, an influential place in the local economy, and an impressive array of appointed and elected officials. Yet even in greater Detroit, Arab Americans provoke anxiety and are easy targets of harassment and abuse. The DAAS and DAS were designed to make sense of this unusual combination of acceptance and exclusion, which renders Arab

Detroit exceptional in ways that challenge popular conceptions of what American citizenship can mean.

We argue throughout this book that Arab Americans are caught up in highly ambivalent relationships with their own nation-state. As transnational models of human rights and global citizenship flourish in diverse sectors of American society, Arab Americans must continually struggle to assert credible and secure attachment to domestic models of U.S. citizenship. As more and more Americans assert cultural identities that connect them, legally and emotionally, to nation-states and regional cultures that lie outside the borders of the United States, Arab Americans must prove to a larger American society that their first loyalty is to the United States, and that whatever ties they maintain to Arabs and Muslims abroad are not a threat to Americans at large. Along these and other dimensions, it is clear that Arab Americans do not experience citizenship in ways common among their fellow nationals. Understanding the culture of crisis in which Arab (and non-Arab) Americans now live is key to assessing this misfit and changing it.

We began this introduction by claiming that the Detroit Arab American Study intervenes in a process of normalization that obscures the dangers, opportunities, and sociopolitical transformations now reshaping the post-9/11 world. This intervention operates at the level of theory and analysis, but it also operates at the level of method. Our ability to administer the survey—even as the FBI conducted its own interviews and the U.S. military invaded Iraq—depended on culturally sensitive engagements with Detroit's Chaldean and Arab populations and effective collaboration with key representatives of their communities. For these reasons, the DAAS itself can be seen as an experiment in citizenship, conducted in a moment of political crisis. Its strengths and weaknesses are very much a product of the special conditions in which the study was conducted. We are confident, however, that the significance of our findings will outlive these conditions. The work of citizenship is unrelenting, and for Arab Americans it is difficult work at best. If the past is a reliable guide, we can assume that Detroit's Arab and Arabic-speaking communities will face new political crises in the future. The DAAS, as a historical benchmark, will provide information and analytical insights that can help people understand these new conditions, when they come, and respond to them intelligently.

NOTES

1. This section is a digest of earlier research done by members of the DAAS team and by other scholars at work in Arab Detroit. Most numerical claims are based on U.S. Census figures or are derived from Kim Schopmeyer's demographic profile of Detroit's Arab population (2000). Our more general depictions of Arab Detroit are based on research presented in the works of Barbara Aswad (1974), Sameer Abraham and Nabeel Abraham (1983), Ernest McCarus (1994), Barbara Aswad and Barbara Bilge (1996), Michael Suleiman (1999), Nabeel Abraham and Andrew Shryock (2000), and Sally Howell and Andrew Shryock (2003).

2. Social distance refers to the degree of acceptance or closeness that members of one group have for another group. The findings about social distance and Arab Americans are based on data from the 2004 Detroit Area Study, a representative survey of the adult (eighteen and older) general population living in Wayne, Oakland, and Macomb counties (Farley, Krysan, and Couper 2006). Social distance may be measured in several ways; here, it is the percentage of respondents who excluded each racial-ethnic group (Arab Americans, whites, African Americans, Asians, and Hispanics) as contiguous neighbors in the neighborhood that has their ideal mix.

3. About 1.2 million of the total U.S. population of 281.4 million reported Arab ancestry, according to the 2000 census brief on the Arab population (de la Cruz and Brittingham 2003). This population grew by 41 percent in the 1980s and 38 percent in the 1990s. About half of the Arab population is concentrated in five states: California, Florida, Michigan, New Jersey, and New York.

4. The 2000 U.S. Census estimated the total number of Arab Americans in the three counties to be about 100,000. However, some researchers and community leaders claim that the U.S. Census substantially undercounts people of Arab descent and that the population could be as large as 300,000 (Schopmeyer 2000; David Shepardson, "Metro Detroit Leaders Claim Numbers Undercounted," *Detroit News,* June 4, 2002).

5. Chaldeans are a linguistic, ethnic, and religious group (almost all are Catholic) from the Middle East, mainly Iraq. They are mentioned by name in the eligibility protocol for several reasons. First, Chaldeans share life experiences and cultural traits with Arabs, and most speak Arabic as well as Syriac and English. Second, some Chaldeans identify as Arab American and some do not, the proportions of which we wanted to determine with data. Third, greater Detroit is home to one of the largest expatriate Chaldean populations in the world.

REFERENCES

Abraham, Nabeel, and Andrew Shryock, eds. 2000. *Arab Detroit: From Margin to Mainstream.* Detroit, Mich.: Wayne State University Press.

Abraham, Sameer, and Nabeel Abraham, eds. 1983. *Arabs in the New World: Studies on Arab-American Communities.* Detroit, Mich.: Wayne State University Press.

Aleinikoff, T. Alexander, and Douglas Klusmeyer. 2002. *Citizenship Policies for an Age of Migration.* Washington, D.C.: Carnegie Endowment for International Peace.

Anderson, Benedict. 1991. *Imagined Communities: Reflections on the Origin and Spread of Nationalism,* rev. ed. London: Verso Books.

Aswad, Barbara, ed. 1974. *Arabic Speaking Communities in American Cities.* New York: Center for Migration Studies.

Aswad, Barbara, and Barbara Bilge, eds. 1996. *Family and Gender Among American Muslims: Issues Facing Middle Eastern Immigrants and Their Descendants.* Philadelphia: Temple University Press.

Bauböck, Ranier. 2003. "Reinventing Urban Citizenship." *Citizenship Studies* 7(2): 139–60.

Baumann, Gerd. 1999. *The Multicultural Riddle: Rethinking National, Ethnic, and Religious Identities.* New York: Routledge.

Benhabib, Seyla. 2001. *Transformations of Citizenship: Dilemmas of the Nation State in the Era of Globalization.* Amsterdam: Kohinklijke Van Gorcum.

———. 2004. *The Rights of Others: Aliens, Residents and Citizens.* Cambridge: Cambridge University Press.

Cainkar, Louise. 2002. "No Longer Invisible: Arab and Muslim Exclusion after September 11." *Middle East Report* 224(fall): 22–29.

Carens, Joseph H. 2000. *Culture, Citizenship, and Community: A Contextual Exploration of Justice as Evenhandedness.* Oxford: Oxford University Press.

Castles, Stephen. 2005. "Hierarchical Citizenship in a World of Unequal Nation-States." *Political Science and Politics* 38(4): 689–92.

Cesari, Jocelyne. 2004. *When Islam and Democracy Meet.* New York: Palgrave MacMillan.

Clemens, Judi, Mick P. Couper, and Kathy Powers. 2002. *The Detroit Area Study: Celebrating 50 Years.* Ann Arbor: University of Michigan Press.

Cole, David. 2003. *Enemy Aliens: Double Standards and Constitutional Freedoms in the War on Terrorism.* New York: The New Press.

Davila, Arlene. 2001. *Latinos, Inc.: The Making and Marketing of a People.* Berkeley: University of California Press.

de la Cruz, G. Patricia, and Angela Brittingham. 2003. "The Arab Population: 2000." Census 2000 Brief. Washington: U.S. Bureau of the Census.

Dudziak, Mary, ed. 2003. *September 11 in History: A Watershed Moment?* Durham, N.C.: Duke University Press.

Espiritu, Yen Le. 1992. *Asian American Panethnicity.* Philadelphia: Temple University Press.

Ewing, Katherine, ed. 2008. *Being and Belonging: Muslims in the United States Since 9/11.* New York: Russell Sage Foundation.

Farley, Reynolds, Maria Krysan, and Mick Couper. 2006. "Attitudes about Arab-Americans: Detroiters' Views." Paper presented at the Sixty-First Annual Conference of the American Association for Public Opinion Research. Montreal, Canada (May 16–18).

Fischer, Claude S., Michael Hout, and Jon Stiles. 2006. "How Americans Prayed: Religious Diversity and Change." In *Century of Difference,* edited by Claude Fischer and Michael Hout. New York: Russell Sage Foundation.

Flores, William V., and Rina Benmayor. 1997. "Constructing Cultural Citizenship." In *Latino Cultural Citizenship: Claiming Identity, Space, and Rights,* edited by William V. Flores and Rina Benmayor. Boston: Beacon Press.

Garcia, Jorge. 2000. *Hispanics/Latinos in the United States: Ethnicity, Race, and Rights.* New York: Routledge.

Goffman, Erving. 1963. *Stigma.* Englewood Cliffs, N.J.: Prentice Hall.

Hagopian, Elaine, ed. 2004. *Civil Rights in Peril: The Targeting of Arabs and Muslims.* Ann Arbor, Mich.: Pluto Press.

Hammar, Tomas. 1989. "Comparing European and North American International Migration." *International Migration Review* 23(3): 631–37.

Hartmann, Douglas, and Joseph Gerteis. 2005. "Dealing with Diversity: Mapping Multiculturalism in Sociological Terms." *Sociological Theory* 23(2): 218–40.

Heisler, Martin. 2001. "Now and Then, Here and There: Migration and the Transformation of Identities, Borders, and Others." In *Identities, Borders, Orders: Rethinking International Relations Theory,* edited by Mathias Albert, David Jacobson, and Yosef Lapid. Minneapolis: University of Minnesota Press.

———. 2005. "Introduction—Changing Citizenship Theory and Practice: Comparative Perspectives in a Democratic Framework." *Political Science and Politics* 38(4): 667–70.

Higham, John. 2002. *Strangers in the Land: Patterns of American Nativism 1860–1925.* New Brunswick, N.J.: Rutgers University Press.

Howell, Sally, and Andrew Shryock. 2003. "Cracking Down on Diaspora: Arab Detroit and America's 'War on Terror.' " *Anthropological Quarterly* 76(3): 443–62.

Huntington, Samuel P. 2004. *Who Are We?* New York: Simon and Schuster.

Ibish, Hussein, and Anne Stewart. 2003. "Report on Hate Crimes and Discrimination Against Arab Americans: The Post-September 11 Backlash." Washington, D.C.: American-Arab Anti-Discrimination Committee.

Irons, Peter. 1983. *Justice at War.* New York: Oxford University Press.

Jacobson, David. 1996. *Rights Across Borders: Immigration and the Decline of Citizenship.* Baltimore, Md.: Johns Hopkins University Press.

Jackson, Sherman. 2005. *Islam and the Blackamerican: Looking Toward the Third Resurrection.* New York: Oxford University Press.

Jamal, Amaney, and Nadine Naber, eds. 2008. *Race and Arab Americans and Race Before and After 9/11: From Invisible Citizens to Visible Subjects.* Syracuse, N.Y.: Syracuse University Press.

Joseph, Suad. 1999. "Against the Grain of the Nation—The Arab." In *Arabs in America: Building a New Future,* edited by Michael Suleiman. Philadelphia: Temple University Press.

Kymlicka, Will. 1995. *Multicultural Citizenship: A Liberal Theory of Minority Rights.* New York: Oxford University Press.

Lowe, Lisa. 1995. *Immigrant Acts: On Asian American Cultural Politics.* Durham, N.C.: Duke University Press.

Maddox, Richard. 2004. "Intimacy and Hegemony in the New Europe." In *Off Stage/On Display: Intimacy and Ethnography in the Age of Public Culture,* edited by Andrew Shryock. Palo Alto, Calif.: Stanford University Press.

Marshall, Thomas H. [1950]1964. "Citizenship and Social Class." In *Class, Citizenship, and Social Development.* New York: Doubleday.

McAlister, Melani. 2001. *Epic Encounters: Culture, Media, and U.S. Interests in the Middle East, 1945–2000.* Berkeley: University of California Press.

McCarus, Ernest, ed. 1994. *The Development of Arab American Identity.* Ann Arbor: University of Michigan Press.

Modood, Tariq. 2005. *Multicultural Politics: Race, Ethnicity, and Muslims in Britain.* Minneapolis: University of Minnesota Press

Naber, Nadine. 2005. "Muslim First, Arab Second: A Strategic Politics of Race and Gender." *The Muslim World* 95(4): 479–95.

———. 2006. "The Rules of Forced Engagement: Race, Gender, and the Culture of Fear Among Arab Immigrants in San Francisco Post-9/11." *Cultural Dynamics* 18(3): 235–67.

Omi, Michael, and Howard Winant. 1994. *Racial Formations in the United States: From the 1960s to the 1990s.* New York: Routledge.

Ong, Aihwa. 1996. "Cultural Citizenship as Subject Making: Immigrants Negotiate Racial and Cultural Boundaries in the United States." *Current Anthropology* 37(5): 737–62.

———. 2003. *Buddha is Hiding: Refugees, Citizenship, the New America.* Berkeley: University of California Press.

Pakulski, Jan. 1997. "Cultural Citizenship." *Citizenship Studies* 1(1): 73–84.

Park, Robert E. 1950. *Race and Culture.* Glencoe, N.Y.: Free Press.

Park, Robert E., and Herbert A. Miller. 1921. *Old World Traits Transplanted.* Chicago: University of Chicago Society for Social Research.

Read, Jen'nan Ghazal. 2007. "Multiple Identities and Post 9-11 Discrimination." In *Race and Arab Americans and Race Before and After 9/11: From Invisible Citizens to Visible Subjects,* edited by Amaney Jamal and Nadine Naber. Syracuse, N.Y.: Syracuse University Press.

Reimers, David. 1998. *Unwelcome Strangers: American Identity and the Turn Against Immigration.* New York: Columbia University Press.

Rodriguez, Richard. 2003. *Brown: The Last Discovery of America.* New York: Penguin.

Rosaldo, Renato. 1997. "Cultural Citizenship, Inequality, and Multiculturalism." In *Latino Cultural Citizenship: Claiming Identity, Space, and Rights,* edited by William V. Flores and Rina Benmayor. Boston: Beacon Press.

Saito, Natsu. 2001. "Symbolism under Siege: Japanese American Redress and the 'Racing' of Arab Americans as 'Terrorists.'" *Asian Law Journal* 8(1): 1–12.

Salaita, Steven. 2006. *Anti-Arab Racism in the USA: Where It Comes from and What It Means for Politics Today.* Ann Arbor, Mich.: Pluto Press.

Sassen, Saskia. 1996. *Losing Control? Sovereignty in an Age of Globalization.* New York: Columbia University Press.

Schlesinger, Jr., Arthur A. 1991. *The Disuniting of America: Reflections on a Multicultural Society.* New York: W. W. Norton.

Schopmeyer, Kim. 2000. "A Demographic Portrait of Arab Detroit." In *Arab Detroit: From Margin to Mainstream,* edited by Nabeel Abraham and Andrew Shryock. Detroit, Mich.: Wayne State University Press.

Shryock, Andrew. 2004. "In the Double Remoteness of Arab Detroit: Reflections on Ethnography, Culture Work, and the Intimate Disciplines of Americanization." In *Off Stage/On Display: Intimacy and Ethnography in the Age of Public Culture,* edited by Andrew Shryock. Palo Alto, Calif.: Stanford University Press.

Silvestrini, Blanca G. 1997. "The World We Enter When Claiming Rights." In *Latino Cultural Citizenship: Claiming Identity, Space, and Rights,* edited by William V. Flores and Rina Benmayor. Boston: Beacon Press.

Solomos, John. 2001. *Culture and Citizenship*. London: Sage Publications.

Soysal, Yasemin. 1994. *Limits of Citizenship: Migrants and Postnational Membership in Europe*. Chicago: University of Chicago Press.

———. 1997. "Changing Parameters of Citizenship and Claim Making: Organized Islam in European Public Spheres." *Theory and Society* 26(4): 509–27.

Suarez-Orozco, Marcelo, and Mariela Paez, eds. 2002. *Latinos: Remaking America*. Berkeley: University of California Press.

Suleiman, Michael, ed. 1999. *Arabs in America: Building a New Future*. Philadelphia: Temple University Press.

Takaki, Ronald. 1989. *Strangers from a Different Shore: A History of Asian Americans*. New York: Penguin.

Taylor, Charles. 1991. "Shared and Divergent Values." In *Options for a New Canada*, edited by Ronald Watts and Douglas Brown. Toronto: University of Toronto Press.

———. 2001. "Democracy, Inclusive and Exclusive." In *Meaning and Modernity: Religion, Polity and the Self*, edited by Richard Madsen, William M. Sullivan, Ann Swidler, and Steven M. Tipton. Berkeley: University of California Press.

Traugott, Michael W., Robert M. Groves, and Courtney Kennedy. 2002. "How Americans Responded: Public Opinion after 9/11/01." Paper presented at the Fifty-Seventh Annual AAPOR Conference. St. Pete Beach, Fl. (May 17).

Turner, Bryon S. 2001. "Outline of a General Theory of Cultural Citizenship." In *Culture and Citizenship*, edited by Nicholas Stevenson. London: Sage Publications.

United Nations Development Programme. 2003. *Human Development Report*. New York: Oxford University Press.

Warner, William Lloyd, and Leo Srole. 1945. *The Social Systems of American Ethnic Groups*. New Haven, Conn.: Yale University Press.

Waters, Mary. 1999. *Black Identities: West Indian Immigrant Dreams and American Realities*. New York: Russell Sage Foundation.

Weglyn, Michi. 1976. *Years of Infamy: The Untold Story of America's Concentration Camps*. New York: Morrow.

Wu, Frank. 2003. *Yellow: Race in America Beyond Black and White*. New York: Basic Books.

PART I

Community in Crisis

CHAPTER 2

Arab American Identities in Question

Andrew Shryock and Ann Chih Lin

Detroit's Arab communities have attracted global attention not only for their size, age, and cultural vibrancy, but also for their symbolically charged location between the West and the Arab Muslim world. As a geopolitical interface, located at the edges of what are widely believed to be civilizations in a state of clash, Arab Detroit is valuable (and often contested) territory. It is courted by politicians, investigated by the media, tapped by ethnic marketers, developed as a tourist destination and a conduit for overseas trade, monitored by U.S. government agencies, and studied by social scientists. Until the 1990s, however, very few people outside Michigan knew anything about its Middle Eastern immigrant and ethnic groups. In 1983, Sameer and Nabeel Abraham began their groundbreaking study, *Arabs in the New World*, by noting that Arab Americans were, until recently, "largely unnoticed in American society":

> The reasons behind their lack of visibility lay partly in their small numbers relative to most ethnic groups in America and partly in the fact that they were generally well integrated, acculturated, and even assimilated into mainstream society. If Arab-Americans as a group had an ethnic presence at all, it was on the local level, in the vaguely defined "Little Syrias" which formed part of the larger ethnic quilt that characterized much of urban-industrial America (Abraham and Abraham 1983, 1).

When these words were written, Arabic-speaking immigrants had been coming to Detroit for a hundred years. They were no longer a small population, and the harsh glare of Middle East politics had already turned them into an object of local fascination and concern. Beginning in the 1960s, a complex array of regional conflicts—between Israel and neighboring Arab states, between Egypt and Saudi Arabia, between Iraq and Iran, between U.S. client states and their enemies—brought thousands of new immigrants to greater Detroit. According to the U.S. Census, there were 52,800 people of Arab descent living in the region in 1980. By 1990, the figure had risen to 62,699. By 2000, when their census numbers had reached 124,263, Detroit's Arab communities were locally prominent and influential, but it was still possible to claim, as did the editors of *Arab Detroit: From Margin to Mainstream,* that "Metropolitan Detroit is home to one of the largest, most diverse Arab communities outside the Middle East, yet the complex world Arabic-speaking immigrants have created there is barely visible on the landscape of ethnic America" (Abraham and Shryock 2000, back cover). After September 11, 2001, this assessment came quickly to sound like the wisdom of a bygone era. Arab Detroit was suddenly a focus of national anxiety. It was highly visible, even overexposed, but its residents could not always control how they were depicted in national and international media. Being seen did not mean being understood.

The ease with which people now acknowledge Detroit's Arab American community—routinely calling it "the" community, as if it were a cohesive, unified constituency—is not merely a by-product of the 9/11 attacks. Arab Detroit's notoriety is based instead on a peculiar concentration of historical trends. As we argued in chapter 1, Arab and Muslim Americans have attained high visibility before, almost always in moments of political crisis, during which they are cast as a vulnerable, potentially threatening population. This powerful association with crisis and political threat obscures the extent to which Arab and Muslim Americans, both today and in the past, have adjusted quite effectively to life in the American mainstream. The story of Arab American identity, and likewise the story of Arab Detroit, is one in which a practical sense of American national belonging is continually undermined by suspicion and geopolitical conflict, especially when demand for "authentically American" Arabs and Muslims is high.

In this chapter, we consider several ways in which the realities of Arab American socioeconomic integration are rendered invisible, or irrelevant, by a crisis orientation that determines how Arabs and Muslims can enter American multicultural politics and how they can represent themselves as both generic citizens and members of a distinctive ethnic group. This process has been shaped by U.S. foreign policy, by dominant hierarchies of ethnicity and race, and by the organizing skills of local activists and community advocates who, in responding to these forces, have built the infrastructure of Arab American identity in Detroit over the last forty years. The 9/11 attacks intensified the interaction of these factors, each of which has a unique history and logic. To understand the dynamic relationship between citizenship and crisis in Arab Detroit, this history (of identity) and logic (of community) need first to be explored.

MAKING IDENTITY (IN) PUBLIC

Like most ethnic communities that have attained wide recognition, Arab Americans in Detroit can be plotted on maps. They can be treated as a population with densities, growth rates, and varying estimates of size. As a rule, such communities are described using ecological metaphors. They come in waves, enter niches, evolve over generations, and adapt to new environments. This naturalizing language implies that ethnic communities automatically appear wherever and whenever their members settle in large numbers. We think it is more helpful to consider ethnic communities as products of sustained, intentional, creative effort. They have leaders and members, stakeholders and interests. They are marked by unity and internal disagreements, and they are even said to have views and beliefs that must be communicated widely so that members of the larger society can know them. As a community of this kind, Arab Detroit is continually made and remade through a collaborative process akin to public performance. It is not a group of people recognized simply because they are "really out there," or because they have a shared culture, or because they seem different from other Americans. As this chapter will show, there are countless ways in which Arab Americans are not similar to each other, are not different from other Americans, and are not "really out there" in quite the ways (stereotypical or commonsensical) they are thought to be.

The terms *Arab* and *American* carry diverse historical associations, and combining the two produces a hyphenated identity whose expressive potential is vast. Most of this potential is never explored; much of it is constrained by assumptions about what Arabs and Americans can be. In Detroit, the expressive potential of Arab American identity is narrowed and expanded constantly.

When we say this process is public and performed—that it unfolds, quite literally, on stages and screens, in books, newspapers, museums, public opinion polls, and in the process of democratic governance—we do not mean to imply that Arab Americans are without private lives, or habitual behaviors they take for granted, or beliefs and attitudes they do not share with strangers. Like other people, Arab Americans live much of their lives in settings that might be described as in-group and "off stage" (Shryock 2004), in "back regions" (Goffman 1959), and characterized by "cultural intimacy" (Herzfeld 2004). These settings are rich sites of identity formation in Arab Detroit; much scholarship has already been done in them, and we will make reference to this work throughout our chapter.

The Detroit Arab American Study (DAAS), by contrast, was constructed in ways that make other kinds of knowledge possible. As scholarship, its significance lies in its ability to bring a marginal zone, defined as Arab and American and poorly understood, into a highly authoritative, mainstream context of evaluation: the social scientific survey. Whether one accepts the claims to objectivity and rigor that predictably accompany this type of knowledge production, its power as a form of collective representation in contemporary societies is impossible to ignore. The DAAS was conceptualized, and explicitly presented to its funders and potential subjects, as a chance to gauge Arab American views on a wide range of topics and to disseminate reliable information about their community. Interviewees were generally sympathetic to these goals—a factor that explains the survey's 74 percent response rate—and most participants realized that their answers would be translated into public knowledge that might change how members of the larger society perceive them.

In short, the DAAS findings are ideally suited to the analysis of Arab American identity in its most public forms. Because citizenship is itself public in character, and is commonly understood as a kind of identity (and not simply a legal status), we can treat Arab American identity and larger, more general models of citizenship as discourses that intersect in the American public sphere, sometime overlapping neatly, sometimes generating troublesome contradictions. The bulk of this chapter is devoted to the analysis of Arab Detroit as a social field, a community, in which certain forms of identity enter the public domain and become key elements of a specifically Arab American citizenship. This process is clearly visible when Arab Americans are placed in demographic frameworks used to measure social status and cultural belonging in the United States. To show how Arab Detroit has assumed its current shape over time, we have created three backdrops against which both nuanced and generalized aspects of Arab American identity can be discerned: immigrant characteristics (attachments and attributes people bring to the United States), incorporation measures (how people adapt to life in the United States), and ethnoracial identifications (labels people use to define themselves in the United States).

The demographic analysis we offer here treats Arab Americans in much the way other ethnoracial groups are treated by social scientists, but it also shows why a specific history of political crisis has made treatment of this kind unusual, and inadequate, in the Arab American case. Citizenship is a moral project rooted in notions of loyalty, collective values, the equality of persons, and commitment to shared political goals; for this reason, our analysis of Arab Detroit's internal composition will have a double purpose. At one level, it produces a reliable demographic portrait of a population whose contours are frequently distorted in popular media. At another level, it explains how particular regimes of cultural citizenship are producing a highly distinctive ethnoracial community made up of equally distinctive subcommunities, all of them marked (and moralized) by a problematic relationship to American identity. The numerical data and the moral projects are locked in a conversation we would like to listen to carefully, and perhaps amplify, to improve our understanding of what is being said, and why.

Backdrop 1: Immigrant Characteristics

Despite their long tenure in the United States, Arab Americans are widely perceived as an immigrant population. American-born Arabs often take offence at this image, especially when it is used to paint all Arabs in the United States as alien, but the percentage of foreign-born Arab Americans has been rising for decades. Nationwide, according to the 2000 census, the figure is now 54 percent. In Detroit, the trend is more pronounced—75 percent of DAAS respondents were born overseas. Because those under eighteen were not included in the study, however, we can safely assume that American-born Arabs are more numerous in Detroit than our figure suggests. Still, the centrality of new immigration to the creation and maintenance of Arab American identity is impossible to ignore. Much of the early and most influential scholarship on Arab Americans engages directly with the immigrant experience (Younis 1961; Aswad 1974; Kayal 1975; Abraham and Abraham 1983; Naff 1985; Hooglund 1987; Orfalea 1988). Likewise, the field of Arab American letters is replete with memoirs, poetry, and novels that explore the lives of immigrants (see Orfalea and Elmusa 1988; Kadi 1994; Majaj 1996; Mattawa 2000; Kaldas and Mattawa 2004). Scholars and artists are not unlike lay people in their fascination with the experience of arrival. The differences, imagined and real, between relatives born in the United States and those who grew up in Arab countries can be elaborately catalogued by Arab Americans (Ajrouch 1999, 2004). When people came to the United States, where they came from, why they came, and who else in their family is coming are standard topics of conversation in Arab Detroit.

Although they express this belief in diverse ways, most Arab Americans subscribe to the popular notion that key aspects of personal and group identity are brought to the United States from homelands and that being more or less American is a matter of relative distance (in time and space) from foreign points of origin and foreignness in general. The following characteristics—country of origin, time spent in the United States, religion, and gender—are especially significant and, as we will see, they play a fundamental role in determining the kind of citizen an Arab immigrant is likely to become.

COUNTRY OF ORIGIN   Arab Detroit is not a miniaturized version of the Arab world (see figure 2.1). Only six of the Arab League's twenty-two member states have sizeable immigrant populations in Detroit. Seventy-two percent of DAAS respondents trace their origins to Lebanon, Syria, or Iraq. Those from Palestine, Jordan, and Yemen account for 21 percent. Lebanese/Syrians are the single largest group (37 percent), followed closely by Iraqis (35 percent), then Palestinians/Jordanians (12 percent), and Yemenis (9 percent). The remaining 7 percent are from other Arab countries or have plural origins that typically include ancestors from one or more of the four largest national groups.

TIME IN THE UNITED STATES   Detroit's Arab and Chaldean population is simultaneously old and new. The city's Syrian Colony was well established by 1900, when it was featured in a *Detroit Free Press* article on February 6. The community's first church was built in 1916; its first mosque, in 1921 (see chapter 4). Descendants of these early Lebanese and Syrian immigrants still live in Detroit, but they are a small portion of the larger Arab American community, which has doubled in size since the 1980s, principally as a result of new migration.

Social scientists commonly speak of first-, second-, and third-generation Americans and associate particular beliefs and practices with each category

Figure 2.1   Country of Origin

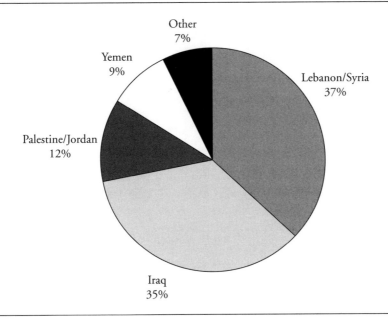

Source: Baker et al. 2004.

(Portes and Rumbaut 2001; Alba and Nee 2003). This approach has numerous drawbacks, including its inability to assess differences in real time spent in America. What, for example, do we make of a nineteen-year-old, third-generation Arab American who grew up in Beirut, or his seventy-year-old, first-generation Arab American grandmother, who was born in Beirut, but has lived continuously in the United States since she was five years old? Despite obvious kinks in generational models, it is still widely assumed among Arabs in Detroit, and among scholars who study them, that time spent in America and being born in the United States have crucial effects on a person's identity and opportunities. The elaborate jargon Arab Americans use to describe each other as newer or older shows how important time on the ground can be. Detroit is home to thousands of "American borns," "Amreeks," "born heres" (BHs), "born theres" (BTs), "old liners," "boaters," "Arab Arabs," "American Arabs," "real Arabs," "immigrants," and "FOBs" (fresh off the boats).

To assess the effects of time in the United States, we have divided the DAAS sample into first-, second-, and third-generation cohorts (see figure 2.2). The

Figure 2.2   Generation and Decade of Arrival in United States

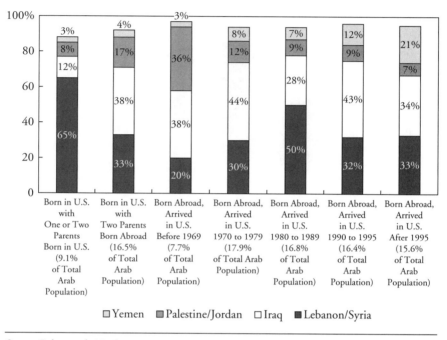

Source: Baker et al. 2004.

third generation, made up of individuals born in the United States with one or two parents also born in the United States, represents only 9 percent of Arab Detroit. The second generation, individuals born in the United States with two parents born abroad, is 17 percent. The first generation, those born abroad, is the largest group numerically, so we have broken it down by decade: arrived in United States before 1969 (8 percent), between 1970 and 1979 (18 percent), between 1980 and 1989 (17 percent), between 1990 and 1995 (16 percent), and after 1995 (16 percent).

Note that 67 percent of Detroit's adult Arab and Chaldean population arrived after 1970. Overall, the community is remarkably new. Temporally, the oldest, most well-established national subgroup is the Lebanese/Syrians; the newest are the Yemenis. DAAS respondents of Lebanese or Syrian ancestry are 31 percent U.S.-born, followed by Palestinians/Jordanians (27 percent), Iraqis (21 percent), and Yemenis (11 percent). Of the 91 third-generation Arab Americans in our sample, 65 percent are Lebanese or Syrians. By con-

Figure 2.3   Religion

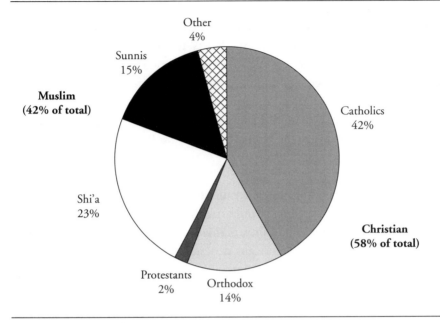

Source: Baker et al. 2004.

trast, more than half of Yemenis (58 percent) are immigrants who arrived after 1990.

RELIGION   In matters of religious affiliation, as with national origin, Arab Detroit is by no means representative of the Arab world (see chapter 4). Roughly 95 percent of Arabs living in the Middle East are Muslim, whereas those living in greater Detroit are majority Christian. About 58 percent of DAAS respondents are Christian and 42 percent are Muslim (see figure 2.3). The general non-Arab population in the Detroit area is more Christian (81 percent) but far less Muslim (only 2 percent). Twelve percent of the larger population belongs to other religious traditions, or claims no religious affiliation at all, whereas fewer than 1 percent of Arabs and Chaldeans do not identify as Christian or Muslim. Among Arab Christians, Catholics are the largest group (73 percent), followed by Orthodox (24 percent), and Protestants (3 percent). Arab Muslims have a Shi'i majority (56 percent), whereas Sunnis, who make up the vast majority of Muslims in the Arab countries and worldwide, are 35 percent.

Yemenis are the most Muslim of the national subgroups at 98 percent, followed by the Lebanese/Syrians (66 percent), the Palestinians/Jordanians (18 percent), and the Iraqis (11 percent). In terms of U.S. residence, Christians are temporally the older community. Thirty-two percent of Christians were born in the United States, versus only 15 percent of Muslims. Among DAAS respondents who are second- and third-generation American citizens, 75 percent are Christian. Among immigrants, the percentage of Christians has declined over time and that of Muslims has risen. Christians represent 86 percent of those who came to the United States before 1970, but only 28 percent of those who arrived after 1996.

GENDER   The immigrant experience differs markedly for males and females, and prevailing models of gender and sexuality—which affect job and educational opportunities, social mobility, marriage choice, and religious practice—vary greatly among Arab Americans depending on when a person came to the United States, from what country of origin, and from what religious background (Aswad and Bilge 1996; Shakir 1997; Abdulhadi, Naber, and Alsultany 2005). The DAAS sample is 46 percent male and 54 percent female. Gender distributions are similar for the immigrant characteristics already discussed; variations between men and women become apparent against the identity backdrop we develop next.

Backdrop 2: Incorporation Measures

Issues of adaptation and incorporation are the bread and butter of ethnoracial politics in the United States, and a ubiquitous subtext for talk of citizenship as well. When people discuss integration, both in scholarly circles and among lay people, they tend to emphasize political status, class position, and cultural belonging. Money and membership are handy gauges for measuring incorporation because they allow for easy, mechanical comparisons between "us" and "them." "Them," in most cases, is other ethnoracial populations—Latinos, Asians, whites, African Americans, and so on—or the larger society, a "them" that does (and does not) include "us." The essentially comparative, competitive nature of this analytical backdrop says important things about American identity, which we will explore shortly. For now, we focus on four points of comparison—legal citizenship, language acquisition, education, and income—that are widely assumed to enhance (or diminish) a sense of practical citizenship and belonging to the national community.

LEGAL CITIZENSHIP   Among Arab Americans, U.S. citizenship is a highly prized status. It opens up new job and educational opportunities, provides new legal protections, enables people to bring kin to the United States, and, in many cases, makes travel within and outside the United States easier. Although 75 percent of DAAS respondents were born outside the United States, more than 79 percent are U.S. citizens. By contrast, 90 percent of Detroit's general population is American-born and 95 percent claim U.S. citizenship. The importance of U.S. citizenship to Arab Americans is evident not only in that so many of them have it, but also in that, controlling for time of arrival, citizenship rates do not differ by country of origin, religion, or gender. Nearly everyone, it seems, wants to be a citizen. Time, however, is a crucial factor in itself. More than 90 percent of immigrants who have been in the United States since 1989 are now American citizens. Sixty-nine percent of those in the United States between eight and thirteen years have received citizenship— a very high percentage, given that five years must elapse between becoming a permanent resident and applying for citizenship.

LANGUAGE ACQUISITION (ENGLISH FLUENCY)   Ability to speak English is essential to full participation in U.S. society. The American economy, its political and educational systems, popular media, and cultural mainstream are hegemonically Anglophone. In Detroit, Arab Americans are already part of this mainstream. Eighty-three percent say they speak English very well or well. Figures for reading (78 percent) and writing (74 percent) English very well or well are only slightly lower. At the same time, an overwhelming majority (85 percent) say they speak a language other than English at home (see figure 2.4). For 69 percent, this other language is Arabic, but 14 percent speak dialects of Aramaic (variously referred to as Chaldean, Assyrian, Athury, or Aramaic) instead. Another 13 percent speak both Arabic and an Aramaic dialect, and the remaining 4 percent speak Arabic along with another third language (French, Spanish, or Greek, to name just a few). These rates of multilingualism are much higher than the average for the Detroit area: in the general population, only 12 percent speak a second language at home, with Arabic and Spanish (each representing just under 3 percent) being the most commonly spoken.

EDUCATION   The benefits of education—of a high school diploma or a college degree—are preached from nearly every rostrum of American public

Figure 2.4   Second Language at Home

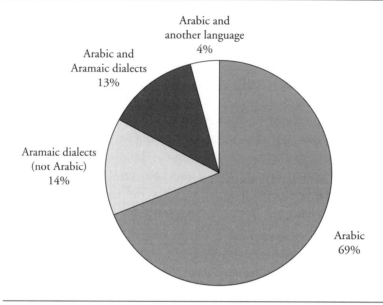

Source: Baker et al. 2004.

opinion, and most Americans take it as an article of faith that less education means less opportunity. The extent to which growing up in America changes educational opportunities is evident in the DAAS results (see figure 2.5). Among American-born Arabs and Chaldeans, only 6 percent are not high school graduates, whereas more than one-third of those born abroad (36 percent) have not completed high school. Seventy-three percent of the American born have acquired at least some college education, a 29 percentage point differential compared to immigrants. Yemenis are the least likely to have higher education (only 4 percent do), followed by Iraqis (16 percent), then by Palestinians/Jordanians (26 percent), and Lebanese/Syrians (28 percent). Men are substantially more likely than women to have higher education.

Twenty-nine percent of DAAS respondents, versus 13 percent of the general population, do not have a high school degree. Fourteen percent have college degrees and 9 percent report advanced degrees (versus 17 percent and 10 percent in the overall population). Rates of college and advanced degrees among American-born Arabs and Chaldeans are about the same as the general population.

Figure 2.5   Education by Place of Birth

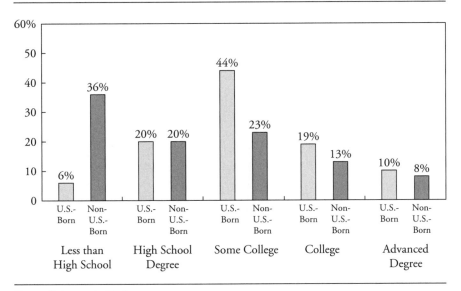

Source: Baker et al. 2004.

INCOME   Immigrants and their children tend to be overrepresented among both the poorest and the wealthiest of Americans, and Arabs are no exception (see figure 2.6). The relatively high number of Arabs and Chaldeans without a high school degree is reflected by the 25 percent with an annual family income of less than $20,000. The proportion of the general population that is this poor is 7 percentage points lower. On the other hand, 25 percent report total family incomes of $100,000 or more per year, compared to 16 percent in the larger population. Arabs and Chaldeans born in the United States are more affluent still: 40 percent report an annual total family income of $100,000 or more, and only 8 percent report less than $20,000 a year.

Uncommon Denominators

Backdrop 1 (immigrant characteristics) and backdrop 2 (incorporation measures) play critical roles in Arab American identity formation. They narrow the meaning of Arab and American in ways that are useful to individuals and groups, yet they also represent divisions and (invidious) distinctions that can make collective action, and pan-Arab solidarities, hard to achieve. In Detroit, it is clear that a wealthy, college-educated, Anglophone, Christian, third-generation

Figure 2.6   Total Family Income in Metropolitan Detroit

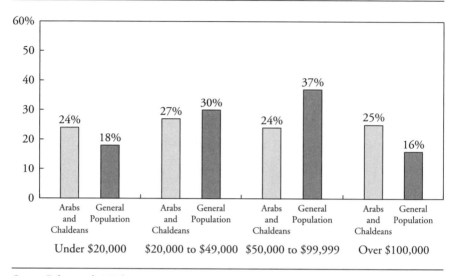

Source: Baker et al. 2004.

Lebanese American man is located in social fields dramatically unlike those open to a poor, Arabic-speaking, Muslim, first-generation, Yemeni immigrant woman who is neither a high school graduate nor a U.S. citizen. These individuals cannot speak to each other without a translator; they do not live in the same neighborhood; they would encounter great resistance from their families if they tried to marry each other. In all likelihood, their paths will never cross. Yet, as we will see, odds are very good that both believe they are Arab Americans, that they belong to a community, and that they share a broad range of sensibilities and attachments.

Backdrops 1 and 2 also expand the meaning of Arab and American in ways that are useful and complicated. Whatever our Yemeni woman and Lebanese man have in common as Arab Americans, it is clear that they have just as much and perhaps more in common with other people who live in the United States. They belong to larger Christian and Muslim communities that cannot be described simply as Arab. They have values and skills that connect them to working-class Americans or to suburban professionals. The Lebanese man posts comments on the *New York Times* website; the Yemeni woman shares food and babysitting responsibilities with her Bangladeshi and African American

neighbors. In short, their immigrant characteristics and incorporation measures make them part of communities and identity spaces filled with non-
Arabs. Their personal location within these larger, overlapping social fields is
what makes them part of American society, which is empirically diverse and
plural. Yet only the Lebanese man would seem (to most readers of this chapter) to be living in the mainstream, a cultural domain that is less diverse and
less plural than most Americans like to admit.

Statistical analyses underscore the extent to which entrance into the
American mainstream is shaped by just a few characteristics. As illustrated in
table 2.1, English fluency and educational achievement are consistently lower
for Iraqis and Yemenis. Although a slightly larger proportion of men than
women are fluent in English, once other factors are controlled, being male
actually predicts less fluency. English fluency increases with time in the United
States, and it in turn predicts education and income. Education and income,
unsurprisingly, predict each other; more surprisingly, being Muslim significantly increases the probability of having the lowest, rather than the highest,
household income even after controlling for education. Being born in the
United States or having American citizenship has exactly the opposite effect.
Demographic variations within the Arab and Chaldean communities are thus
significant predictors of life chances. Despite these differences, however, Arab
Americans are often portrayed—and portray themselves—as sharing a common experience of inclusion or marginalization from America society.

A third backdrop, ethnoracial identification, provides the ideological tools
needed to close the gaps, and limit the tactical possibilities, created by backdrops 1 and 2. In learning to think of themselves as Arab American, or white,
or racially "other," people of diverse national, religious, socioeconomic, and
linguistic backgrounds learn to represent themselves, and to be represented,
using identity labels that make sense to millions of Americans. Fluent, con-
vincing use of these labels is proof of Americanization, because little of this terminology is brought to the United States from Arab homelands.

Backdrop 3: Ethnoracial Identification

Ethnic and racial identities are indispensable features of American life. People
are expected to have one, and those who explicitly deny having one are thought
to be unusual, politically and personally. Some racial identities—white, black,
Asian, American Indian or Alaska Native, Pacific Islander—are officially recognized by the U.S. government and are used in counting Americans, distributing

Table 2.1   Coefficients from Regression of English Fluency, Education, and Income on Immigrant Characteristics (Backdrop 1) and Incorporation Measures (Backdrop 2)

	English Fluency (Immigrants Only)	Education				Income		
		Less than High School	High School	Some College	College Degree	Less than $20,000	$20,000 to $49,999	$50,000 to $99,999
Iraqi	-1.17*	2.84***	1.16*	1.39**	.41	.35	-.25	-.35
	(.535)	(.800)	(.576)	(.530)	(.546)	(.569)	(.442)	(.413)
Yemeni	-1.52**	3.73***	1.82*	-.96	-.87	.19	.03	-.82
	(.579)	(1.085)	(.919)	(.899)	(1.094)	(.667)	(.565)	(.620)
Palestinian	.11	2.50**	1.25	1.04	.75	-.23	-.26	-.21
	(.633)	(.872)	(.652)	(.611)	(.620)	(.637)	(.484)	(.447)
Lebanese/Syrian	.17	2.16**	.45	.47	-.17	.18	-.11	-.28
	(.548)	(.792)	(.553)	(.503)	(.513)	(.570)	(.436)	(.404)
U.S. Citizen	—	-.59	-.42	-.49	-.21	-1.12***	-.92**	-.28
		(.508)	(.510)	(.496)	(.529)	(.309)	(.307)	(.347)
U.S.-Born	—	-.81	.52	1.06***	.45	-1.24***	-.83***	-.37
		(.439)	(.352)	(.325)	(.357)	(.324)	(.245)	(.222)
Muslim	-.86**	-.59	-.19	.10	.14	.79**	.20	-.05
	(.292)	(.409)	(.388)	(.364)	(.392)	(.309)	(.271)	(.267)
Male	-.70***	.98**	.79**	.64*	.29	.001	.06	-.03
	(.206)	(.317)	(.304)	(.287)	(.313)	(.227)	(.205)	(.202)
Years in U.S.	.05***	—	—	—	—	—	—	—
	(.010)							

English fluency	—	-17.76***	-15.99***	-15.28***	-14.9***	-.82**	.28	1.35**
		(.592)	(.627)	(.655)	(.000)	(.316)	(.377)	(.475)
Income $50,000 +	—	-3.08***	-2.75***	-2.33***	-2.13***	—	—	—
		(.494)	(.486)	(.655)	(.496)			
College	—	—	—	—	—	-2.00***	-1.04***	-.51*
						(.355)	(.242)	(.219)
Constant	2.56***	17.42***	17.12***	16.59**	16.56***	1.57*	1.13	-.34
	(.638)	(1.162)	(1.051)	(1.039)	(13.29)	(.738)	(.640)	(.713)
R^2	.229			.399			.282	
N	706			856			856	

Source: Authors' compilation.

Notes: English fluency is a dummy variable, 1 = speaking English well or very well, 0=speaking English not very well or not well at all. The coefficients result from a binary logit model. Results for reading English and writing English are similar, and thus not shown here. Because 99 percent of those born in the U.S. report speaking English well or very well, this analysis is performed only for immigrants.

The coefficients result from a multinomial logit model, where the reference category is education = advanced degree (post-BA).

The coefficients result from a multinomial logit model, where the reference category is total family income = $100,000 +.

Years in U.S. is a continuous variable, measured by years since immigration to the United States.

When used as an independent variable, income is measured as a dummy variable, family income >$50,000 = 1 and family income <$50,000 = 0. Results are consistent with income measured as a four-category variable (under $20,000, $20,000 to $49,999, $50,000 to $99,999, and $100,000 +).

When used as an independent variable, education is measured as a dummy variable, BA or higher =1, less than a BA = 0. Results are consistent with education measured as a five-category variable (less than a high school diploma, high school graduate, some college, BA, and advanced degree).

Nagelkerke R^2

*** $p < .001$, ** $p < .01$, * $p < .05$. Standard errors in parentheses.

resources, and monitoring patterns of discrimination, social inequality, and achievement. The massive effort the U.S. Census puts into updating and analyzing its racial categories—which divide 300 million Americans into only five groups, with a residual slot for "other"—is proof enough that what we call race is a creation of the political process. In 2000, census coders managed to define 92 percent of Americans as belonging to one of the five named racial categories; 6 percent were identified as belonging to some other race; and only 2 percent claimed to belong to more than one race (U.S. Bureau of the Census 2001). These figures suggest that there are real consequences, socially and politically, for citizens who cannot be located, or cannot locate themselves, on the existing ethnoracial grid (Shryock 2008).

DAAS findings suggest that Arab Americans and Chaldeans cannot be neatly placed on American ethnoracial grids. They are far more likely to identify as other than most people in Detroit, and 30 percent reject Arab American identity altogether, even though many of these rejecters speak Arabic, were born in Arab countries, and have close friends and family who do identify as Arab Americans. This ambiguity reflects, more tellingly than any other factor, the vulnerable location this population occupies in the politics of American citizenship. Our analysis of backdrop 3 centers on race and ethnicity as labeling devices. Because these concepts are used to categorize U.S. citizens and sort them into nominally distinct groups, we give our closest attention to the sorting terms used to describe individuals and groups in publicly acceptable ways—namely, identity labels that are officialized either by their appearance on government forms or by their appearance in the names of Arab and Muslim organizations—and the labels individuals embrace as alternatives to public, official identities.

ETHNICITY   The DAAS includes two questions that address ethnic identification, and each acknowledges that Arab American is not the only label people in our sample use to explain who they are: "Do you feel the term *Arab American* describes you? Is there any other term like *Arab American* that better describes you?" If respondents said yes to the second question, they were asked to specify.

A solid majority of DAAS respondents were willing to call themselves Arab American. Seventy percent said the term describes them, but 30 percent wanted to be called something else. People offered roughly 100 alternative identities when asked if there were "another term, like Arab American, that

Figure 2.7   Percentage Accepting Arab American by Country of Origin and Religion

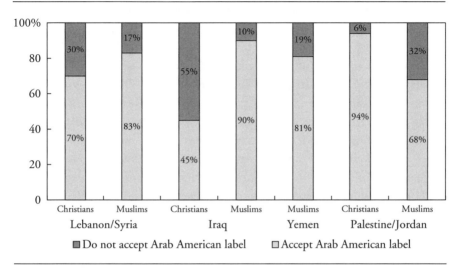

Source: Baker et al. 2004.

describes you better." Their responses included Chaldean, just American, Iraqi, Egyptian Christian, Arabic, Lebanese American, American Lebanese, and other permutations of national, regional, and religious labels.

Christians were less likely than Muslims to accept the Arab American label, and this distinction is related to the large number of Christians who are of Iraqi origin (see figure 2.7). Although 61 percent of all Christians in the DAAS sample thought the term described them accurately, only 45 percent of Iraqi Christians did. Iraqi Christians in the Detroit area are mostly Chaldean Catholics, an Aramaic and Arabic-speaking group whose leaders and organizations are known locally for insisting on their non-Arab status. If Chaldeans are factored out of the sample, the proportion of DAAS respondents who accept Arab American identity rises to more than 80 percent. Moreover, half of all Chaldeans born abroad accept the Arab American label; it is American-born Chaldeans who, at 74 percent, overwhelmingly reject it. By contrast, only 30 percent of Christians from Lebanon and Syria (mostly Maronites) and Egypt (mostly Copts) wanted to be called something other than Arab American. Muslims, regardless of national origin, welcomed the term. More than 80 percent said it described them.

With the exception of Iraqis, half of whom resist the Arab American label, more than 75 percent of those from Yemen, Palestine/Jordan, and Lebanon/Syria embrace it. Citizens and noncitizens accept the label at a rate of 70 percent; the same is true of those born in the United States (71 percent) and those born abroad (66 percent). In statistical analyses, the appeal of Arab American identity seems not to be affected by levels of income or education, by levels of English fluency, or by citizenship and birthplace. Table 2.2 shows that only being Muslim or Palestinian significantly increases the potential for accepting an Arab American identity. As a platform on which to build panethnic solidarities, Arab American identity currently has no rival in Detroit. Yet, in its most generic and inclusive forms, Arab Americanness contains, overlaps, and is frequently at odds with dozens of identity options that do not privilege Arabness, Chaldean being the most prominent.

RACE   The DAAS examined racial identities by first asking a question drawn from the U.S. Census: "What is your race? (Check all that apply): 1. White; 2. Black, African American, or Negro; 3. American Indian or Alaska Native; 4. Asian; 5. Pacific Islander; 6. Other (Specify)." (U.S. Bureau of the Census 2003)

Arabs are officially defined as white by the U.S. Census—80 percent were coded as such in the 2000 census (U.S. Bureau of the Census 2003)—but not all Arab Americans accept or are even aware of this status. Scholars who study Arab American identity have shown how flexible and contested the labels applied to Arabic-speaking immigrants have been over the last century, ranging from Asian to Semite to Caucasian (Samhan 1999; Naber 2000; Gaultieri 2001). To avoid forced categorizations, the DAAS race question was analyzed

Table 2.2   Coefficients from Regression of Arab American and White Racial Identity on Immigrant Characteristics (Backdrop 1) and Incorporation Measures (Backdrop 2)

	Arab American Identity	White Racial Identity
Iraqi	−1.045** (.360)	−.224 (.365)
Yemeni	−.449 (.466)	−.144 (.445)
Palestinian	1.102* (.459)	−.059 (.397)
Lebanese/Syrian	.053 (.369)	.427 (.366)

Table 2.2   (continued)

	Arab American Identity	White Racial Identity
U.S. citizen	.281 (.221)	.410* (.208)
U.S.-born	−.127 (.210)	−.009 (.216)
Muslim	.739*** (.232)	−.747** (.258)
Male	−.044 (.166)	−.219 (.164)
English fluency	−.217 (.269)	.066 (.252)
Family income		
Less than $20,000	.265 (.268)	.728** (.261)
$20,000 to $49,999	.192 (.235)	.080 (.230)
$50,000 to $99,999	.387 (.233)	.620** (.238)
Education		
Less than high school	.136 (.361)	−.627 (.378)
High school	.190 (.350)	−.545 (.369)
Some college	−.157 (.327)	−.648 (.353)
College degree	.057 (.362)	−.202 (.383)
Dearborn resident	—	−.953*** (.226)
Complexion		
Dark	—	−1.406*** (.331)
Medium	—	−.897*** (.169)
Constant	.777 (.571)	1.809** (.587)
R^2	.184	.220
N	844	827

Source: Authors' compilation.

Notes: Arab American identity is a dummy variable, 1 = "The term 'Arab American' describes me" and 0 = "The term 'Arab American' does not describe me." The coefficients come from a binary logit model.

White racial identity is a dummy variable, 1 = "white" checked in answer to the question, "What is your race?" and 0 = "white" not checked. The coefficients come from a binary logit model.

Family income is measured as a four-category variable; the reference category is income = $100,000+.

Education is measured as a five-category variable; the reference category is education = advanced degree.

Complexion is determined by the interviewer's assessment of the respondent's complexion in three categories: dark or very dark, medium, and light or very light. The reference category is complexion = light or very light.

Nagelkerke R^2

*** $p < .001$, ** $p < .01$, * $p < .05$. Standard errors in parentheses.

Figure 2.8   Racial Identity

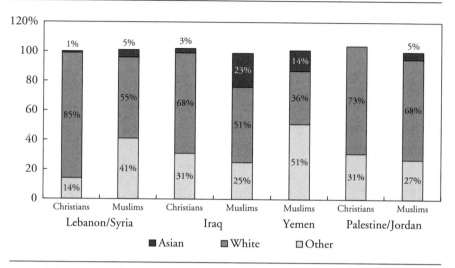

Source: Baker et al. 2004.

Note: Percentages do not add up to 100 percent because some people chose more than one identity.

differently from that asked by the U.S. Census. The DAAS did not recode write-in responses—Arab, Palestinian—as white when the respondent did not check the white box. A DAAS respondent who described herself as other, then specified that she was Iraqi, would not be placed in the white category (as she would be by U.S. Census coders) but would be recorded as other (and Iraqi).

The choice of white or other is not random (see figure 2.8). Well over 90 percent of Arab Americans chose one of these two identities, but only 2 percent chose both. Those choosing two identities are counted in both categories. The 64 percent majority who identified as white were more likely to be Christians and to live in middle- and upper middle-class suburbs, interspersed among a white majority population. The 33 percent who identified as other were more likely to live in the heavily concentrated Muslim enclaves of Dearborn, Dearborn Heights, and adjacent neighborhoods. In the Dearborn area, 46 percent of respondents called themselves other, versus 27 percent who live elsewhere. Whereas 73 percent of Christians identify as white, only 50 percent of Muslims do.

Religion and residence are not the only important variables. Arabs and Chaldeans born in America, and those with U.S. citizenship, are more likely to identify as white than noncitizens and those born abroad. Also, those who said the label Arab American does not describe them were more likely to identify as white (71 percent); among those who accepted the Arab American label, only 60 percent considered their race white. Country of origin produces marked differences in racial identification. Only 36 percent of Yemenis call themselves white, whereas 66 percent of both Lebanese/Syrians and Iraqis do. The highest levels of whiteness are found among Palestinians, 72 percent of whom describe themselves using this term.

The preference for white or other is nearly exclusive. Only 6 percent of Arabs and Chaldeans called themselves Asian. Only two individuals said they were black. When asked to specify what kind of other they might be, most DAAS respondents suggested variants of Arab (43 percent), Middle Eastern (29 percent), or Chaldean (16 percent). A smaller number (9 percent) opted for a national identity, with Lebanese (4 percent) being the most common. In short, individuals who chose other were sending two clear messages: they do not consider themselves white, and they do not accept the racial categories on offer in the U.S. Census. It is worth noting that, in a control sample of 508 members of greater Detroit's general population, 68 percent of respondents identified as white, a figure only four percentage points higher than the Arab sample. In Detroit, it is preference for "otherness" that makes Arabs highly unusual. Only 3 percent of Detroit's larger population described themselves as other.

Regression analyses show that the determinants of racial identification are substantially and surprisingly different from the determinants of ethnicity. Although country of origin is an important predictor of Arab American identity (for Iraqis and Palestinians), it is not significant for racial identity controlling for additional predictors. Instead, table 2.2 shows that income, darker complexions, and residence in Dearborn or Dearborn Heights are the most significant predictors of racial identity. The only significant predictor in common for ethnicity and race is Islam: Muslims are more likely to consider themselves Arab American and less likely to consider themselves white.

TWO ZONES OF ARAB AMERICAN CITIZENSHIP

Having set our three backdrops in place, we are now better equipped to understand the social fields in and across which Arab American citizenship is developing in Detroit. First, it is clear that Arab Detroit consists of several communities at once, each with a distinctive relationship to things Arab, things American, and things Arab American. The DAAS findings suggest two large, partially overlapping zones in which heavy identity construction has already been done.

The larger of the two zones (in area, population size, and temporal presence) can be portrayed as Christian, suburban, and likely to identify as white. It has a higher percentage of American-born members and people who have spent more time in the United States. Incomes are generally higher here, as are education levels, and fewer people speak English poorly. Lebanese, Syrians, Iraqis, Palestinians, and Jordanians predominate in this zone.

The other Arab Detroit is smaller (in area, population size, and temporal presence) but highly visible and politically prominent. This second zone can be portrayed as Muslim, residing predominantly in or near Dearborn and Detroit, and more likely to identify as other. The foreign-born are more numerous here, as are those who have spent less time in the United States. Incomes are generally lower, as are education levels. More Arabic is spoken in this zone, and more people have limited fluency in English. Lebanese Muslims and Yemenis predominate in this zone.

One could argue—as many Arab Americans in Detroit do (Shryock and Abraham 2000)—that the inhabitants of zone 1 are substantively closer to the American mainstream, whereas the inhabitants of zone 2 are widely perceived as outsiders who must prove they are American. It is hardly coincidental that the public performance of Arab American identity is carried out more elaborately, and with greater urgency, in zone 2. The most prominent and effective Arab American institutions—ACCESS (Arab Community Center for Economic and Social Services), ADC (American-Arab Anti-Discrimination Committee), the Arab American National Museum, two of the largest mosques in North America, the *Arab American News,* the Arab International Festival, and the American Arab Chamber of Commerce—are all located in Dearborn, which has been dubbed, in popular media, the capital of Arab America.

Arab Americans who live outside the Dearborn area, about 70 percent of the DAAS sample, are also invested in their identities; they too have a vigorous organizational scene. Yet for all its churches, social clubs, journals, newspapers, cable television shows, and social service agencies, zone 1 has a surprisingly low profile. It is seldom compelled to be publicly Arab—and it cannot be publicly Muslim—in the way zone 2 is compelled to be. This relative invisibility can itself be taken as proof that zone 1, self-identified as white and Christian, is more securely located in the American mainstream. Although it is no longer exclusively Christian or white, most Arab immigrants correctly assume that the mainstream is not hospitable territory for Muslims or for Arabs who consciously identify as other. The statements of Arab American leaders frequently confirm this view. In an op-ed piece written by James Zogby, head of the Arab American Institute, the scrutiny aimed at Arab Americans by journalists after the 9/11 attacks is cast as an opportunity to (re)assert the Americanness of Arabs living in the United States (2001). Note what counts as evidence of diversity.

> Arab Americans are being discovered, or should I say being rediscovered, by the same papers and networks that have discovered us twice before in just the past decade. As I speak to those assigned to do the story, they discover yet again the diversity of my community. The fact that we are not a new ethnic group in America (we've been here for 120 years), that most Arab Americans are not Muslims (in fact, only 20% are). That most Arab Americans are not recent immigrants (in fact, almost 80% are born in the U.S.). And that many Arab Americans have achieved prominence and acceptance in America (two proud Arab Americans, Spencer Abraham and Mitch Daniels, serve in President [George W.] Bush's cabinet, and Donna Shalala served in Bill Clinton's cabinet) (Zogby 2001).

The numbers, proportions, and terminologies are all debatable, but Zogby's narrative is flawless in its ability to map out the terrain of mainstream acceptance many Arab Americans would like to enter and many already occupy. In directing our attention to the American born, the Christian, the well established, and the politically incorporated, Zogby replicated perfectly the characteristics that prevail in zone 1. By contrast, the Arab communities Zogby set up as his implicit points of contrast are new, Muslim, born overseas, unknown, accented, and culturally peculiar. This profile corresponds closely to Detroit's zone 2. It is zone 2 that, as Zogby would predict, attracts greater attention (both favorable and hostile) from politicians, mass media, federal authorities, and the public at large. Ironically, the prominence and acceptance enjoyed by the Arab Americans of zone 1 is enhanced and, at the same time, threatened by the stigmatized traits that mark off zone 2 as other.

To complicate matters, Detroit's zone 1 is home to tens of thousands of Iraqi Americans who reject Arabness entirely. The Chaldean community might even be considered a zone 3, historically and culturally distinct from the others, but carving out this jurisdiction would require that we overlook the many Chaldeans, Assyrians, Syriacs, and other Iraqi Christians (roughly 45 percent) who are willing to identify as Arab Americans. It would also require us to ignore the fact that half of all Chaldeans speak Arabic, that Chaldeans have come from and maintain active ties to a nation-state that has an Arab majority culture, and that many of Detroit's secular Arab American organizations, even those associated with or dominated by Muslims, have prominent Chaldean members. The Chaldeans of Detroit, in their vexed stance toward Arabness, which ranges from active acceptance to vehement rejection, are best understood as a border community. They are neither historically nor culturally separate from the larger Arab populations that surround them in Detroit and Iraq. They insist on their separateness, however, when Arabness threatens them, either as a stigmatized identity associated with Muslims in the United States or as an oppressive and Muslim-dominated majority culture in Iraq. They also take offense when their ancient pre-Islamic heritage, often described as Babylonian or Assyrian or Christian, is ignored by members of the larger society, who quickly assume Chaldeans, like so many other Iraqis and Arabic-speaking immigrants, are Arab Muslims.

CRITICAL ASPIRATIONS
AND COMMON DESIRES

The existence in Arab Detroit of at least two distinct zones of identity formation has not resulted in a polarized, functionally divisive community. Instead, these populations are held together by a cohesive sociopolitical matrix. Whatever their individual and group particularities might be, the majority of DAAS respondents are U.S. citizens (79 percent); most call themselves Arab American (70 percent); and most are foreign born (75 percent). If community, as Gerald Creed recently suggested, "is an aspiration envisioned as an entity" (2006, 22), what are the aspirations that enable so many inhabitants of Detroit to see themselves as part of an entity called "the Arab American community"? Answers to this question are on display in the open-ended responses DAAS respondents gave when asked to list three pressing needs facing the local Arab and Chaldean community. About 21 percent said they wanted the larger society to understand them better in order to fight stereotypes and foster a less hostile environment for Arabs in America. Sixteen percent said the community needs to achieve better representation in the media and government to attain these goals. Twenty-seven percent expressed a desire to keep Arab culture alive in America and build stronger cultural institutions.

The latter category also included those who called for greater Arab and Chaldean unity and wanted more community gatherings. Twenty percent said unity between Arabs and non-Arabs in the Detroit area was a pressing need, and many called for programs that educate people about cultural issues. Many said Arabs and Chaldeans should try harder to accept American culture and assimilate or be open to life in mainstream society.

Framed as needs, this wish list is a concise manifesto of community-generating aspirations. Its desires are rooted in shared experiences of foreignness (real and assumed), citizenship (as a legal status and a contested identity), and Arabness (as a source of pride and stigma). Whether they can be easily sorted into zone 1 or zone 2, most DAAS respondents want to be recognized as U.S. citizens or to become citizens, they want to manage their cultural differences in a language of mutual respect, and they want to be seen as simultaneously American and Arab. These desires are the common cloth of multicultural pluralism. They are hardly unrealistic ambitions. Other Americans of immigrant and ethnic backgrounds would immediately understand these aspirations, as would members of polite society, a trend-setting elite whose political and economic investments in diversity are now vast. Yet for Arab Americans, open access to the cultural mainstream is consistently denied, and many Americans (including members of polite society) think Arabs—especially Muslim Arabs—are being unrealistic when they ask to be treated like everyone else. This discontinuity in our national ideology of multicultural inclusion is a direct outgrowth of U.S. foreign policy in the Middle East, and complicates the Arab American experience by adding to it a set of immigrant characteristics that have politicized the community in debilitating ways.

The heavy flow of immigrants to Detroit that began in the late 1960s was not simply a result of the liberalized immigration laws that, since 1965, have brought millions of people to the United States from Asia, Africa, and Latin America. For Arabs, this flow was also triggered, and has been periodically increased, by complicated, often horrific, geopolitical events. Many Palestinian are in Detroit today because Israel, with U.S. support, has occupied their home villages, displaced local populations, and made life in Gaza and the West Bank increasingly unbearable for Arabs (Seikaly 1999). Many Lebanese are in Dearborn because of a bloody civil war, in which the United States had its proxies, and several U.S.-backed Israeli invasions and occupations of southern Lebanon (Aswad 1992). Many Yemenis came to Detroit to escape a civil war (in which the United States backed the loser), then to escape border conflicts between North and South Yemen (the United States supported the North), then to avoid a civil war between northern and southern factions in the Yemeni government (Abraham 1978; Friedlander 1988; Sarroub 2005). Many Iraqis came to Detroit to escape persecution under Saddam Hussein's Ba'ath regime (which the United States supported for many years) and to avoid Saddam's disastrous Gulf Wars (one against Iran, two against the United States); others came as refugees after participating in a failed, U.S.-instigated uprising against Saddam; others still are in Detroit because U.S. sanctions against Iraq (and its present occupation of that country) have led to economic collapse, pervasive violence, and civil war (Walbridge and Aziz 2000; Sengstock 1982, 2005).

In short, Arabs and Chaldeans in Detroit belong to larger, transnational communities that have been adversely affected by U.S. foreign policy. Throughout the cold war, this policy was distinguished by its strong support for Israel, its backing of autocratic oil states and client regimes, and its opposition to Arab nationalism and other popular sovereignty movements in the Middle East. Since then, these policies have expanded to include direct U.S. military occupation of Arab and Muslim lands. Insofar as Arab and Muslim people have resisted U.S. policy, they have been consistently portrayed in U.S. news and entertainment media as enemies (Abraham 1994; Stockton 1994; Shaheen 2001). Arab-Israeli wars, oil embargoes, the 9/11 terror attacks, armed struggle against U.S. forces in Iraq and Afghanistan, support for Hizbullah or Hamas—these and other forms of organized resistance to U.S. and Israeli interests in the region have effectively turned "the Arabs" and "the Muslims" into cultural enemies—even when most Arab and Muslim regimes are U.S. allies, even when forms of resistance to U.S. policy are not morally equivalent and not uniformly supported by Arabs and Muslims. Unless they loudly and insistently declare their loyalty to the United States, and because they are expected to do so, Arab Americans are associated with cultural others, with a hostile civilization that is said to reject the liberation of women, oppose religious freedom, hate democracy, deny Israel's right to exist, refuse the separation of church and state, and that cannot therefore be treated as modern. These classically Orientalist assumptions have been subject to intense critique for more than thirty years, by authors ranging from Edward Said (1978) to Melani McAlister (2001), but they remain firmly in place, and they have become even more ornate in their current role as ideological props for the war on terror (see Mamdani 2004).

Before World War II, when the United States did not have extensive imperial interests in the Arab world and before its principal ally in the region, Israel, had been established as a nation-state, Detroit's Arabic-speaking immigrants did not figure as a politically sensitive population, nor did they need to build infrastructure for a durable, panethnic Arab identity. Except for a handful of mosques and churches, none of the institutions and organizations that represent Arab Americans in Detroit today existed before 1970, and the term Arab American was itself seldom used. People were more likely to call themselves Syrian or Lebanese and, before the 1970s, were more likely to *be* Syrian or Lebanese. In Detroit, most of these early immigrants (and certainly their children) came to think of themselves as white and ethnic—akin to Italians, Jews, Irish, and Poles—and they became de facto Americans just as predictably, facing similar indignities and discriminations and opportunities, as other immigrants admitted to provisional forms of whiteness.

In a historical process now well known to scholars and community activists, Arab American identity began to take its current shape in the aftermath of the 1967 Arab-Israeli War, in response to a U.S. cultural and political climate that was increasingly anti-Arab and anti-Muslim (Suleiman 1994; Terry 1999; Ahmed 2006). After forty years in the enemy box, many Arab Americans have lost, and many have explicitly rejected, their hold on normative whiteness, a status that functions well as an index of their hold on normative American citizenship. This transformation has left vivid traces in the DAAS findings. It explains why Muslim Arabs are more likely to identify as other than Christians Arabs are, and why second-generation Arab Americans, regardless of religious affiliation, are more likely to call themselves other than immigrants are (a choice that reflects a pervasive sense of alienation and in-betweenness). The same process also explains why Arabs who have lived in the United States for longer periods, have parents born in America, speak English well, and are not Muslim, are more likely to see themselves as white, and why those who see themselves as white are less likely to call themselves Arab American. As a site of identity formation, Arab Detroit is caught between margin and mainstream, its mood an ambivalent mix of pride and stigma, influence and exclusion, recognition and invisibility. These contradictions make Arab Detroit a difficult place to represent, especially for scholars and activists who want to represent it either as a place of victimization and fear or as an economic and political success story. It is both. In zone 1, zone 2, and in the spaces between them, it is both.

CONCLUSION: CITIZENSHIP IN CRISIS, CITIZENSHIP AS CRISIS

Within this larger historical context, the 9/11 attacks and the backlash that followed were not radical, transformative moments for Arab Americans, their community, or their sense of identity. Instead, 9/11 was an unusually intense episode in a series of crises that have come to define Arabness and Islam in America. The rich organizational and institutional landscape of Arab Detroit, which is discussed in more detail in chapter 3, has served well as a defensive shield against crisis, and has grown stronger with repeated use. As a public good, one might liken this community network to scar tissue; it is protective, often stronger than the tissue it replaces, but it remains clear evidence of a wound. Edward Said, in one of his final essays, confessed that "I don't know a single Arab or Muslim American who does not now feel that he or she belongs to the enemy camp and that being in the United States at this moment provides us with an especially unpleasant experience of alienation and widespread, quite specifically targeted hostility" (Gabriel 2002, 23). This pessimism might seem inconsistent with certain DAAS findings—namely, that 86 percent of those interviewed agreed that they feel at home in America, or that 91 percent agreed that they were proud to be American—but these positive responses can also be viewed as the public flip side of Said's personalized estrangement. The deep ambivalences that structure the DAAS findings are evident in the life experience of Said himself, an Arab Christian who felt acutely marginal even though he was affluent, highly educated, successful, politically influential, culturally privileged in almost every calculable way, and admired around the globe. Like Said, the Arab Christians of Detroit's zone 1 are never far from stigma; they cannot and usually do not wish to disengage from the political struggles that place them—alongside the Arab Muslims of zone 2—on "the wrong side" of U.S. foreign policy. In Detroit, Arab American identity and the community organizations that have grown up around it are unifying expressions of this widely shared experience.

A binary or doubled sense of belonging and exclusion is a leitmotif of minority consciousness in the United States. Among Arab Americans, this sensibility does not end in second-class citizenship. It calls citizenship into question (Joseph 1999; Howell and Shryock 2003; Shryock 2004). Because Arabs and Muslims cannot be neatly classed as us or them—because they might be us and them—they exist in a "state of exception." According to Giorgio Agamben, this paradoxical condition materializes when boundaries lose their ability to divide and contain.

The exception is that which cannot be included in the whole of which it is a member and cannot be a member of the whole in which it is always already included. What emerges in this limit figure is the radical crisis of every possibility of clearly distinguishing between membership and inclusion, between what is outside and what is inside, between exception and rule (Agamben 1998, 25).

The crisis defined so precisely here is akin to challenges that confront Arabs and Chaldeans in Detroit. They are seen by others, and often see themselves, as being in the United States but not of it, as being of the Arab world but not in it (Abraham 1989). As limit figures, they are denied a credible sense of normative citizenship, yet they are expected to display their (suspect) American identity publicly, incessantly, and convincingly. In chapters to come, we examine these themes in closer detail, in hopes of unsettling some of the assumptions that make Arab American citizenship so difficult to imagine and achieve.

REFERENCES

Abdulhadi, Rabab, Nadine Naber, and Evelyn Alsultany, eds. 2005. "Gender, Nation, and Belonging: Arab and Arab American Feminist Perspective." *The MIT Electronic Journal of Middle East Studies* (Spring). Available at: http://web.mit.edu/cis/www/mitejmes/intro.htm.

Abraham, Nabeel. 1978. *National and Local Politics: A Study of Political Conflict in a Yemeni Immigrant Community of Detroit, Michigan.* Ann Arbor, Mich.: University Microfilms.

———. 1989. "Arab-American Marginality: Mythos and Praxis." In *Arab Americans: Continuity and Change,* edited by Baha Abu-Laban and Michael Suleiman. Belmont, Mass.: Association of Arab-American University Graduates Press.

———. 1994. "Anti-Arab Racism and Violence in the United States." In *The Development of Arab American Identity,* edited by Ernest McCarus. Ann Arbor: University of Michigan Press.

Abraham, Nabeel, and Andrew Shryock, eds. 2000. *Arab Detroit: From Margin to Mainstream.* Detroit, Mich.: Wayne State University Press.

Abraham, Sameer, and Nabeel Abraham, eds. 1983. *Arabs in the New World: Studies on Arab-American Communities.* Detroit, Mich.: Wayne State University Press.

Agamben, Giorgio. 1998. *Homo Sacer: Sovereign Power and Bare Life.* Palo Alto, Calif.: Stanford University Press.

Ahmed, Ismael. 2006. "Michigan Arab Americans: A Case Study of Electoral and Non-electoral Empowerment." In *American Arabs and Political Participation,* edited by Philippa Strum. Washington: Woodrow Wilson International Center for Scholars.

Ajrouch, Kristine. 1999. "Family and Ethnic Identity in an Arab American Community." In *Arabs in American: Building a New Future,* edited by Michael Suleiman. Philadelphia: Temple University Press.

———. 2004. Gender, Race, and Symbolic Boundaries: Contested Spaces of Identity among Arab American Adolescents. *Sociological Perspectives* 47(4): 371–91.

Alba, Richard, and Victor Nee. 2003. *Remaking the American Mainstream: Assimilation and Contemporary Immigration.* Cambridge, Mass.: Harvard University Press.

Aswad, Barbara, ed. 1974. *Arabic Speaking Communities in American Cities.* New York: Center for Migration Studies.

———. 1992. "The Lebanese Muslim Community in Dearborn, Michigan." In *The Lebanese in the World: A Century of Emigration,* edited by Albert Hourani and Nadim Shehadi. London: I. B. Tauris.

Aswad, Barbara, and Barbara Bilge, eds. 1996. *Family and Gender Among American Muslims: Issues Facing Middle Eastern Immigrants and Their Descendants.* Philadelphia: Temple University Press.

Baker, Wayne, Sally Howell, Amaney Jamal, Ann Chih Lin, Andrew Shryock, Ronald Stockton, and Mark Tessler. 2004. "Preliminary Findings from The Detroit Arab American Study." Ann Arbor: University of Michigan Institute of Social Research and University of Michigan–Dearborn Center for Arab American Studies.

Creed, Gerald, ed. 2006. *The Seductions of Community: Emancipations, Oppressions, Quandries.* Santa Fe, N.M.: School of American Research.

Friedlander, Jonathan, ed. 1988. *Sojourners and Settlers: The Yemeni Immigrant Experience.* Berkeley: University of California Press.

Gabriel, Judith. 2002. "Edward Said Speaks Out Before and After 9-11: Muffling the Arab Voice." *Aljadid* 8(39): 23, 26.

Gaultieri, Sarah. 2001. "Becoming 'White': Race, Religion and the Foundations of Syrian/Lebanese Ethnicity in the United States." *Journal of American Ethnic History* 20(4): 29–58.

Goffman, Erving. 1959. *The Presentation of Self in Everyday Life.* New York: Anchor.

Herzfeld, Michael. 2004. *Cultural Intimacy: Social Poetics of the Nation-State.* New York: Routledge.

Hooglund, Eric, ed. 1987. *Crossing the Waters: Arabic-Speaking Immigrants to the United States Before 1940.* Washington, D.C.: Smithsonian Institution Press.

Howell, Sally, and Andrew Shryock. 2003. "Cracking Down on Diaspora: Arab Detroit and America's 'War on Terror'." *Anthropological Quarterly* 76(3): 443–62.

Joseph, Suad. 1999. "Against the Grain of the Nation: The Arab." In *Arabs in America: Building a New Future,* edited by Michael Suleiman. Philadelphia: Temple University Press.

Kadi, Joanna, ed. 1994. *Food for Our Grandmothers: Writings by Arab American and Arab Canadian Feminists.* Boston: South End Press.

Kaldas, Pauline, and Khaled Mattawa. 2004. *Dinarzad's Children: An Anthology of Contemporary Arab American Fiction.* Fayetteville: University of Arkansas Press.

Kayal, Philip. 1975. *The Syrian-Lebanese in America: A Study in Religion and Assimilation.* Boston: Twayne Publishers.

Majaj, Lisa. 1996. "Two Worlds Emerging: Arab American Writing at the Crossroads." *Forkroads* 3(Spring): 64–80.

Mamdani, Mahmood. 2004. *Good Muslim, Bad Muslim: America, the Cold War, and the Roots of Terror.* New York: Pantheon.

Mattawa, Khaled. 2000. *Post-Gibran: Anthology of New Arab American Writing.* Bethesda, Md.: Kitab, Inc.

McAlister, Melani. 2001. *Epic Encounters: Culture, Media, and U.S. Interests in the Middle East, 1945–2000.* Berkeley: University of California Press.

Naber, Nadine. 2000. "Ambiguous Insiders: An Investigation of Arab American Invisibility." *Journal of Ethnic and Racial Studies* 23(1): 37–61.

Naff, Alixa. 1985. *Becoming American: The Early Arab Immigrant Experience.* Carbondale: The Southern Illinois University Press.

Orfalea, Gregory. 1988. *Before the Flames: A Quest for the History of Arab Americans.* Austin: University of Texas Press.

Orfalea, Gregory, and Sharif Elmusa. 1988. *Grape Leaves: A Century of Arab American Poetry.* Salt Lake City: University of Utah Press.

Portes, Alejandro, and Rubén Rumbaut. 2001. *Legacies: The Story of the Immigrant Second Generation.* Berkeley: University of California Press.

Said, Edward. 1978. *Orientalism.* New York: Random House.

Samhan, Helen. 1999. "Not Quite White: Racial Classification and the Arab-American Experience." In *Arabs in America: Building a New Future,* edited by Michael Suleiman. Philadelphia: Temple University Press.

Sarroub, Lukia. 2005. *All American Yemeni Girls: Being Muslim in a Public School.* Philadelphia: University of Pennsylvania Press.

Seikaly, May. 1999. "Attachment and Identity: The Palestinian Community of Detroit." In *Arabs in America: Building a New Future,* edited by Michael Suleiman. Philadelphia: Temple University Press.

Sengstock, Mary. 1982. *The Chaldean Americans: Changing Conceptions of Ethnic Identity.* New York: Center for Migration Studies.

———. 2005. *Chaldeans in Michigan.* East Lansing: Michigan State University Press.

Shaheen, Jack. 2001. *Reel Bad Arabs: How Hollywood Vilifies a People.* Northampton, Mass.: Interlink Publishing.

Shakir, Evelyn. 1997. *Bint Arab: Arab and Arab American Women in the United States.* Westport, Conn.: Praeger.

Shryock, Andrew. 2004. "In the Double Remoteness of Arab Detroit: Reflections on Ethnography, Culture Work, and the Intimate Disciplines of Americanization." In *Off Stage/On Display: Intimacy and Ethnography in the Age of Public Culture,* edited by Andrew Shryock. Palo Alto, Calif.: Stanford University Press.

———. 2008. "The Moral Analogies of Race: Arab American Identity, Color Politics, and the Limits of Racialized Citizenship." In *Race and Arab Americans Before and After 9/11: From Invisible Citizens to Visible Subjects,* edited by Nadine Naber and Amaney Jamal. Syracuse, N.Y.: Syracuse University Press.

Shryock, Andrew, and Nabeel Abraham. 2000. "On Margins and Mainstreams." In *Arab Detroit: From Margin to Mainstream,* edited by Nabeel Abraham and Andrew Shryock. Detroit, Mich.: Wayne State University Press.

Stockton, Ron. 1994. "Ethnic Archetypes and the Arab Image." In *The Development of Arab American Identity,* edited by Ernest McCarus. Ann Arbor: University of Michigan Press.

Suleiman, Michael. 1994. "Arab Americans and the Political Process." In *The Development of Arab American Identity,* edited by Ernest McCarus. Ann Arbor: University of Michigan Press.

Terry, Janice. 1999. "Community and Political Activism among Arab Americans in Detroit." In *Arabs in America: Building a New Future,* edited by Michael Suleiman. Philadelphia: Temple University Press.

U.S. Bureau of the Census. 2001. *Census 2000 Brief: Overview of Race and Hispanic Origin.* Washington: U.S. Department of Commerce.

———. 2003. *Census 2000 Brief: The Arab Population, 2000.* Washington: U.S. Department of Commerce.

Walbridge, Linda, and T. M. Aziz. 2000. "After Karbala: Iraqi Refugees in Detroit." In *Arab Detroit: From Margin to Mainstream,* edited by Nabeel Abraham and Andrew Shryock. Detroit, Mich.: Wayne State University Press.

Younis, Adele. 1961. *The Coming of the Arabic-Speaking People to the United States.* Ann Arbor, Mich.: University Microfilms.

Zogby, James. 2001. " 'Rediscovering' Arab Americans." Posted November 12. Available at: http://www.aaiusa.org/washington-watch/1587/w111201.html (accessed May 12, 2009).

CHAPTER 3

The Aftermath of the 9/11 Attacks

Sally Howell and Amaney Jamal

National and international media often turn their attention to Detroit when exploring connections between the United States and the Middle East. So too do federal authorities. In the immediate aftermath of the 9/11 attacks, the "special relationship" between Arab Detroit, the media, and law enforcement agencies intensified significantly. America was in crisis, and prevailing anxieties were felt by and projected onto Arab and Muslim citizens in unique ways. The Detroit suburb of Dearborn, with its heavy concentration of newly arrived Lebanese, Iraqi, Yemeni, and Palestinian immigrants, was an early target of investigation and concern. Here, journalists and Arab community leaders were already on a first-name basis, fear of a backlash was palpable, and an alleged sleeper cell was identified and raided within days of the attacks. Working-class mosques, colorful Arabic storefronts, women and girls wearing headscarves, and Arabic speakers gathering to watch al-Jazeera broadcasts made Dearborn an alluring backdrop for initial coverage of the war on terror. The images these stories purveyed, whatever the intentions of the reporters and their agencies, encoded two contradictory assumptions: that Detroit's Arab communities and their experiences after 9/11 were somehow representative of the experiences of Arab Americans nationwide, and that Detroit's Arab communities, by virtue of their visibility, accessibility, and concentrated otherness, were in fact exceptional to national patterns. In this chapter we examine the post 9/11 backlash in Detroit in light of both assumptions.[1]

The tension between Detroit as representative of Arab America and Detroit as exceptional to Arab America has a long history among Arab American activists and Arab Americanist scholars (Shryock and Abraham 2000). Like so much else concerning Arabs in America, this tension acquired a political urgency after 9/11 that has not waned. When President George W. Bush uttered his famous challenge on September 20, 2001, "Either you are with us, or you are with the terrorists,"[2] many in Michigan felt that the statement targeted their community quite specifically. Were local Arabs with us, or with the terrorists? County, state, and municipal officials, business leaders, and clergy rushed in to assure Arab Americans that their loyalty was not in doubt and that discrimination against local Arabs and Muslims would not be tolerated. Arab Detroiters donned protective American flags, held large, televised memorial services for the victims of the attacks, and issued strongly worded condemnations of the attacks and the motivations behind them. Although thousands of suddenly vulnerable Arabs suffered insults or abuse at the hands of their fellow citizens, thousands more received gestures of goodwill and support from non-Arab neighbors. These local experiences of protection and solidarity contrasted sharply with events transpiring on the national stage, where the president's challenge appeared to elicit a different response, where the USA PATRIOT Act was swiftly passed by Congress, and where Arab and Muslim Americans (as well as those who resembled them) suddenly found themselves humiliated on airplanes, detained and deported (if lacking citizenship) without legal counsel, and subjected to unprecedented surveillance and governmental scrutiny. It appeared that the federal government and national media both had less certain, and certainly less affirmative, answers to the president's challenge than leaders in Detroit had.

To frame Arab Detroit as exceptional, we must go beyond portraying it as a demographic anomaly and ask instead whether the local experience of the 9/11 backlash was qualitatively different from that experienced elsewhere. If the answer is yes, it is also imperative that we consider how and why Detroit achieved this exceptional status. In his cautionary analysis of the myth of American exceptionalism, Seymour Lipset pointed out that the city on the hill was never a beacon of freedom to all; rather, the rights and privileges of American citizenship have always been distributed unequally, based on racial and class formations held in place by dominant ideologies and by violence

(1996). We argue that Detroit's exceptionalism is also a double-edged sword that defies binary representations of Arab Americans as either proof of the American dream—of egalitarianism, the rule of law, and tolerance—or proof of the American nightmare—of discrimination, violence, and bigotry. Rather, it suggests a complex amalgam of both realities, in which ignorance, fear, and exploitation live side by side with solidarity, expediency, and progress. Arab Detroit is exceptional, we argue, because of the power of a local community—with its own local history and political culture—to insulate itself from a national public culture that sees Arabs (and Muslims) as a problem and has difficulty separating "good" Arabs from "bad."

Michigan's Arabs, through the work of myriad individuals and the efforts of many successful ethnic institutions, have been incorporated to a remarkable degree into local structures of economic, social, and political capital. At the national level, by contrast, Arabs have found their efforts to organize and influence governmental policies, especially foreign policies, blocked (Samhan 2006; Suleiman 2006). This power differential between local and national arenas, which has become more critical since 9/11, gives special significance to the question of Detroit's role as *an* Arab American community versus its role as exemplar of *the* Arab American community. Drawing on data from the Detroit Arab American Study, from national surveys, from conversations with Arab American community leaders,[3] and from our observations of local events, we will examine the social, political, and economic repercussions of the war on terror in Arab Detroit. Insofar as Detroit's experience in the aftermath of the 9/11 attacks was a departure from the norm, what are the factors that account for this difference? More critical, what are the consequences of this difference? Has the crisis experienced in Detroit since 9/11 threatened the security of this community's hard-won political profile? Given the size, longevity, and genuine incorporation of this diverse community, the question of its representational status has profound implications for the future of Arab and Muslim communities nationwide.

SETTING THE DEMOGRAPHIC STAGE: "MICHIGAN IS OUR NEW YORK"

Among scholars and Arab American community leaders, Detroit's exceptional nature has been highlighted for multiple, often conflicting purposes.[4] On the one hand, Detroit, and specifically Dearborn, is cast as the golden city of assimilationist desires, where, in the late 1990s, Arab Americans included in their ranks the CEO of Ford Motor Company, a U.S. senator, and the head of the United Auto Workers. At the same time, however, Detroit is home to a large number of recently arrived Arabs. Many have found success as professionals, or as gas station and liquor store owners. Many languish in low-income jobs, cleaning the homes of others, working as busboys in Detroit's casinos, providing nonunionized labor to Detroit's shrinking industrial sector, or driving ice cream trucks. Dearborn is often viewed as little more than an Arab ghetto, where pressure to Americanize is minimal and almost all one's social and consumer needs can be met in the Arabic language. Alternatively, Dearborn's thriving Lebanese business district has become a tourist destination for non-Arabs eager to sample the enclave's wares. Affluent suburban Arabs flock to Dearborn on weekends to shop for bargain vegetables, freshly butchered halal meat, and the delicacies of a half dozen bakeries. The Dearborn enclave has also produced two of the oldest, most influential mosques in America, along with the country's most celebrated Arab American community organization: ACCESS (the Arab Community Center for Economic and Social Services). These organizations have gained for Dearborn Arabs a measure of political clout and influence at the state level that is unrivaled elsewhere.

Arab Detroit is distinctive nationally largely because of its unique immigrant characteristics, bringing together old, well-established populations with a high percentage of the recently arrived. Chapter 2 analyzed some of the internal components of Arab American identity formation in Detroit, but Arab Detroit is unlike Arab America at the national level in many other ways as well. We explore several of Detroit's distinguishing features and analyze how these demographics have contributed to an exceptionally well-enfranchised ethnic American enclave.

Religion

Arab Detroit has far more Muslims than Arab America as a whole, and a larger percentage of Shi'a Muslims in particular. About 58 percent of Arabs and Chaldeans in Detroit identify as Christian, and 42 percent as Muslim. Among Arab Christians, Catholics are the largest group (73 percent), followed by Orthodox (24 percent), and Protestants (3 percent). Arab Muslims have a Shi'a majority (56 percent) and a Sunni minority (35 percent), though Sunnis make up the majority of Muslims in the Arab countries and worldwide. Arab Christians outnumber Arab Muslims in Detroit, as they do nationally, but the margin locally is not large. Muslim Arabs represent less than a third of Arabs nationwide (23 to 33 percent).[5]

Concentration

Arab Detroit contains America's best-known Arab immigrant enclave, Dearborn, where a large number of mostly Muslim Arabs live in very high concentration. No other American city includes such a highly visible and large Arab enclave. Arab Detroit is not famous simply for the size and diversity of its Arab communities. It is known primarily for the high concentration of Arabs, a solid 35 percent of the city's 99,000 residents who live in Dearborn (U.S. Bureau of the Census 2007). The adjacent township of Dearborn Heights and several Detroit neighborhoods that abut Dearborn are also home to sizable populations of Arabs. This immigrant enclave, with its thriving business districts, residential neighborhoods that are more than 90 percent Arab, old and new mosques, multitude of community activists, and well-known organizations has put Dearborn at the center, nationally and locally, of all things Arab American. This singular enclave, however, is by no means the totality of Arab Detroit. In fact, only 29 percent of the DAAS sample live in Dearborn and Dearborn Heights. Nine percent live in Detroit and Hamtramck, an enclave of growing significance, but the majority of local Arabs (62 percent) are scattered throughout Detroit's suburbs, typically in much smaller concentrations. In general, Muslims and Christians tend not to live in the same neighborhoods. About two-thirds of Arab Muslims (64 percent) live in the Dearborn area, whereas very few Christian Arabs (only 5 percent) do.

Affluence and Poverty

Arabs in Detroit are both richer and poorer than the general population. Compared to other Arab Americans nationally, those living in Detroit are less well educated and more recently arrived. Although nationally Arabs have achieved high educational and economic success, the heavily immigrant Arab population in Detroit (75 percent of adults), often arriving from rural and war torn regions of the Middle East, makes the economic and educational profile of Detroit distinctive. Only 72 percent of Arab Detroiters have high school degrees, compared to 88 percent of Arabs nationwide, and where more than 43 percent of Arab Americans nationally have a bachelor's degree or higher, only 23 percent in the Detroit area do (Arab American Institute Foundation 2006). The relatively high number of Arabs and Chaldeans without a high school degree is reflected in income figures. Twenty-four percent claim an annual family income of less than $20,000, compared to 18 percent of the general Detroit population.[6] On the other hand, 25 percent report annual family incomes of $100,000 or more, compared to only 16 percent in the larger population. Arabs and Chaldeans born in the United States are more affluent still: 36 percent report an annual family income of $100,000 or more, and only 7 percent report less than $20,000. Finally, Arabs and Chaldeans own their own businesses in greater numbers (19 percent and 14 percent respectively) and are more likely to be self-employed (31 percent and 16 percent). When compared to Arab Americans nationally, however, 37 percent of whom own their own businesses, Arab Detroiters look more like others in Detroit and less like Arab Americans in general (Arab American Institute 2002).

The socioeconomic gaps that divide those educated in the Middle East from those educated in the United States are stark and have led to a higher poverty rate among Arabs in Detroit than elsewhere. Yet the presence of an Arab working class in Detroit has had positive consequences for the population as whole. Low-income Arabs have two effective, increasingly prominent organizations that lobby for their concerns. ACCESS and the Arab American and Chaldean Council (ACC) opened their doors in the early 1970s in reaction to new immigration from distressed Arab countries and a series of economic downturns in the auto industry that had left immigrant workers vulnerable. Both ACCESS and ACC have built successful alliances between Arab immigrants in need, Arab immigrant professionals and human service providers, and American-born Arabs committed to community-based activism. Although many Arab and Chaldean service organizations have developed since the 1970s, ACCESS and ACC have the strongest track records. Each has an annual operating budget of more than $12 million, and each is well connected to state and local governments. These organizations bring together rich and poor, immigrant and American born, enclave dwellers and suburbanites, Christians and Muslims. More significant, they collaborate extensively with non-Arab organizations and governmental agencies in the Detroit area and nationally as well. They have done significant work to bring Arab Americans into the mainstream of local public culture (Howell 2000; Shryock 2004).

Public Service

Arab Detroit has an unprecedented number of elected officials, law enforcement officers, appointed government officials, and other public servants. Arab Detroiters are uniquely situated in positions of local power and influence. The City of Detroit, for example, is a border town, home to the Ambassador Bridge and the Detroit-Windsor Tunnel, which carry between them nearly one-third of all traffic crossing the U.S.-Canada border (Canada-U.S.-Ontario-Michigan Border Transportation Partnership 2004). The Ambassador Bridge is rare among American border crossings in that it is privately owned and operated. It is rarer still for being owned by an immigrant from Lebanon, Manuel Maroun. Likewise, when international travelers arrive at the Detroit Metropolitan Airport, they pass through a terminal bearing the name of another Lebanese American, former Wayne County Road Commissioner Michael Berry. Flight schedules and ground traffic at the airport are managed by Hassan Makled, director of Airfield Operations, who, like Berry, is a member of the Islamic Center of America.[7] All this coming and going is carefully monitored by Detroit and Wayne County Homeland Security Task Forces, both of which are led, in part, by Lebanese American law enforcement officers who are also Shi'a Muslims. These men are among more than sixty deputized Arab Americans in Wayne County alone, where Azzam Elder, a Palestinian American, was recently named deputy Wayne County executive and his wife, Charlene Makled Elder, a Lebanese American Muslim, now serves as a circuit court judge. The Elders are two of at least thirty-six Arab Americans in Michigan to hold political appointments, and the state is home to at least twenty-three Arab American judges and elected officials.[8] This list, with its perhaps surprising inclusion of Arab Americans who work for Homeland Security task forces, is perfectly mundane in Detroit. It does not include the much larger number of Arab Americans who sit on the boards of local hospitals and the United Way, serve as regents of state universities, or are active participants in the local ACLU (American Civil Liberties Union), UAW (United Auto Workers), Civil Rights Board, or many of the state's important nonprofit organizations. Although no other state can rival Michigan's high number of Arab public servants, similar patterns of community service by Arab Americans can be found across the United States.

Clearly, Detroit is quite unlike Arab America as a whole. It is more recently arrived, more bilingual, more Muslim, less well educated, has a higher percentage of economically marginal households, is home to the largest, most visible Arab American enclave, and its members have a higher level of representation in municipal, county, and state government. In the words of Ismael Ahmed, former director of ACCESS, "Michigan can and should be a model of political participation" (2006, 50), making it, in the words of another well-known Arab American activist, James Zogby, "our New York." But do these differences make Detroit exceptional to Arab America in other ways as well? Given, for instance, that many of Detroit's distinctive demographic features are associated nationally with increased vulnerability to hate crimes and discrimination, it should follow that Arab Detroiters were more vulnerable to the 9/11 backlash than other Arab Americans. We show, in the section that follows, that this was not the case. Likewise, we might assume that the federal crackdown on Arab and Muslim transnational networks, fueled in part by the PATRIOT Act (Howell and Shryock 2003), would have had a greater impact on Detroit's large immigrant and Muslim population. Our findings do not contradict this assumption, but suggest that the impacts are ambiguous and difficult to assess.

BACKLASH PART 1: ARAB AMERICAN SECURITY

9/11 occurred on a Tuesday. By Wednesday we started receiving phone calls in our mosque, at our parochial school on Ford Road, threatening to come bomb our buildings, kill the school kids in retaliation for 9/11. I have to admit that I got a little scared myself. . . . That was Wednesday. We shut the school down in the middle of the day. . . . By Thursday morning, then Sheriff Robert Ficano became aware of the threats that were being made to the most visible place probably in the country—Arab American Dearborn. . . . ACCESS started getting phone calls making threats, the mosques did, several of the mosques, some of the other organizations. You know the temperament of the country was—you had to take them seriously. . . . So Ficano and myself and a few other Arab officers got together and we called a meeting of the imams of all of the mosques in Dearborn and some of the surrounding mosques that border Dearborn in Detroit. . . . Ficano offered to set up protection for the mosques for the prayer that was coming up on Friday, the next day, and it was agreed. What we did is we went out and sought volunteers from the sheriff's department who would work a few hours every Friday, beside their regular shift, at the various mosques. We did that and we were able to put at least two police officers at every mosque in Dearborn for the Friday prayer and every mosque that requested it. (Ronald Amen, former Wayne County deputy sheriff, interview, January 8, 2005)

When we examine the post 9/11 backlash data from the DAAS and national studies we find stark contrasts between Detroit and Arab America as a whole, contrasts that suggest the efforts of Ron Amen, Robert Ficano, and thousands of concerned and well-placed citizens like them did indeed make a tremendous difference throughout the Detroit area. The percentage of DAAS respondents who reported having a bad experience after the 9/11 attacks because of their race or ethnicity was 15 percent, significantly less than the 25 percent reported in a national Zogby poll (Arab American Institute 2002).[9] The majority of these discriminatory acts (61 percent) involved verbal insults or threats. Some 43 percent of DAAS respondents reported worrying more about the future facing their families in the United States after the attacks, but this number is also significantly lower than the 66 percent who reported such worries nationwide. The gap between Arab Detroit and the rest of Arab America also extends to questions regarding willingness to exchange civil liberties for more security. By and large, the national Arab American community was much more likely (at 49 percent) to selectively forgo their civil liberties than Arabs in Detroit were (20 percent).

These numbers suggest that Detroit fared better after 9/11 than Arab America as a whole, a finding that alternately surprised, disturbed, and reassured the Arab Detroiters we shared it with, especially those who work in frontline occupations directly affected by the backlash and the war on terror. Rena Abbas-Chami, deputy director of the American-Arab Anti-Discrimination Committee (ADC) in Michigan, reported that the number of discrimination complaints her office received skyrocketed from four to five a week to several hundred in September and October of 2001 (interview, February 7, 2005). ADC's staff was so overwhelmed they began referring their clients directly to their national office and to a hate crimes hotline they established with Wayne County immediately after the attacks. "Dearborn seemed to be the epicenter of the threats to avenge 9/11," reflected the former Wayne County deputy sheriff Ron Amen in an interview on January 8, 2005. Dearborn and Arab Detroit more generally were indeed vulnerable. The public visibility the community gained in the 1990s, when multicultural inclusion was the order of the day, now made Arab Americans feel exposed and prone to attack. Rumors flew about young men being dragged from their cars and beaten up on the outskirts of Dearborn. People stayed at home as much as they could. One *Detroit Free Press* story, which circulated nationally, claimed that Dearborn was placed under martial law (Niraj Warikoo, "Rumor Mill Spins Fast and Furious: Some Are Harassed," September 12, 2001, 12A). Law enforcement agencies in Michigan were also concerned about the vulnerability of Arab Americans and responded, especially in Dearborn and Wayne County, with unprecedented patrols of Arab American neighborhoods, business districts, and houses of worship to provide a sense of security and calm (Thacher 2005).

Likewise, the number of DAAS respondents who reported gestures of kindness from non-Arabs after the attacks was twice as high (33 percent) as those who reported discrimination (15 percent). This informal support was matched by local officials, corporate leaders, educators, and other opinion makers. Imad Hamad, director of ADC-Michigan, found himself meeting with Dearborn Mayor Mike Guido and Chief of Police Greg Guibord just before noon on September 11 to discuss the possibility of a backlash and how best to thwart troublemakers while reassuring the community at large (interview, April 31, 2005). These local policing efforts were highly successful, with only two hate crimes reported in Dearborn (with a population of roughly 34,000 Arabs) in 2001 and 2002. Human Rights Watch called these local campaigns exemplary and has since encouraged other cities to follow Dearborn's lead (Singh 2002). It seemed as though every elected official in the state issued a statement about tolerance.[10] The breadth and depth of public support shown to Arab Detroit went a long way toward making Dearborn residents feel, in the words of Maysoun Khatib, a Michigan Civil Rights Commission program officer, that the city wore an "invisibility cloak" protecting it from hostility and attack (interview, February 19, 2005). "People know us," explained attorney Bill Swor. "My intuition, my experience tells me that because the Arab community in Detroit has been here 100 years, 120 years, has been a greater part of the fabric [of the city] for a longer period of time and is integrated in the [local] infrastructure . . . then I guess you buy the good as well as the bad and it is harder, even if you don't like the guy, it is harder to be overtly hostile" (interview, November 9, 2004).

By examining which parts of Detroit's Arab community were most vulnerable after the attacks, and which witnessed the greatest solidarity from non-Arabs, we can illustrate how the public outpouring of support for Arab Detroiters after 9/11 helped ensure the security of this population. Nationally, it was immigrants and Muslims who reported the largest percentages of bad experiences after the attacks (immigrants 29 percent and Muslims 42 percent), or those with a poor command of English (Zogby International 2002). In Detroit, however, despite its unusually large percentage of foreign-born and Muslim Arabs, the numbers look very different. Not only was the overall backlash in Detroit less severe, but Michigan's most vulnerable populations fared better than their counterparts in other states (on vulnerable Arab populations in California and Illinois, see especially Naber 2006; Cainkar 2006). Foreign-born Arabs in Detroit reported fewer bad experiences (14 percent) than their U.S.-born counterparts (19 percent) (see figure 3.1).

Figure 3.1   9/11 Backlash and Place of Birth

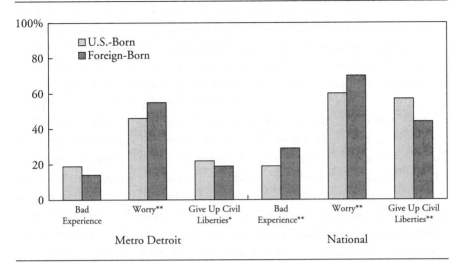

Source: Authors' compilation.
Note: *** $p < .001$, ** $p < .01$, * $p < 0.5$.

Likewise, the percentage of negative experiences reported by Muslims, 20 percent, though higher than those reported by Arab Christians (13 percent) is less than half of those reported nationwide, 42 percent (Muslim) and 16 percent (Christian) (DAAS 2003, Zogby International 2002). And, in an unusual turn of events, the more fluent in English DAAS respondents were, the more likely they were after the attacks to report having had a bad experience related to their race or ethnicity (see figure 3.2).

Similarly, although Muslims in Detroit (71 percent) and elsewhere (82 percent) report greater worries about their future in the United States than Christian Arabs (39 percent in Detroit and 57 percent nationally), Michigan Arab populations overall report significantly less (43 percent) than the national average (66 percent). Christians nationally (58 percent) and in Detroit (30 percent) were more willing to trade civil liberties for security than Muslims were, presumably because they did not feel as implicated in the 9/11 attacks (see chapter 7). Detroit Muslims, however, were significantly less likely (6 percent) to accept this compromise than Muslims nationwide (35 percent). Finally, although the percentage of foreign-born Arab Detroiters (55 percent) who worry about their future is greater than that of the American-born (46 percent),

Figure 3.2   Backlash and Religion

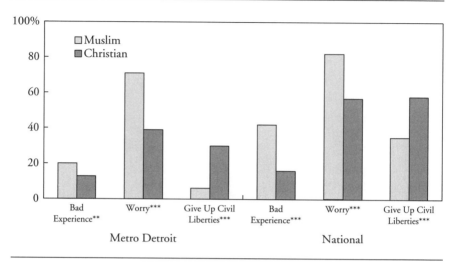

Source: Authors' compilation.
Note: *** $p < .001$, ** $p < .01$, * $p < 0.5$.

this percentage is still significantly lower than national figures. Only 19 percent of Detroit's foreign-born Arab population was willing to trade civil liberties for security, less than half the national average of 51 percent (DAAS 2003, Zogby International 2002).

DAAS findings suggest that participation in ethnic associations correlates directly to greater empowerment among Arab Detroiters. Of DAAS respondents, 39 percent report being involved in an Arab ethnic association, including advocacy groups like ADC, the Yemeni Benevolent Association, or the Chaldean Federation. These organizations act as gateways to a larger political world, linking local residents to mainstream institutions at the local, regional, and national levels. Police departments, elected officials, service providers, churches, universities, marketers, and many others go through Detroit's community organizations when hoping to reach local Arab Americans. Sometimes ethnic associations act as surrogates for the communities they represent, monopolizing contacts and resources, but they also act as conduits through which incorporation is pursued (Howell 2000; Jamal 2005; Shryock 2004). Among DAAS respondents, participation in ethnic associations is linked to both positive and negative post-9/11 outcomes. The 39 percent who reported

Figure 3.3   Participation in Ethnic Associations

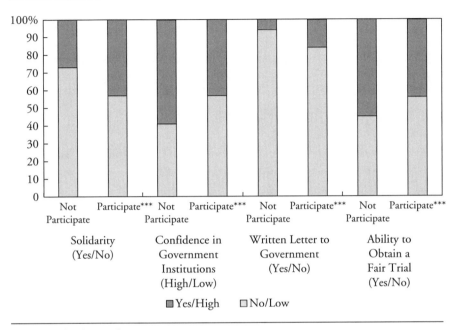

Source: Authors' compilation.
Note: *** $p < .001$, ** $p < .01$, * $p < 0.5$.

participating in ethnic associations had different experiences than those who reported active membership (or regular attendance) in churches, mosques, or village clubs. For example, when compared to nonmembers, members of ethnic associations were 15 percent more likely to have reported experiencing an act of solidarity by a non-Arab after the 9/11 attacks (43 percent to 27 percent), less likely to express confidence in the federal government (43 percent to 59 percent), and less likely to think Arabs and Muslims accused of supporting terrorism could receive a fair trial (44 percent to 55 percent). Nonetheless, members of ethnic associations were also far more likely to contact a government official to express an opinion on a political issue (16 percent) than Arabs who do not belong to such groups (6 percent). Membership in an Arab ethnic association brings with it greater skepticism about the American political system. It also brings increased opportunity to engage, sometimes productively, with mainstream political institutions (see figure 3.3).

Overall, our data suggest that Arab Detroit weathered the post-9/11 backlash with fewer scars than the Arab American community nationwide and that Arab Detroiters, relative their counterparts elsewhere, are more confident about their future in the United States and more assertive of their rights as citizens. These findings are most pronounced among those Arab populations—immigrants and Muslims—that are most vulnerable nationwide.

BACKLASH, PART 2: THE FEDERAL LAW ENFORCEMENT AGENDA

Everybody saw George Bush go to the mosque in Washington, D.C., and take his shoes off and enter the prayer room, the masjid area, as a show of solidarity with the Muslims in this country. And certainly, initially, we all thought that was a really good thing for him to have done and we appreciated that and really looked to him to defend our civil rights. And then it all appeared to be a dog and pony show. As the situation evolved a few weeks later we started to see Muslims and Arabs just disappearing from the country. Actually they were being arrested, incarcerated, held without charge, without contact, without an attorney, just kind of disappearing. . . . And then, the infamous PATRIOT Act came into existence and we could actually see in black and white that all those things that George Bush said to us when he was running for office prior to 9/11, about how he was going to do away with profiling, about how he was going to do away with secret evidence, turned out to be a lie. Not only did he not do away with those things, he actually put his attack dog, John Ashcroft, in a position to strengthen those violations of our civil rights as Arab Americans, as Muslim Americans. (Ronald Amen, former Wayne County deputy sheriff, interview, January 8, 2005)

When Arab Detroiters talk about the impact of the 9/11 attacks, their greatest concern, echoing Ron Amen, is the erosion of their civil liberties and the profiling of their communities by law enforcement and the media. They speak of the silencing effect on those who want to criticize Israeli and U.S. policies in the Middle East.[11] They worry about the constriction of economic and cultural flows that connect the United States and the Arab world, and the simultaneous expansion of U.S. military campaigns in the Muslim world. It is not always easy to see but, in Washington and in U.S. national media, Arab Americans are portrayed as potential threats to American security and as potential assets in the Bush administration's campaign to reshape the Middle

East and fight the war on terror (Hagopian 2003). This situation has yielded a heady mix of opportunity and constraint for Arab Americans, just as it has delivered an especially violent mix of opportunity and destruction to the Arab world. Nowhere in America has the two-edged nature of increased federal attention been more apparent than in Detroit's well-established and recently arrived Arab communities. If Arab Detroit's exceptional nature sheltered it from angry, intolerant individuals bent on revenge, did it also protect Arab Americans from ill-informed federal agents who saw culprits and conspirators around every corner? Did it situate Detroit's Arab organizations to capitalize on new economic and cultural possibilities that followed (and were a part of) the backlash or did it force them to redirect their energies toward defensive educational and legal campaigns? Did it empower Arab Americans to influence policy on the national level now that many Arab ethnic associations were working closely with federal agencies? We next explore how Detroit has responded to what Hussein Ibish, former spokesperson for ADC, has described as the Bush administration's message to Arab Americans: "Private citizens should not and cannot discriminate against Arabs and Muslims, but we [the federal government] can and will" (2003).

The Hunt for Terrorists in Detroit Courtrooms

In the days immediately following the 9/11 attacks, the Federal Bureau of Investigation (FBI), the Immigration and Naturalization Service (INS), and local law enforcement agencies rounded up and detained without charge more than 1,100 Arab, South Asian, and Muslim men as part of Investigation PENTTBOM, which sought out individuals who were suspected, on the most speculative of evidence, of having pre-knowledge of the 9/11 attacks or planning additional terror attacks (U.S. Department of Justice 2003). For the most part, these men were held without charges and in complete secrecy, often in solitary confinement. More than half were eventually deported, though none have been linked, directly or indirectly, to the 9/11 conspiracy. As the investigations widened over several months, the numbers grew to more than 5,000 detained, 155 of them in Detroit (Cole 2003). Detroit may not have been the epicenter of the public backlash against Arabs and Muslims in the United States, but it was in many ways the epicenter of the Justice Department's campaign to apprehend terror suspects and reassure the public that it was doing all it could to hunt down and prosecute those with terrorist ties. On the anniversary of the 9/11 attacks, for example, Mark Corallo, a Justice Department spokesman in Washington, announced that the FBI office in Detroit had more than doubled in size, that their agents were receiving full cooperation from "wary community leaders acting as cultural guides into the local Arab world," and that the Detroit office was at the forefront of "the largest investigation in the history of the United States" (Tamar Audi, "Secret Sweep: Detroiters Caught in Widening Investigation," *Detroit Free Press,* November 12, 2002, 1A). This vast deployment of man hours and new powers of surveillance yielded not the terrorists Bush was hoping for, but a tripling of the arrest rate of local Arab and Muslim petty criminals and visa over-stayers (Greg Krupa and John Bebow, "Immigration Crackdown Snares Arabs," *Detroit News,* November 3, 2003, 1A). As Detroit Attorney Bill Swor, who has worked on several prominent terrorism-related cases, pointed out to us, these investigations had a chilling effect on the community: "When every federal investigation involving an Arab, whether a citizen or a resident alien, is vetted through the terrorism unit . . . and every illegal act treated as a federal offense . . . and each case is charged at grotesque levels, finding the most serious charges we can bring, the community remains traumatized because the community knows that it is being not only watched, but targeted" (interview, November 9, 2004).

On September 17, 2001, five days after the attacks, the FBI raided a house in Detroit. They were looking for Nabil Almarabh, a noncitizen whose name had appeared on a pre-9/11 terrorism watch list. Almarabh was not in Detroit, but his four noncitizen housemates were each detained after a cache of false identity papers and other "suspicious" Arabic documents were found in their apartment. They were quickly dubbed an "operational combat sleeper cell" of "al-Qaida terrorists" by John Ashcroft, a label referenced frequently in news stories about Detroit for the next several years. Farouk Ali-Haimoud, Ahmed Hannan, Karim Koubriti, and Abdel-Ilah Elmardoudi were eventually indicted on terrorism charges when a former housemate testified, in exchange for a plea bargain, that they had attempted to recruit him for a terrorist cell. Ali-Haimoud and Hannan were acquitted of terror-related charges in 2003, but a year later, to much public fanfare, Elmardoudi and Koubriti were convicted of conspiring to provide material support and resources to terrorists. The case was not yet closed, however. The convictions were overturned a few months later and the charges against both men were thrown out when the U.S. Attorney's Office in Detroit was forced to admit that their former lead prosecutor, Richard Convertino, had withheld "impeachment and exculpatory material" from the defense (U.S. Attorney Stephen Murphy, personal communication, May 20, 2005). Convertino quickly resigned, but after three years of unprecedented investigative work and relentless international publicity, the government had failed to prove that anything remotely resembling a sleeper cell of al-Qaida terrorists had resided in Detroit.[12]

A former Special Agent in Charge of the FBI in Michigan admitted that in 2001 and 2002, the Detroit FBI office strongly encouraged the public to volunteer terror-related tips, many of which proved to be misleading and to have been motivated by personal vendettas. "Terrorism is the hot button right now," said John Bell. "If you want to get law enforcement on someone, you accuse him of being a terrorist" (Bay Fang, "Under Scrutiny, Always," *U.S. News and World Report,* December 30, 2002, 26). Bill Swor described the resulting legal cases as both "frivolous and insidious, a waste of resources . . . a witch hunt" (personal communication, 2004). In its own defense, the U.S. Attorney's Office in Detroit claims to "have had a number of other successful prosecutions that are aimed at disrupting terrorism that have not specifically charged crimes of terrorism, per se, but nonetheless, helped prevent terrorist attacks. These prosecutions generally fall into two categories: cases based on intelligence information, and cases that protect vulnerabilities in our homeland security" (Stephen Murphy, personal communication, 2005). When pressed for information on the number of such cases tried in Detroit, or anywhere else for that matter, local officials have been unwilling to provide further answers. The White House has been less cautious about reporting such numbers. In 2005 President Bush claimed that more than half of the 400 suspects against whom terrorism-related charges had been filed since 9/11 had been successfully convicted. His use of these numbers drew heavy criticism. On June 14, 2005, the *Washington Post* asserted that only 39 people, not 200, had been convicted of crimes related to terrorism or national security, and only a few of these cases involved plots against the United States. The overwhelming majority of cases involved convictions on minor crimes, such as making false statements or violating immigration law. The median sentence meted out regardless of the charges brought to trial was eleven months, a sentence that seemed unlikely to deter people genuinely involved in campaigns against the United States or its allies (Dan Eggan and Julia Tate, "In Terror Cases, Few Convictions," *The Washington Post,* June 12, 2005, A01). To date, six Arab Americans with ties to Detroit have been found guilty on charges related to providing material support for terrorism. All had connections to Hizbullah, not al-Qaida.[13]

Although Arab Detroiters were relieved to see the sleeper cell convictions overturned, they are nonetheless alarmed by the prejudicial manner in which these cases and many others like them have been handled and by the inflammatory news coverage that accompanied each arrest and trial (Jamal 2004). The FBI's local antiterrorism unit, renamed the national security unit in 2006, continues to surface when Arab or Muslim Americans are under investigation for offenses unrelated to terrorism. In August of 2006, for example, five young men who were buying large quantities of discounted cell phones for resale in other markets were also accused of providing material support to terrorists. That all five were Arab Muslims did not go unnoticed by attorneys or the media. In one case, the men were in possession of photographs of the Mackinac Bridge. News headlines accused them of plotting to blow up the famous Michigan landmark. The other young men were found with a manual from Royal Jordanian Airlines in their car and, on the basis of this, were accused of plotting to infiltrate the airline, also for terror-related purposes. The manual, like the car, belonged to an employee of the airline, the mother of one of the accused. All charges against each of the five men were eventually dropped, but not before damning headlines, such as "2 Dearborn Men Linked to Terrorism" (*Detroit Free Press,* August 10, 2006) or "3 Arraigned on Terror Charges" (*Detroit Free Press,* August 13, 2006) had done their work. Local Arab and Muslim leaders in Detroit were furious with federal authorities for how the cases were handled and very publicly bungled, accusing law enforcement agents and those who reported on the young men as being equally guilty of racial profiling (see *Detroit Free Press* articles from August 10 to August 16, 2006).

These cases, based on the flimsiest of circumstantial evidence, have done little to strengthen public trust in federal agencies that now regularly justify their investigations, prosecutions, and deportations of Arab and Muslim defendants with intelligence reports that are not made public. The U.S. Attorney for Eastern Michigan, Stephen Murphy, admitted that "it would not be surprising to learn that the arrest rate of Arab Americans has increased since 9/11 in light of our investigative priorities" (personal communication, May 20, 2005). And, rather than tapering off over the years as investigations in Detroit have yielded scant return on the money and man hours invested, or as Congress and the Supreme Court have finally begun to challenge the Bush administration's interpretations of First Amendment protections, homeland security and antiterrorism are considered among the few growth sectors in Michigan's rapidly shrinking economy. In 2006, shortly after the White House revealed its program of domestic surveillance and wiretapping operations,[14] the FBI announced another doubling—the third since 9/11—of the number of their Michigan agents who are pursuing terror-related investigations. They also broke ground on a new facility in Detroit in 2007, planning to triple the square footage of their local office space and increase their security (Joe Swickard, "FBI to Have New Offices in Detroit," *Detroit Free Press,* August 29, 2006, 1A). The U.S. Attorney's Office in Detroit, likewise, added two attorneys to their terrorism unit in 2006 (Paul Eggan, "Terror Unit to Boost Staffing," *Detroit News,* March 21, 2006, 1B), and Governor Granholm has made attracting new homeland security jobs to the state a key anchor of the state's 21st Century Jobs Fund (State of Michigan 2006). The growth of this economic niche has Arab leaders in Detroit worried that federal agents are interested in their communities only insofar as they are useful for "propaganda purposes," military recruitment, and "spying" (Caroline Drees, "In Terror War, American 'Outreach' has US Muslims Wary," Reuters, May 2006).

A Damper Against Discrimination?

A tally of abuses meted out by government agencies against Arabs and Muslims and legal briefs filed in response[15] would say little, however, about the larger transformations Arab institutions have undergone in reaction to the war on terror and the new political realities it has generated. It is often difficult to determine whether these changes are driven by rewards or punishments, by a sense of belonging or exclusion. Amid the profiling and attempts to marginalize Arab Americans as a political constituency that prevails at the national level, changes taking place on the ground in Michigan have often had positive effects, strengthening an Arab community that was already confident and well connected before September 2001.

Churches and mosques in Michigan, like those across the country, have made a concerted effort to welcome outsiders, hosting film crews, open houses, and ecumenical events. They have also strengthened their support for one another. Human service organizations like ACCESS and ACC have provided hundreds of cultural sensitivity workshops for journalists, law enforcement agencies, corporations, lawyers, and school districts. The list is long and impressive and includes training for State Department officials and the U.S. military. ADC-Michigan, the Council on American-Islamic Relations (CAIR), and the Michigan Civil Rights Commission now provide regular workshops on civil rights issues of relevance to Arabs and other citizens. Although many of these educational programs are more than a decade old, the funds available to support them have grown exponentially since the 9/11 attacks (for a careful analysis of culture work before and after 9/11, see Shryock 2004). Millions of dollars have been spent on these efforts in recent years by a variety of corporate, government, and foundation sponsors. This largess enabled the Arab American National Museum, the first of its kind in the United States, to open its doors in Dearborn in 2005. Likewise, ADC-Michigan broke ground on a new, multimillion-dollar Arab American Center for Civil and Human Rights in 2007. New funding has also been made available to scholars resulting in the Detroit Arab American Study and a plethora of edited volumes, including this one, published by presses and funded by foundations that had little interest in niche communities like Arab and Muslim Americans before September 11, 2001. Mosques, too, continue to invest in public outreach; their construction projects and educational programs have yielded equally impressive results. Since the 2001 attacks, more than a dozen mosque building projects have been completed, more than doubling the square footage of prayer space available in Dearborn and Detroit.[16] This climate of growth and success is welcomed by Arab Detroiters. They recognize that each of these developments improves their ability to assert and defend their claims to full American citizenship. Community leaders are equally aware, however, that these developments bring with them significant costs.

National and local foundations are not the only parties with a newfound interest in sponsoring research on Arab Americans or supporting events and publications that reach Arab American audiences. A motley array of individuals and organizations are lining up to benefit from these opportunities. The number of weekly and monthly newspapers and magazines published by Arabs in Detroit has doubled in recent years, for example, and most are financed, in no small part, by the full-cost, full-page recruitment ads placed in them by the U.S. Army, the FBI, the Central Intelligence Agency (CIA), and businesses operating in and out of occupied Iraq. Likewise, the CIA has become a prominent, if unlikely, sponsor of the Dearborn Arab International Festival since 2004, their information booth conspicuous among the falafel stands and carnival rides. Such sights have become commonplace at Arab events in the Detroit area, especially those organized by the American Arab Chamber of Commerce and ACCESS, both of which have developed close ties to the U.S. Departments of State, Homeland Security, and Commerce in recent years.

Together with the League of Arab States and the Gulf Cooperation Council, these otherwise local organizations hosted an event in 2003 called the U.S.-Arab Economic Forum. Intended to increase trade between the Arab Gulf states and Detroit, the event drew heavy criticism from local activists. "The feeling in the region that the United States is on a crusade against Arabs and against Islam is as bad as I have ever seen it," said Osama Siblani, publisher of the *Arab-American News*. "This is not the time to be having this summit. . . . Who in his right mind is going to come and invest from the Arab world when he knows if he comes here he's going to be stripped, searched and humiliated at the airport?" (Jennifer Brooks, "Division Cloud Promise Surrounding Arab Forum," *Detroit News,* September 26, 2003, 1A). Forum organizer Ahmed Chebanni adamantly defended the project, arguing that "peace and prosperity go hand in hand. By using Arab-Americans as a business vehicle, we will establish a real, meaningful dialogue and create a basis for long-term dialogue" (Brooks 2003). In a political climate where actual economic ties between everyday American citizens and their relatives and communities in the Middle East were being seriously curtailed and support for Islamic charities was dwindling due to U.S. seizures and political posturing (Howell and Shryock 2003), this optimism proved difficult to sustain. Even Wayne County Executive Robert Ficano could mention only another round of seven digit contributions to the Arab American National Museum, a division of ACCESS, as a tangible, realized benefit of this partnership (Haimour 2005). "We do not wish to judge others. We do not wish to preach to others. We certainly do not wish to coerce others. We wish to help others, and by so doing, help ourselves," said Colin Powell in his address to the forum (2003). Yet his speech also cautioned Arabs, both American and foreign, to check their criticisms of Israel and opposition to the U.S. invasion of Iraq at the door. If coercion does not account for this partnership, then the opportunism of community leaders offers little solace to those who are left on the margins of the post-9/11 boom in all things Arab American.

Just as Arab organizations have been met halfway in their educational and civil liberties campaigns by concerned foundations, corporations, public institutions, and government agencies, Arab Americans have also met federal law enforcement agencies halfway—some would say more than halfway—in their many investigations in the Arab American community. Within a week of September 11, 2001, more than 4,000 Arabs from Detroit called to volunteer their services to the FBI and CIA as translators of stockpiled communications intercepts ("Arabic Speakers Answer U.S. Need," *Detroit Free Press,*

September 19, 2001, 7A).[17] Arab Americans were no less eager to catch genuine terror suspects than other Americans. They had a special interest and often specialized skills that could be of help in this regard. It was in this spirit that ADC-Michigan pulled together a coalition of fifteen Arab American organizations for monthly meetings with the regional leadership of the FBI, the U.S. Attorney's Office, and an additional dozen federal agencies after the 9/11 attacks. Imad Hamad, director of ADC-Michigan, and John Bell, then special-agent-in-charge of Detroit's FBI office, had already worked together through the National Conference for Community and Justice. It was through this relationship that Building Respect in Diverse Groups to Enhance Sensitivity (BRIDGES) was established as a forum for dialogue where "both sides" could communicate freely (Imad Hamad, personal communication, July 6, 2005).

The first major accomplishment of this task force was to create a series of best practice guidelines that the FBI in Michigan followed in November 2001 when it began questioning more than 500 of the state's Arab and Muslim noncitizens as part of a national effort that included 7,600 noncitizens nationwide. ADC was able to monitor these investigations locally, both in 2001 and on the three subsequent occasions the FBI repeated the process, making pro bono attorneys available, providing a helpline for those with questions, ensuring that interviewees received advance letters to explain the program's voluntary nature, providing translators, and insisting that federal agents not confront respondents at school or in the work place. U.S. Attorney Stephen Murphy asserted that the process also enabled law enforcement to conduct these investigations without alienating the Arab community, and to be more efficient and effective by pairing federal agents with local law enforcement officers (John Bell, personal communication, July 9, 2005).[18] Although the process was inherently discriminatory—profiling informants along religious and national lines—and the best practice guidelines were reached only after extensive and heated debate, the execution of these interviews in Michigan was significantly less disruptive of individual lives and community-law enforcement relations than elsewhere. In particular, Eastern Michigan was one of only four districts in which letters were uniformly mailed in advance to interviewees and one of only two districts in which the U.S. Department of Immigration and Naturalization was kept out of the interview process (Ramirez, O'Connell, and Zafar 2004, 24).

In 2005, several of the people we interviewed for this project were cautiously, if also strategically, optimistic about the benefits that flowed from the BRIDGES alliance, pointing to a sustained dialogue between the state and the community that enabled all parties to clarify legal, linguistic, and cultural matters in ways that improved the application of federal laws on the ground. Arab leaders argued that the process made the law enforcement community more accountable to Arab concerns, and law enforcement agreed, adding that it also brought greater trust and public support. Both sides recognized that the familiarity encouraged by an ongoing airing of principles, concerns, and grievances was able to produce better law enforcement and greater cooperation among those involved and provided a list of Arab Americans who sought and received assistance from law enforcement agencies. Several individuals, for example, had their names removed from federal no-fly lists, several hate crimes against Arab Americans were prosecuted with speed and efficiency, and a few federal detainees who posed no threat or flight risk were freed while their cases were pending trial (Imad Hamad and Stephen Murphy, personal communication, May 20, 2005).

Although some are encouraged to see Arab American complaints handled in this face-to-face terrain where justice can occasionally be facilitated, BRIDGES has not yet been able to challenge the status quo in which the presumption of innocence seems to have been reversed and due process is lacking for Arab and Muslim defendants. As time passes, the volatility of the BRIDGES alliance has made it less effective and less easy to sustain. Kenwah Dabaja, then Michigan field director of the Arab American Institute, described BRIDGES as too inconsistent in its efforts, meeting less and less frequently, often in reaction to the latest crisis (personal communication, 2007). Even when the group met according to schedule, outside events frequently sidetracked their discussions. In September 2006, for example, the head of the Department of Justice's Civil Rights Division, Assistant U.S. Attorney Wan Kim, was scheduled to address BRIDGES members in a public forum. After he outlined the progress his department had made prosecuting hate crimes and other forms of discrimination against Arabs and Muslims since 9/11, the meeting was completely overrun by comments about the cell phone cases mentioned earlier and angry complaints about a raid on Life for Relief and Development (LIFE), an Islamic charity headquartered in the Detroit area that took place the day before the BRIDGES meeting and just before the onset of Ramadan. Daniel Roberts, special agent in charge of Detroit's FBI office, argued that the raid had been timed to take place before rather than during this month of fasting and charitable giving to be "sensitive to community concerns." LIFE was not closed down, nor were its assets frozen, but it took the FBI most of the month of Ramadan to issue a public statement to this effect. Dabaja summed up the

FBI's participation in the BRIDGES alliance saying, "I don't get the feeling they are listening" (Kenwah Dabaja, personal communication, May 19, 2007).[19]

Despite these tensions, BRIDGES is now considered an ideal model of community-law enforcement relations by observers outside Michigan, and it is being replicated in other parts of the country (Ramirez, O'Connell, and Zafar 2004), a process that is supported by Arab American activists and by the Department of Justice alike. In a study of such community-law enforcement initiatives nationwide, the Soros Foundation attributes the success of BRIDGES to the remarkable degree of institutional incorporation the Arab community in Michigan has achieved. The BRIDGES story is the latest chapter in a long history of local activism in which Arab Americans have made political gains by working with city hall, as it were, while actively fighting against it (Ahmed 2006; Terry 1999). Imad Hamad lamented the fact that BRIDGES, though replicated in other locations, has met with only local success in eastern Michigan and has been able to intervene positively only on a case-by-case basis. "Of course, the dialogue needs to be with policy makers and not just those who implement policies," he argued. "For BRIDGES to make a difference outside Michigan, we need to communicate with those in D.C. and not only those who are in Detroit" (interview, July 6, 2005).

CONCLUSION

Imad Hamad's appeal was echoed by each of the Arab Americans we interviewed, who suggested that the federal government, especially the law enforcement agencies managing the state of exception created of our ongoing crisis, would benefit tremendously from the insight of Arab and Muslim professionals, not simply as translators, role-playing actors, field agents, or civil rights watchdogs, but as intelligence officers, presidential advisors, and policymakers.[20] Arabs in Michigan have achieved genuine political incorporation. At the state level, they shape the way social services are delivered, health data is collected, automobiles are designed and manufactured, world music is packaged, homeland security measures are implemented, and gasoline, milk, and other goods are distributed and sold. As in other ethnic communities, most of this work is accomplished without reference to collective identities, and ethnic institutions stand by to carefully catalog and augment these efforts, ensuring that Arabs are a political constituency local governments must acknowledge and support. This process has been decades in the making, but the events that transpired on and after September 11, 2001, compelled officials to recognize that the fate of Michigan and of Dearborn in particular are intertwined now with the fate of their Arab citizens. This is why the public backlash in Michigan was significantly less severe than in other communities.

At the national level, Arabs have not achieved this sort of inclusion, and until they do, the exceptional privileges they have gained in Detroit will remain fragile. Arab leaders in Detroit are acutely aware of the limitations of this status, as is Imad Hamad, whose sensitivity to the difference between the local and the national is rooted in personal experience. In September 2003, the FBI in Washington sought to recognize Hamad's singular contribution to the BRIDGES effort by awarding him its highest civilian honor, the Exceptional Public Service award. Hamad soon found himself slandered by a national media campaign that described him as "a man who supports terrorism and was himself a suspected terrorist" (Schlussel 2003). He was further humiliated when the FBI declined to award him the honor they had already announced to the media. As the public controversy around the award escalated, Arab American members of the BRIDGES alliance threatened to withdraw. Hamad was forced to defend his past, reassure the public that he is not a terrorist, and plead with BRIDGES partners to continue their collaboration with a government agency that was clearly ambivalent about Hamad and insensitive to the community he represents.[21]

Awareness of the difference between local and national politics is keen among Detroit's major Arab American institutions, each of which has found itself performing the defensive maneuvers described earlier—defending their pasts and promoting their institutional histories, investing vast resources in reassuring the public that they are not and do not support terrorists, and urging their constituents to not lose faith as they collaborate in increasingly complex ways with the FBI, CIA, Department of State, and other federal agencies that are interested in Arab Americans only as potential threats to U.S. security or potential allies in the U.S. war on terror. In Arab Detroit today, local social service providers, arts presenters, civil liberties advocates, and Muslim charities find themselves working closely with, and often accepting the patronage of, federal agencies that specialize in security issues, foreign and domestic espionage, criminal investigations, and other forms of governmental discipline and control. Occasionally, Arab American groups are enlisted, mostly as window dressing, in U.S. campaigns to transform the Middle East, economically, politically, and militarily.[22] This work stands at a remove from the bread and butter efforts of Detroit's Arab ethnic associations to provide services and address community needs, activities that have garnered them strong grassroots support. When Arab organizations are included in public diplomacy and community policing efforts but are not treated as full partners with a voice in setting agendas and negotiating strategies, they risk weakening their grassroots strength and eroding Arab confidence in American public institutions and government. The new status quo suggests that, at the national level, Arab Detroit is being reconfigured as a constituency defined not by its genuine integration with a city and its society, but by its imputed associations with foreignness and danger. If this odd feature of Arab Detroit's political incorporation continues to receive institutional support, it may produce tragic (and unintended) consequences for a community that has withstood the 9/11 backlash and now looks forward, longingly, to a more stable era of acceptance.

NOTES

1. An earlier, and lengthier, version of this chapter was published in *Being and Belonging: Muslims in the United States Since 9/11,* edited by Katherine Ewing and published by the Russell Sage Foundation in 2008.
2. George W. Bush, Address to a Joint Session of Congress and the American People, United States Capitol, September 20, 2001.
3. Bill Swor, Rena Abbas-Chami, Maysoun Khatib, Ron Amen, and Imad Hamad participated in lengthy interviews with Sally Howell. Most of these conversations were recorded on tape. Several others, who prefer to remain anonymous, provided details and helped formulate the ideas in this paper. Barbara McQuade, from the U.S. Attorney's Office in Detroit, responded helpfully to an earlier draft of this paper. Steven Murphy, U.S. Attorney, Eastern Michigan region, and John Bell, former FBI Special Agent in Charge, Detroit, both replied in writing to questions we submitted to the U.S. Attorney's Office in Detroit. We thank each of the individuals, named and unnamed, who contributed to this research and analysis.
4. Ismael Ahmed attributes the quote "Michigan is our New York" to James Zogby, adding that Arab Detroiters "can and should be a model of political participation" for Arab Americans nationwide (2006, 50).
5. The U.S. Census does not collect information on religion. The national breakdown cited here is drawn from surveys of Arab Americans conducted in 2000 and 2002 by Zogby International (see http://www.aaiusa.org/demographics and Zogby 2002).

6.   Respondents were asked about the total family income for the respondent and all family members residing in the household.

7.   Hassan Makled retired from his position at the Detroit Metropolitan Airport in 2006.

8.   These numbers are the authors' calculation based initially on the Arab American Institute's 2007 "Roster of Arab Americans in Public Life" and updated as new appointments have been announced and approved. Ronald Amen provided the number of deputy sheriffs for Wayne County.

9.   The DAAS was conducted in 2003 and the Zogby International polls in 2002. It may appear that the Zogby poll numbers are higher than the DAAS numbers because of the timing of these studies; however, hate crimes across the nation have been on the rise each year since 9/11, as reported by both ADC (2002, 2003) and CAIR (2001, 2002, 2004, 2005, 2006).

10.   When Governor John Engler visited Arab American leaders in Dearborn on September 27, 2001, and assured them that "there is never any excuse for discrimination against anyone", the timing of his visit received local criticism, following, as it did, rather than preceding President Bush's visit with Arab American leaders in Washington ("Engler, Arab Americans Talk," *Detroit Free Press,* September 28, 2001, 3B).

11.   This silencing effect predates the 9/11 attacks, but has become more pronounced since. It was especially apparent in the Detroit area during the 2006 Israeli-Hizbullah War when Arab American leaders were routinely described as Hizbullah supporters in the media and then dismissed. This smear campaign reached its peak when gubernatorial candidate Dick DeVos cancelled his planned appearance at an Arab American Political Action Committee (AAPAC) dinner in Dearborn after the editor of the *Detroit Jewish News* argued in an editorial that "no legitimate candidate for public office should go before the Dearborn-based [PAC] . . . because its leadership has defended Hezbollah" (Robert Sklar, September 6, 2006, 7). The president of AAPAC was likewise introduced publicly by the head of Michigan's FBI Field Office, as a "supporter of Hezbollah" (Osama Siblani, personal communication, October 26, 2006).

12.   Hannan and Koubriti were recently reindicted, this time on a charge of insurance fraud. The new case is pending.

13.   The guilty pleas include U.S. v. Makki and U.S. v. Kourani. A third man, Nemr Ali Rahal, was arrested in May 2005 for raising $600 to support the families of suicide bombers connected to Hizbullah ("Dearborn Man to be Tried in Terror Case," *The Detroit News,* May 4, 2005, 3B). Finally, four men pleaded guilty in

Detroit in 2006 to a variety of racketeering and counterfeiting charges related to a money-making scheme intended to benefit Hizbullah—Youssef Bakri, Imad Hamadeh, Theodore Schenk and Karim Nasser. For many Lebanese and other Arabs, Hizbullah's status on the U.S. State Department's list of foreign terrorist organizations (FTO) is problematic. Hizbullah has had a violent past, but the organization's political party today plays a significant role in the Lebanese parliament and its social service arm has long aided the disenfranchised Shi'a of the South. Hizbullah is credited with forcing Israel, after a grueling twenty years, to end their occupation of South Lebanon, and with defending this same territory against the full force of an Israeli air, sea and land assault in 2006 (Deeb 2006). At a 2005 public forum in Dearborn, "Charitable Giving and Terrorism Sanctions," Chip Poncy, of the U.S. Treasury Department, warned Arab and Muslim Americans that they must regulate themselves to ensure that their charitable donations are not being rerouted to support terror. The audience objected to Hizbullah's inclusion on the FTO list along with other organizations that oppose Israel but are not seen as a threat to the United States or to American citizens.

14. This program was challenged in court by the ACLU of Michigan, with support from several of the Arab and Muslim organizations mentioned elsewhere in this paper. It was found unconstitutional in a Detroit courtroom ("Ruling on Wiretaps Faces Fierce Challenge," *Detroit Free Press,* August 18, 2006, 1A).

15. ADC Michigan and ACCESS, for example, joined the ACLU of Michigan in filing the first challenge to the USA PATRIOT Act in July of 2003 (ACLU Press Release, July 30, 2003) and have continued to advocate on behalf of local Arab and Muslim defendants in years since.

16. This exponential growth in mosque construction corresponds to a precipitous drop in the funds given to international Islamic charities. Six of the largest and best-known Islamic charities operating between the United States and the Muslim world have been closed and their assets have been frozen since September 2001 (David Ashenfelter and Joe Swickard, "Muslim Charity Sues Treasury Dept.," *New York Times,* December 12, 2006, 24).

17. The FBI does not use volunteer labor. Between 2001 and 2005 the Detroit office of the FBI hired fifteen Arabic translators. Hundreds applied, but the hurdles to employment are many. The agency has no tests for competency in Arabic beyond their classical Arabic written exam (Laura Waters, Detroit FBI recruitment officer, personal communication, 2005). The Department of Homeland Security has also had a difficult time hiring and retaining Arab Americans in its

Michigan offices, according to an anonymous former officer, although details have been impossible to track down. Independent security contractors have also sprung up in Michigan to handle work outsourced by federal agencies. They seem to have a better track record at hiring Arabic speakers. The former deputy director of ADC-Michigan, Rana Abbas, left her post in 2008 to become the co-director of one such private contractor, Global Linguistic Solutions.

18. For an excellent account of how the local and federal law enforcement pairings came about, how they were received by Arab activists, and the problematic role local police were able to play in this process, see also David Thacher (2005).

19. As of Ramadan 2007, six major Muslim charities in the United States have been closed and had their assets frozen, three from Michigan. Several others are under investigation. Very few charges have been levied against any of these agencies or their employees, and the evidence against them has not been shared with those under investigation. Muslim community leaders now assert that the Treasury Department is among the least forthcoming federal agencies, indicating the significance of this financial warfare to the operationalization of the war on terror (see Muslim Public Affairs Council 2007).

20. Iraqi Americans in the Detroit area are now regularly flown to U.S. military bases in several states to act the part of Iraqi insurgents, innocent civilians, and government ministers for military training exercises (see Associated Press story by John Milburn, October 15, 2007 or the *New York Times* story by Robert Worth, December 27, 2003).

21. Hamad's alleged crime was to support Palestinian nationalist aspirations— through legal channels—when he was not yet a citizen. Like the thousands of Arab and Muslim men who have been detained and deported since 9/11, Hamad's deportation proceedings and citizenship appeal dragged on for years, and the evidence used against him was kept secret for security reasons.

22. This trend has been especially pronounced in relation to the U.S. invasion and occupation of Iraq (see, for example, "Bush Shares Hopes for Iraqi Homeland," *Detroit Free Press,* April 29, 2003).

REFERENCES

Ahmed, Ismael. 2006. "Michigan Arab Americans: A Case Study of Electoral and Non-Electoral Empowerment." In *American Arabs and Political Participation*, edited by Philippa Strum. Washington: Woodrow Wilson International Center for Scholars.

American-Arab Anti-Discrimination Committee (ADC). 2002. "The Arab American Experience after September 11: Healing the Nation." Washington, D.C.: Arab American Institute.

American Community Survey. 2005. "Data Profile Highlight, Dearborn, Michigan." Washington: U.S. Bureau of the Census.

———. 2003. "Muslim/Arab Employment Discrimination Charges Since September 11." EEOC Fact Sheet. Washington, D.C.: Arab American Institute. Available at: http://www.adc.org/index.php?id=1682 (accessed May 1, 2007).

Arab American Institute. 2002. "Profiling and Pride: Arab American Attitudes and Behavior Since September 11." Washington, D.C.: Arab American Institute. Available at: http://www.aaiusa.org/resources/opinion-polls (accessed May 1, 2007).

———. 2007. "Roster of Arab Americans in Public Life and Public Service." Washington, D.C.: Arab American Institute. Available at: http://www.aaiusa.org/resources/400/campaigns-elections (accessed May 1, 2007).

Arab American Institute Foundation (AAIF). 2006. "Select Social and Demographic Characteristics for Arab Americans." Washington, D.C.: Arab American Institute.

Cainkar, Louise. 2006. "The Social Construction of Difference and the Arab American Experience." *Journal of American Ethnic History* 25(2–3): 243–78.

Canada-U.S.-Ontario-Michigan Border Transportation Partnership. 2004. *Planning/Need and Feasibility Study Report.* Detroit, Mich.: URS Corporation. Available at: http://www.partnershipborderstudy.com/pdf/a_PNFStudyReport_FINAL_updated pgnumbers.pdf (accessed May 1, 2007).

Cole, David. 2003. *Enemy Aliens: Double Standards and Constitutional Freedoms in the War on Terrorism.* New York: The New Press.

Council on American-Islamic Relations (CAIR). 2001. *Accommodating Diversity.* Washington, D.C.: Council on American-Islamic Relations.

———. 2002. *Stereotypes and Civil Liberties.* Washington, D.C.: Council on American-Islamic Relations.

———. 2004. *Unpatriotic Acts.* Washington, D.C.: Council on American-Islamic Relations.

———. 2005. *Unequal Protection.* Washington, D.C.: Council on American-Islamic Relations.

———. 2006. *The Struggle for Equality.* Washington, D.C.: Council on American-Islamic Relations.

Detroit Arab American Study (DAAS). 2003. Unpublished dataset. Ann Arbor, Mich: Institute for Social Research.

Deeb, Lara. 2006. "Hizballah: A Primer." *Middle East Report Online,* May 31. Available at: http://www.merip.org/mero/mero073106.html (accessed May 1, 2007).

Hagopian, Elaine. 2003. "The Interlocking of Right-Wing Politics and U.S. Middle East Policy: Solidifying Arab/Muslim Demonization." In *Civil Rights in Peril,* edited by Elaine Hagopian. Chicago: Haymarket Press.

Haimour, Muhannad. 2005. "Michigan Leaders Pave Way for Business in the Middle East." *Forum and Link* 1(16): 14–16.

Howell, Sally. 2000. "Cultural Interventions: Arab American Aesthetics Between the Transnational and the Ethnic." *Diaspora* 9(1): 59–82.

Howell, Sally, and Andrew Shryock. 2003. "Cracking Down on Diaspora: Arab Detroit and America's 'War on Terror.'" *Anthropological Quarterly* 76(3): 443–62.

Ibish, Hussein. 2003. "The Civil Liberties of Arab Americans Post 9/11." Presented at the University of Michigan. Ann Arbor (October 17).

Jamal, Amaney. 2004. "Religious Identity, Discrimination and 9/11: The Determinants of Arab American Levels of Political Confidence in Mainstream and Ethnic Institutions." Presented at the American Political Science Association 2004 Annual Meeting. Chicago (September 2–5).

———. 2005. "The Political Participation and Engagement of Muslim Americans: Mosque Involvement and Group Consciousness." *American Politics Research* 33(4): 521–44.

Lipset, Seymour Martin. 1996. *American Exceptionalism: A Double-Edged Sword.* New York: W. W. Norton.

Muslim Public Affairs Council. 2007. "Ramadan and Anxiety over Charity." Available at: http://www.mpac.org/article.php?id=528 (accessed May 1, 2007).

Naber, Nadine. 2006. "The Rules of Forced Engagement: Race, Gender, and the Culture of Fear Among Arab Immigrants in San Francisco Post-9/11." *Cultural Dynamics* 18(3): 235–67.

Powell, Colin. 2003. "Remarks at U.S.-Arab Economic Forum." Detroit (September 29). Available at: http://www.accessmylibrary.com/coms2/summary_0286872746_ITM (accessed May 1, 2007).

Ramirez, Deborah, Sasha Cohen O'Connell, and Rabia Zafar. 2004. *A Promising Practices Guide: Developing Partnerships Between Law Enforcement and American Muslim, Arab, and Sikh Communities.* New York: Open Society Institute.

Samhan, Helen. 2006. "Losing the Battle: How Political Activism Guarantees Ethnic Integration (in Spite of Defeats Along the Way)." In *American Arabs and Political Participation,* edited by Philippa Strum. Washington: Woodrow Wilson International Center for Scholars.

Schlussel, Debbie. 2003. "The FBI's Outrageous Award." Available at: http://www.debbieschlussel.com/columns/column091303.shtml (accessed May 1, 2007).

Shryock, Andrew. 2004. "In the Double Remoteness of Arab Detroit: Reflections on Ethnography, Culture Work, and the Intimate Disciplines of Americanization." In *Off Stage/On Display: Intimacy and Ethnography in the Age of Public Culture,* edited by Andrew Shryock. Palo Alto, Calif.: Stanford University Press.

Shryock, Andrew, and Nabeel Abraham. 2000. "On Margins and Mainstreams." In *Arab Detroit: From Margin to Mainstream,* edited by Nabeel Abraham and Andrew Shryock. Detroit, Mich.: Wayne State University Press.

Singh, Amardeep. 2002. "We Are Not the Enemy: Hate Crimes Against Arabs, Muslims and Those Who Are Perceived to be Arabs or Muslims After September 11." *Human Rights Watch* 14(6)(G): 1–42.

State of Michigan. 2006. "Jobs Today, Jobs Tomorrow: Governor Granholm's Plan to Revitalize Michigan's Economy." Lansing, Mich.: Office of the Governor. Available at: http://www.michigan.gov/gov/0,1607,7-168-46485-,00.html (accessed May 1, 2007).

Suleiman, Michael. 2006. "A History of Arab-American Political Participation." In *American Arabs and Political Participation,* edited by Philippa Strum. Washington: Woodrow Wilson International Center for Scholars.

Terry, Janice. 1999. "Community and Political Activism Among Arab Americans in Detroit." In *Arabs in America: Building a New Future?* edited by Michael Suleiman. Philadelphia: Temple University Press.

Thacher, David. 2005. "The Local Role in Homeland Security." *Law & Society Review* 39(3): 635–76.

U.S. Department of Justice. 2003. *The September 11 Detainees: A Review of the Treatment of Aliens Held on Immigration Charges in Connection with the Investigations of the September 11 Attacks.* Washington: U.S. Department of Justice.

Zogby International. 2002. "What U.S. Arabs Think." Unpublished dataset.

PART II

Beliefs and Bonds

CHAPTER 4

Belief and Belonging

Sally Howell and Amaney Jamal

"The more the immigrants enter into the religious life of America, the better and quicker they become Americans," observed historian Philip Hitti in 1924 (121). He intended the statement as a criticism of the early Syrian immigrants to the United States, whose churches—Maronite, Melkite, and Orthodox—he feared were perpetuating sectarian conflicts among the immigrants and isolating them from other Americans. In Detroit and its suburbs today there are dozens of Arab churches and mosques. Chaldean, Maronite, and Melkite Catholics have their own congregations, as do Egyptian Copts and Syrian, Greek, and Antiochian Orthodox Christians. Among Muslims, the Sunni-Shi'a distinction is only the most obvious divide running through more than two dozen predominantly Arab mosques. The strength, diversity, and overall visibility of these houses of worship have led today's scholars to draw conclusions different from those of Hitti. Andrew Shryock and Nabeel Abraham, for example, argued that Detroit's churches and mosques encourage immigrants and the American-born to interact with one another in a complex dynamic that serves to "mobilize immigrants, provide them with social services, and connect them to the political mainstream" (2000, 202). They take for granted the idea that American immigrant and ethnic communities are "entering the religious life of America" precisely by building religious institutions that are ethnic, sectarian, non-English speaking, non-Protestant, and otherwise new to the United States.

Our findings suggest that the religious experiences of Arabs in greater Detroit exist somewhere between these two realities. Neither uniformly poor nor structurally marginal, two factors to which Andrew Fuligni (1998) and Alejandro Portes and Rubén Rumbaut (1996) attributed the isolation of some immigrant congregations, Arab Detroit's houses of worship better resemble those described by Michael Foley and Dean Hoge (2007), Peggy Levitt (2007), and Stephen Warner and Judith Wittner (1998), for whom economic diversity and a mix of immigrant generations greatly enhances the social, economic, and political incorporation of worshippers. Concern about the religious participation and political incorporation of Arab Americans nonetheless remains, and focuses on two not unrelated questions. First, many scholars have argued that some of Detroit's Christian churches, especially Maronite and Chaldean ones, have worked to isolate their congregations from Arabs and Arab identity, weakening the overall sense of ethnic cohesion and solidarity among Arab Americans (Sengstock 1999; Jones 2000; Ahdab-Yehia 1983) and thereby weakening the political empowerment of Arab Detroit as a whole. Second, since the 1980s especially, observers have suggested that several of Detroit's Arab congregations, especially the mosques of recently arrived immigrants, are marginal for political or ideological reasons rather than (or in addition to) socioeconomic ones. Less is known about how sociopolitical conditions shape the incorporation of immigrants as religious communities, especially those from Arabic speaking countries.

Scholars have paid close attention to the role of religious institutions in the political mobilization of nonimmigrant citizens as well (Harris 1994; Jones-Correa and Leal 2001; Wuthnow 1999). Sidney Verba, Kay Scholzman, and Henry Brady (1995) found that churchgoers are more likely to be engaged in political activities. Churches can potentially increase individual levels of civic skills, political efficacy, and political knowledge. "The acquisition of such civic skills," they wrote, "is not a function of SES [socioeconomic status] but depends on the frequency of church attendance and denomination of the church one attends" (1995, 82). Some studies posit that instead of merely increasing levels of civic involvement, religious institutions can also serve as conduits for direct political mobilization. Steven Rosenstone and John Hansen argued that involvement "in organizations . . . promotes political participation by making people susceptible to mobilization. Politically, organizations stand between national and local political leaders and ordinary citizens" (1993, 87). More recent studies have found that civic skills gained in churches not only influence levels of political participation indirectly, but directly as well by recruiting congregants into the political process (Djupe and Grant 2001). In short, church participation can bolster political engagement. Does it do so equally for Arab mosques and churches?

Ethnohistorical research has produced nuanced accounts of the great investment that Detroit's Arabic-speakers have made in their houses of worship, attesting to the important role they play in supporting ethnic and religious distinctiveness, in shoring up (and sometimes resisting) Arab American pan-ethnicity, and in seeking mainstream accommodation for uncommon religious dietary practices, holiday observances, and ritual obligations (Abraham 2000; Ahdab-Yehia 1983; Elkholy 1966; Haddad and Smith 1993; Howell 2000a; Jones 2000; Sengstock 1999; Walbridge 1997; Wasfi 1971; Wigle 1974). Work on Christian and Muslim congregations has diverged on the question of political engagement. For the most part, scholars agree that church participation facilitates assimilation and political engagement among Arab Christians (Allhof 1969; Besecker-Kassab 1992; Kayal 2002), while scholars who work among Muslim Americans are more reserved in applying straight-line assimilation models (Haddad and Esposito 1998). Ingrid Mattson sorted Muslim religious practices into those associated with incorporation, isolationism, and "resistant engagement" (2003). Others have pointed out that Muslims who participate in the more public and institutionally situated religious activities of their congregations are also more likely to be involved in other forms of civic engagement, patterns that hold across the socioeconomic spectrum (Bagby 2004; Howell 2000a; Jamal 2005; Khan 2003; McCloud 2003; Safi 2006). Likewise, although political empowerment and ethnic identification are by-products of congregational participation for members of other minority faith traditions (Levitt 2004; Rutledge 1992; Wilcox and Gomez 1990), scholars have cautioned that only some types of congregational practice—institutional development, worship, and charity—lead to increased participation in the political sphere. More private and devotional practices correspond, instead, to political disengagement (Ammerman 1997).

For Arab Americans, the nuances of these links between devotional practices (or simple piety) and sociopolitical incorporation have not yet been fully explored. This research gap is due in part to the complexity and diversity of religious identifications among Arabs; it is also caused by the increasingly sensitive political contexts in which Arab American belonging is promoted and challenged. Although this challenge is deeply historical and has long targeted Muslim Americans more directly than Christians, its political ramifications have intensified since 9/11, affecting Arab Americans as a whole and accounting for much of the bifurcation of Muslim and Christian identities that is now visible in Detroit (see Hitti 1924; Naff 1985; Suleiman 2007).

Neoconservative commentators who make alarmist claims describing American mosques as sites of anti-American political and religious radicalization were, in the post-9/11 period, embraced by the Bush administration and other shapers of mainstream political thought; their influence in the mainstream media and within the homeland security establishment was also considerable (Horowitz 2004; Pipes 2003). Daniel Pipes went so far as to describe all forms of Muslim organizational life in the West as part of "lawful jihad," asserting that by "working through the school system, the media, the religious organizations, the government, businesses and the like you can promote radical Islam" (Andrea Elliot, "Battle in Brooklyn," *New York Times,* April 28, 2008, 1). Religiously oriented political activism can direct itself toward many opposing political ends both for mainstream American believers and among immigrant or other minority populations (Tamney 2007; Green 2007; Prashad 2000), a point Muslim critical theorists in the West are especially eager to illustrate (Majid 2007; Mamdani 2004), but in Pipes's extremist perspective no Muslim American activity is palatable or beyond suspicion. In this state of hegemonic paranoia about Islam and Muslims, everyday practices like building mosques or meeting regularly for prayer are taken as insurgent acts rather than as steps taken toward religious and social incorporation.

Scholars working in multiethnic immigrant terrain argue, as did Peggy Levitt, that those "who care more about holy sites and shrines make different kinds of political choices than the person who puts the national flag first and foremost" (2004, 154). But Arab Americans—especially Muslims whose national belonging is challenged, even those who seek to engage in mainstream politics in its most nationalistic and flag-waving varieties, supporting "our troops" or raising funds for presidential candidates, for example—are often questioned about their sincerity or blocked from participation (Howell 2000b; Shryock 2002).[1] Thus, for Arab Americans the links that exist between piety, congregational participation, religious and ethnic identification, and political incorporation are extremely consequential, precisely because they are also dichotomized, difficult to reconcile, and suspect (Joseph 1999; Naber 2005).

We argue in this chapter that the war on terror, by singling out Muslims and Muslim institutions as potential threats to national security, has intensified the distinction between Muslim and Christian Arabs in Detroit, where, in public contexts at least, some Christian populations tend to downplay the Arab content of their ethnic and ethnoreligious identities, and others continue to identify strongly as and with Arabs. Muslims, on the other hand, have found themselves and their mosques under intense public scrutiny; they have seen their religious charities shut down and fellow Muslims detained by law enforcement officers for simple religious observances, like praying in public.[2] Muslim congregations, simply put, have fewer means by which to escape the stigma now associated with Arabness and Islam in America. For both populations, religious piety and congregational participation influence their social incorporation as American citizens, sometimes in contradictory ways. In the pages that follow, we explore the role churches and mosques play in the Americanization process and ask if it has become more difficult for Muslim Arabs to participate as citizens. We also consider how Arab Detroiters, both Muslim and Christian, both observant and nonpracticing, participate in local houses of worship, asking, as Philip Hitti did several generations ago, whether this participation encourages or discourages their incorporation as cultural and political citizens of the United States.

ROUTES TO INCORPORATION

The Detroit area is home to several of America's oldest Arab churches and mosques. It has long been at the fore of campaigns to foster public acceptance of Muslim and Eastern Christian religious traditions. The emigration of the first Christian Arabs to Detroit from the Ottoman province of Syria was set in motion in the late nineteenth century by their encounters with French and American missionaries active in the region. After arriving in the United States, these Arabic-speaking immigrants were able to worship in American churches decades before they built institutions of their own. Some of the first Maronite families to settle in Detroit, for example, joined Christ Church, an Episcopal congregation in the heart of the city. Many of their descendants worship there to this day. For the most part, however, Arabic-speaking Christians were quick to build their own churches. St. Maron's Catholic Church (established 1916), St. George's Antiochian Orthodox Church (established 1918), and Our Lady of Redemption Melkite Catholic Church (established 1929) kept Detroit's Syrian, Lebanese, and Palestinian communities alive during the immigration dry spell that extended from 1924 to 1965. Iraqi Chaldeans established their first parish, the Mother of God Church, in 1947. Today, the Detroit area is home to more than a dozen churches with Arabic and Aramaic-speaking congregations.

Muslim immigration to Michigan, by contrast, began to accelerate at the start of World War I, just as immigration to the United States was becoming more difficult. This pattern effectively held Muslim numbers below a few thousand until the 1960s (Naff 1985; Elkholy 1966). The smaller size of their communities made it difficult for Muslims to build viable religious institutions of their own. Their first effort, the Moslem Mosque of Highland Park, opened its doors to great fanfare in 1921. It was considered an exotic novelty by some, a beacon of Islam in the West by others. With no tradition of supporting a mosque independently and no precedent for resolving sectarian and ethnic disputes among worshippers of diverse origins (Syrian, South Asian, Turkish, and Albanian), the Highland Park mosque closed within a year. Sunni and Shi'a Arabs established separate institutions in Dearborn and Highland Park in the 1930s (Howell 2007a, 2007b).[3] The largest mosques to emerge from these early efforts, the American Moslem Society (established 1938) and the Islamic Center of America (established 1961), have in recent decades become, once again, majority immigrant institutions. Radically altered and reinvigorated in the process, these mosques have given rise to more than a dozen rival and sibling institutions, many of which are now undergoing their own population shifts and ideological upheavals.

Both Christian and Muslim Arabs became religious outsiders when they arrived in the Untied States. Moving from a region with a Sunni Muslim majority to a nation-state in which Protestant Christianity was dominant, both traditions—Islam and Eastern Christianity—became minority traditions. Laurence Moore first used the term *religious outsiders* to illustrate how sectarian, minority, and immigrant traditions have challenged Protestant hegemony in the United States. The claim to outsider status on the part of any faith community, he argued, is simultaneously a demand for mainstream rights and acceptance (1986, 46). According to this logic, outsider status has not disempowered immigrants from Arab Muslim societies; rather, it has sharpened their attention to the dynamics of ethnoreligious solidarity and buffered them from the religious (and secular) mainstream. Despite the many factors that set Arab Muslims apart from Arab Christians, and distinguish both from other Americans, their churches and mosques have played a significant role in the creation of American citizens. By insisting on the right to practice Islam and Eastern Christian rites in the United States, by mirroring American Protestant styles of congregational worship and institutional organization, and by expanding the contexts in which non-Protestant and non-Christian religious practices are accommodated in the American public sphere, Arabic-speaking Christians and Muslims have contributed significantly to the religious pluralism of the United States.

This process has not unfolded in the same way, however, for Muslim and Christian Arabs. Arab-majority churches, both Catholic and Orthodox, made this journey, as Philip Kayal pointed out, in several stages: "Christians in the Middle East, it must be remembered, traditionally defined themselves as members of 'religious nations' rather than citizens/members of secular states. Assimilation then would commence for them after a new identity emerged here which was recognizable to the host society" (1973, 111). Thus Arabic-speaking Christians had to accept a generic Syrian-Arab ethnoreligious identity that overlooked their historical and liturgical differences before they were able to acculturate as American Christians.[4] They had to make similar accommodations within Catholicism by adapting Latin rites in the 1950s, and within Orthodoxy by joining with Greek and Russian patriarchates in the same period. In the 1950s, Arab Muslims established the Federation of Islamic Associations in the United States and Canada, a group that sought to represent and unify Muslims, of diverse national and theological origins, in a similar religious framework. Muslims were such a tiny minority until recent decades, however, that their visibility and influence were marginal. With practices that sometimes differ markedly from those of Christianity (such as Friday rather than Sunday collective worship, holidays that shift dates and even seasons with each calendar year, distinct fasting traditions, unique food and clothing traditions, and fixed times for multiple, distinctive, and very visible daily prayers), Muslims have faced many obstacles to the accommodation of their religious practices by mainstream institutions.

Today, Christian and Muslim Arabs in greater Detroit find their status as majority or minority traditions dramatically reversed relative to their status in the Middle East. More than half (58 percent) of Detroit's Arabs are Christian, whereas in the Arab world less than 5 percent are. Proportions for sectarian affiliations are also reversed: 42 percent of Detroit's Arabs are Catholic, whereas in the Arab world only a minority of the Christian population are. Orthodox Christians are the majority among Christians in the Arab world, but make up only 13 percent of Detroit's Arabs and only 23 percent of its Arab Christians. Similarly, the second largest sectarian population in Arab Detroit is Shi'a, at 23 percent, who make up more than half (56 percent) of Detroit's Arab Muslim population. In the Arab world, only 15 percent of Muslims are Shi'a, and globally an even smaller percentage are. Sunni Muslims are by far the largest faith community in the Arab world, yet in the Detroit area they represent only 35 percent of Arab Muslims, and among Arab Americans as a whole, only 15 percent. As noted earlier, these populations also arrived in the United States at different times. Two-thirds of Catholics arrived in the United States before 1979 or are the children and grandchildren of immigrants. Two-thirds of Detroit's Shi'a, by contrast, immigrated after 1979, and only 18 percent are second- or third-generation Americans. Orthodox Christians made up a solid 33 percent of the migration before 1970, but by the 1990s were less than 10 percent. Of Detroit's Muslim population, only 13 percent were part of the pre-1970 migration (6 percent were Sunni). Of immigrants arriving after 1995, 32 percent are Sunni.

Denominational and sectarian populations are also divided along national lines. Seventy percent of Catholics are Iraqi Chaldeans, the majority of whom arrived in Michigan between 1970 and 1995. Twenty percent are of Lebanese/Syrian origin and are largely of the second and third generation. Only 30 percent of Lebanese Catholics are immigrants. Muslims, again, are more recent immigrants. Half of the Sunnis are Yemenis whose migration has gradually increased since the 1970s. Twenty percent of the Sunni population and the vast majority, 80 percent, of Shi'a are Lebanese immigrants, many of whom came in the 1980s in response to the Lebanese civil war and Israel's 1978 and 1982 invasions of Lebanon and subsequent occupation of the south. A quarter of the Lebanese Shi'a, however, have arrived in the past fifteen years. The other Shi'a are Iraqis, almost all of whom came in the 1990s after the first Gulf War.

Given that Arab Christians have been in Detroit longer, they tend also to be wealthier, better educated, and more integrated into the American middle class than Arab Muslims. One-third of Muslims have not graduated from high school, and Muslims are less likely to have college education than Christians. Muslims are twice as likely, at 34 percent, to have an annual household income of less than $20,000. Thirty-eight percent have incomes of $50,000 or more, which is comparable to the national Muslim average of 41 percent. Detroit's Muslims, however, are unlike Muslim Americans as a whole, who have much

higher education (Pew Forum on Religion and Public Life 2007).[5] The majority of Christian households, in contrast, earn $50,000 or more. Seventy-nine
percent of Muslims live in or near Dearborn or Detroit, which are both home
to large Arab enclaves. The city of Dearborn, in particular, with a population
of 99,000, is now 35 percent Arab American (U.S. Bureau of the Census
2007). Christians, however, are spread fairly evenly throughout the western,
eastern, and northern suburbs of Detroit.

Both Christian and Muslim Arab communities are deeply aware that life in
the United States makes new identities for them possible and that these new
identities need not be strictly religious. Chaldeans, for example, who are a small
Catholic minority in Iraq, have been alternately persecuted and protected by the
Iraqi government. With a cultural heritage that predates Islam and a language
(Aramaic) that ties them to the earliest Christian communities, Chaldeans are
free to reject Arab identity once they settle in the United States, where Arabness
is often stigmatized rather than privileged. As a result, Chaldean ethnonationalism is thriving in southeast Michigan, a trend that has produced a Chaldean
ethnicity unique to Michigan that is both part of and opposed to the sociopolitical dynamics of the region's Muslim and (non-Chaldean) Christian
Arab communities (Sengstock 1999). One question we are interested in concerns whether Chaldean rite churches actively promote this dynamic.

Arab Christian identities in the United States are not always antithetical to
Arab nationalism. Orthodox Christians tend to be proud of their status as Arabs.
In the DAAS survey, 84 percent of Orthodox Christians identified as Arab
American, compared to 54 percent of other Arab Christians. Palestinians in particular, who have a history of colonization, discrimination, and occupation different from that of Iraqis, do not dispute the Arabness of their identities. Local
churches where Palestinians predominate, including a Lutheran congregation
in Dearborn, are adamantly nationalist on questions of Palestinian statehood.
In addition, they provide excellent Arabic language classes for their children,
something most Arab-majority churches (and many mosques) in Detroit have
long forgone. Do these churches then actively promote Arab solidarity to any
measurable extent?

Among Muslims, these processes have evolved differently. A relatively small
and isolated population until the 1970s, Arab American Muslims have embraced
Islam and their Arab ethnicity interchangeably (82 percent of Muslims in the
DAAS population embrace the term Arab American). The Islamic revivalism
that began in Egypt, Saudi Arabia, and Iran in the 1970s played a pivotal role

in reconfiguring how Americans, including Muslim Americans, came to view Islam and its place in North American society. The early Muslim immigrants had worried primarily about the loss of their children to Christianity. They were less concerned about the inherent compatibility of Islam with American values, institutions, foreign policies, or social mores (Aossey 1978; Makdisi 1959; Wolf 1960). For immigrants who arrived after 1970, however, the compatibility of Islam and American culture has been a pressing issue (Bukhari et al. 2004; Leonard 2003). This issue was made more urgent by the presence of ethnic Arabs who had, over several decades, become American Muslims. To newly arrived immigrants, the approaches to Islamic practice favored by Americanized Muslims appeared lax at best and often seemed deviant or heretical (Abraham 2000).

Today, as in the early decades of the twentieth century, Arab Muslims in Detroit are the largest and most visible population of Muslims in a faith community that also includes Africans, African Americans, Bosnians, Albanians, Turks, and South Asians (Bagby 2004; Howell 2007b).[6] Arab Muslims find themselves asking and answering questions about Islam and American life within this larger, multicultural Islamic context, an environment that is often as vexed about Arab nationalism and ethnicity as the larger society is. With the intensification of U.S. diplomatic and military involvement in the Middle East in recent decades, the repercussions of publicly identifying as Arab or Muslim in America have shifted in ways both subtle and obvious. Islam has come to represent not simply the exotic and new but something far more ominous in the collective imagination of Americans (Naber 2008; McAlister 2001; Said 2000; Suleiman 1992). Especially since the 9/11 attacks, the suspicion and stereotyping faced by Arabs have been directed most intensely at Islam and Muslims. Heightened terror alerts and inflammatory news stories that focus on Muslims as a potential threat dominate the popular media.

In the United States and the Arab world alike, many people now believe that a clash of civilizations is occurring (see chapter 8, this volume), rather than a conventional geopolitical struggle over resources, rights, and political power (Pew Global Attitudes Project 2006). Thus the 9/11 attackers are widely seen as representing Islam, and U.S. and British ground forces fighting Islamic insurgencies in Iraq and Afghanistan are seen as representing Christianity or the West. In this new geopolitical space, Muslim Americans, like Muslims in Europe, are a social anomaly (Cesari 2004; Dudziak 2003; Modood 2005). They are also subject, much more so than Arab Christians, to special investigations. In 2005, for example, the FBI announced that it had driven specially-equipped radiation detection vehicles by Detroit mosques (Niraj Warikoo, "Nuclear Search Targets Muslims," *Detroit Free Press,* December 24, 2005). They made no similar claim about local Arab churches. In this climate, belonging to an outsider faith tradition has taken on new meanings that weigh heavily on Muslim American congregations, especially Arab ones. Although Arab Christians might argue that their congregations moved beyond their outsider status a generation or more in the past—sentiments our findings both support and contradict—few Arab Muslims would argue the same.

RELIGIOUS COMMITMENT AND
CHURCH OR MOSQUE ATTENDANCE

Turning our attention to the DAAS findings, we now examine how religious piety and congregational participation affect the political engagement of Arab Americans, their sense of belonging and discrimination, and their identification as ethnic or religious Americans. To guide our understanding of why people participate in religious institutions and how seriously they draw on the lessons taught there, we created a religious commitment (piety) scale that includes three items: praying daily, frequent study of scripture, and tithing or paying *zakat*.[7] Those who value all three practices we refer to as having a high level of piety or religious commitment; those who value one or two of them we describe as having medium commitment; and those who do not value any of them we refer to as having low commitment or as being more secular. We also looked at frequency of church or mosque attendance for purposes other than weddings or funerals.[8] Among Arab Detroiters, levels of piety and church or mosque attendance vary significantly by sectarian affiliation and ethnonational background. Before attempting a detailed analysis of these variations and their effects on political incorporation, we first look at more general patterns in the data.

More than one-third of Christians (38 percent) express a high level of personal commitment to their faith, valuing daily prayer, studying the bible, and tithing to their churches. As the regression on table 4.1 shows, those with high commitment are more likely to be women, to be more recently arrived immigrants, and to have less formal education than other Christians. Conversely, those with low commitment (12 percent of Christians) are better educated and have higher income than those with high or medium commitment (50 percent). Younger Christians and those who have been in the United States longer tend to be more secular and to show less commitment. Those who were born

Table 4.1   Religious Attendance and Religious Commitment

	Attend Religious Institutions (Christians)	Attend Religious Institutions (Muslims)	Religious Commitment (Low-High) (Christians)	Religious Commitment (Low-High) (Muslims)
Gender (female)	−0.348**	0.534***	0.171**	0.113
	(0.131)	(0.164)	(0.069)	(0.078)
Education	−0.027	−0.045	−0.026	−0.013
	(0.059)	(0.070)	(0.029)	(0.035)
Income	0.025	−0.102	−0.033	−0.003
	(0.072)	(0.090)	(0.037)	(0.045)
Immigrant cohort	−0.046	0.111	0.154**	0.011
	(0.105)	(0.134)	(0.060)	(0.070)
Citizen	−0.451*	0.272	0.064	−0.168
	(0.219)	(0.203)	(0.133)	(0.096)
Constant	−3.595***	−3.036***	−0.957***	−1.400***
	(0.390)	(0.459)	(0.229)	(0.229)
Observations	481	351	483	353
R^2	0.03	0.06	0.06	0.02
Adj R^2	0.02	0.04	0.05	0.01

Source: Detroit Arab American Study 2003.
Note: Parentheses contain standard errors.
*** $p < .001$, ** $p < .01$, * $p < .05$.

in the United States, however, are more likely to be in both the highest and lowest commitment categories, a pattern found among immigrant populations generally (Levitt 2004; Warner and Wittner 1998). Lebanese and Syrian Christians are more likely to be in the secular category than others, whereas Iraqis, especially Iraqi Chaldeans, tend more toward the high commitment category, perhaps because their populations are somewhat more recently arrived than Syrian and Lebanese Christian populations are.

In terms of church attendance, 48 percent of Christians attend church almost every week or more than once a week, and those who are most committed to practicing their faith are also more likely to be in this high attendance category. Christians in the most secular category tend to attend church a few times a year or less often than that. Church attendance in general, however, is not linked solely to piety among Christians. The least educated attend the most frequently, and attendance tapers off with higher education. Older adults attend church much more frequently than young adults, and more recently arrived immigrants attend more frequently than those who have been in the United States longer. Recent immigrants attend much more frequently than those who were born here, with Lebanese and Syrians somewhat more likely to attend than others. Chaldeans, despite their high commitment, and Palestinians are the least likely to attend church frequently. When we break this down according to denomination, Catholics and Orthodox express similar patterns in terms of both personal commitment and frequency of church attendance.

Personal religious commitment and frequent mosque attendance work very differently for Arab Muslims than they do for Arab Christians. A larger percentage of Christians (48 percent) attend church frequently than Muslims attend mosque (26 percent), whereas Muslims are more likely to express high personal commitment to their faith (52 percent high, 38 percent medium, and 10 percent low).

Muslims in the highest personal commitment category are found across the demographic spectrum, with gender contributing more than any other single factor to the extent of individual piety. Roughly half of both men and women are highly committed, but women by a margin of 10 percentage points are more likely than men to be less committed. Additionally, those with high personal commitment are found in the income extremes, but those who are more secular are found more in higher income brackets. Younger Muslims are much more likely than others to express high personal commitment to Islamic practices, and young adult Christians are more likely to be secular, both findings that mirror national patterns (Pew Forum on Religion and Public Life 2007). The most recently arrived and those born in Palestine and Yemen are also more likely to be in the high commitment category. Iraqis are not more likely to be highly committed, but they are least likely to be secular.

In terms of mosque attendance, women are more likely to be in the highest attendance categories, a pattern that defies expectations, given that participation in congregational prayers is considered more of an obligation for men than for women and that many of Detroit's mosques do not accommodate women as readily as they do men.[9] Wealthier Muslims are also more likely to attend religious services frequently, and those with the lowest incomes are more likely to attend infrequently if at all. Young adult Muslims attend more frequently than their elders, just as they show higher levels of commitment. Those born in the United States are also more likely to attend frequently, as are Yemeni Americans. Lebanese and Syrian Muslims are less likely to do so, but Iraqis, who have arrived more recently and who have fewer and less well-established mosques, also attend much less frequently than other Muslims. Sunnis are much more likely to attend mosque services frequently and to be in the high commitment category than their Shi'a counterparts, a finding confirmed by historical studies of Arab Detroit (Elkholy 1966; Wasfi 1971) and by national findings among Muslim Americans (Bagby 2004; Pew 2007). Unlike their Christian coethnics, Muslims in the most secular category of our scale rarely attend religious services, and those with a high level of religious commitment attend much more frequently. In other words, Muslim attendance at religious services is much more directly related to individual piety and less to social or other factors than church attendance is for Arab Christians (see table 4.1).

HOW RELIGIOUS COMMITMENT AND CHURCH OR MOSQUE ATTENDANCE MATTER

We now pay closer attention to how religious commitment and church attendance affect political participation, ethnic identity, and perceived levels of discrimination among Arab Detroiters. Does attending a church or mosque encourage people to identify as Arab American? Are the secular or the pious more likely to participate in political protests? Does either piety or attendance contribute to one's sense that Arab Americans or Islam are treated unfairly in the media? We explore these questions using four indicators of political participation: voting, contacting a public official to express a political opinion, participating in a social or political demonstration (in the past year), and contributing financially in support of a political candidate to measure our first set of dependent variables. For Christians, neither religiosity nor church attendance systematically explains greater levels of political participation. Those with stronger religious commitment are more likely to have made contributions to a political candidate. The most systematic factors explaining greater levels of political participation among both Christians and Muslims are education, citizenship, and time in the United States. Those who are more educated, are U.S. citizens, and have lived in the United States longer are more likely to be politically active, regardless of how frequently they attend religious services. More frequent mosque attendance and a high religious commitment among Muslims also encourage

Table 4.2   Political Participation Among Christians

	Vote	Petition	Protest	Contribute	Written
Church attendance	−0.056 (0.092)	−0.080 (0.100)	0.034 (0.165)	−0.120 (0.128)	−0.035 (0.119)
Religious commitment	0.136 (0.195)	0.175 (0.213)	0.572 (0.396)	0.547** (0.245)	0.436 (0.308)
Gender (female)	−0.114 (0.251)	0.200 (0.262)	−0.333 (0.407)	0.255 (0.326)	−0.302 (0.337)
Education	0.548*** (0.110)	0.450*** (0.103)	0.217 (0.125)	0.390*** (0.127)	0.573*** (0.140)
Income	0.086 (0.127)	0.427*** (0.140)	0.134 (0.161)	0.779*** (0.195)	0.359** (0.172)
Immigrant cohort	−0.656*** (0.192)	−1.355*** (0.244)	−0.588 (0.377)	−0.808*** (0.248)	−1.090*** (0.275)
Citizen	3.512*** (1.029)	0.166 (0.654)	0.378 (1.157)	1.068 (1.092)	−0.216 (1.090)
Constant	−4.568*** (1.176)	−2.644*** (0.982)	−3.747* (1.961)	−6.648*** (1.630)	−3.929*** (1.303)
Observations	479	481	481	481	481

Source: Detroit Arab American Study 2003.
Note: Parentheses contain standard errors.
*** $p < .001$, ** $p < .01$, * $p < .05$

political protesting and petitioning, activities that bespeak Muslim frustration with the political system rather than, or in addition to, their active engagement as citizens. This is especially true of both high commitment and more secular Muslims. Those with less religious commitment also vote more frequently when they regularly attend mosques (see tables 4.2 and 4.3).

To look at religious and ethnic identity, our second set of dependent variables, we constructed two indices. The first measured religious identity and the second Arab American ethnicity. Each is constructed using three questions. For religious identity, we included three statements: "I identify with other Muslim/Christian Americans"; "being Muslim/Christian American is a major factor in my social relations"; and "for others to know me as I really am, it is important for them to know that I am Muslim/Christian American."[10] In terms

Table 4.3   Political Participation Among Muslims

	Vote	Petition	Protest	Contribute	Written
Mosque	0.073	−0.836***	−0.480***	0.358*	−0.566
attendance	(0.129)	(0.200)	(0.136)	(0.177)	(0.305)
Religious	−0.068	−1.325***	−0.122	0.223	−0.790
commitment	(0.247)	(0.324)	(0.251)	(0.307)	(0.439)
Gender	0.025	0.689	0.405	−0.059	0.332
(female)	(0.305)	(0.425)	(0.357)	(0.509)	(0.665)
Education	0.027	0.838***	0.273*	0.628***	0.834***
	(0.136)	(0.180)	(0.124)	(0.167)	(0.238)
Income	0.437**	0.575**	0.035	0.835***	−0.193
	(0.170)	(0.217)	(0.169)	(0.266)	(0.367)
Immigrant	−0.374	−0.940***	−0.181	−0.283	−0.810
cohort	(0.237)	(0.303)	(0.284)	(0.337)	(0.481)
Citizen		1.699	0.810	0.841	1.540
	—	(0.894)	(0.490)	(0.887)	(1.184)
Constant	−1.129	−1.943	−1.389	−8.715***	−2.733
	(0.936)	(1.270)	(1.031)	(1.752)	(1.428)
Observations	237	350	349	350	350

Source: Detroit Arab American Study 2003.
Note: Parentheses contain standard errors.
*** $p < .001$, ** $p < .01$, * $p < .05$.

of ethnic identity, we first ask if the term *Arab American* describes the person. If the answer was yes, we asked if the person agreed with the following statements: "I identify with other Arab Americans"; "being Arab American is a major factor in my social relations"; and "for others to know me as I really am, it is important for them to know that I am Arab American."[11] The question about strength of identification as Arab American was not asked of those who do not identify this way (30 percent). Christians with a high level of religious commitment and those who attend church frequently are much more likely to identify as Christian Americans and to identify strongly with other Christians. The same is true of Muslims who are highly committed and attend mosque frequently. They are more likely to identify as and with Muslim Americans. Contrary to expectation, however, strong religious commitment

Table 4.4   Arab and Religious Identity Among Christians and Muslims

	Arab Identity (Christians)	Arab Identity (Muslims)	Religious Identity (Christians)	Religious Identity (Muslims)
Religious attendance	−0.052 (0.042)	−0.120*** (0.041)	−0.152*** (0.034)	−0.192*** (0.036)
Religious commitment (Christians)	0.074 (0.097)		0.201*** (0.065)	
Gender (female)	0.183 (0.109)	0.217* (0.096)	−0.008 (0.089)	0.314*** (0.094)
Education	−0.046 (0.041)	0.058 (0.044)	−0.043 (0.040)	0.052 (0.038)
Income	−0.001 (0.051)	0.094 (0.059)	−0.037 (0.042)	0.024 (0.048)
Immigrant cohort	0.214* (0.094)	0.043 (0.075)	0.092 (0.069)	0.007 (0.071)
Citizen	0.359 (0.199)	−0.005 (0.124)	−0.018 (0.135)	0.014 (0.108)
Religious commitment (Muslims)		0.225*** (0.078)		0.435*** (0.083)
Constant	2.484*** (0.417)	2.566*** (0.324)	3.242*** (0.278)	2.355*** (0.298)
Observations	309	288	471	349
R^2	0.06	0.15	0.13	0.28
Adjusted R^2	0.04	0.13	0.11	0.27

Source: Detroit Arab American Study 2003.
Note: Parentheses contain standard errors.
*** $p < .001$, ** $p < .01$, * $p < .05$.

and frequent church attendance have little bearing on Christian identification with Arab American ethnicity. Pious, mosque-attending Muslims, by contrast, are much more likely to identify strongly as and with Arab Americans. Religiosity among Muslims reinforces Arab American and religious identities simultaneously, but among Christians religiosity and church attendance have mixed consequences for Arab American identification (see table 4.4).

Additionally, we look at how religious commitment and church attendance structure attitudes about discrimination, tapping four dependent variables. One asks whether respondents worry more about their futures in the United States since the attacks of 9/11. One asks whether Muslims and Arabs can obtain a fair trial in the United States since the attacks. The final two ask if the media is biased against Arab Americans, or against Islam and Muslim Americans. Among Christians, church attendance correlates with less worry about the future. In general, neither church attendance nor religious commitment contributes to increased concern about Arabs or Muslims obtaining a fair trial in the United States, except among moderately committed Christians for whom frequent church attendance encourages the perception of media bias against both the Arab community as a whole and Muslims and Islam in particular. Among Muslims, those with a high religious commitment worry more about their future in the United States and are more likely to believe that Muslims and Arabs cannot obtain fair trials. Even controlling for mosque attendance, we find that higher religious commitment contributes to a strong perception of discrimination among Muslims. In other words, mosque attendance may provide Muslims with increased opportunities to express frustration over discrimination or unpopular political policies, but this frustration tracks more to religious piety than to mosque attendance or worship. Arab Muslims in Detroit found the post-9/11 American political climate hostile to Islam and to Muslims, and the more committed they were to the practice of their religious beliefs, the more likely they were to perceive this hostility (see tables 4.5 and 4.6).

ETHNIC AND SECTARIAN DISTINCTIVENESS

It is easy to assume that Arab Christians and Arab Muslims represent unified blocs, when in fact they vary internally in systematic and often contradictory ways. Among Catholics, for example, those who attend church more often are also more likely to vote, and high commitment Orthodox are more likely to have contributed to a political campaign. Among both Catholics and Orthodox, piety and frequent church attendance encourage stronger identification as Christians, but have little bearing on Arab American ethnic identification. High commitment Orthodox are more likely than high commitment Catholics to worry about their futures in the United States, perhaps because the Orthodox feel more distant from the religious mainstream. Orthodox Christians are also much more likely than Catholics to identify as Arab Americans, a pattern that may contribute to their heightened sense of vulnerability.

Table 4.5   Worry, Discrimination, and Bias Among Christians

	Worry	Fair Trial	Media Bias Against Arabs	Media Bias Against Muslims
Church attendance	0.208** (0.097)	0.075 (0.086)	0.139 (0.088)	0.239*** (0.090)
Religious commitment	0.191 (0.198)	0.254 (0.177)	0.119 (0.196)	0.101 (0.180)
Gender (female)	0.351 (0.253)	−0.403 (0.219)	0.403 (0.230)	−0.081 (0.226)
Education	−0.134 (0.106)	−0.021 (0.092)	0.135 (0.097)	−0.009 (0.095)
Income	−0.015 (0.123)	−0.038 (0.112)	0.314*** (0.121)	0.141 (0.115)
Immigrant cohort	0.159 (0.205)	0.291 (0.177)	−0.512** (0.202)	−0.676*** (0.193)
Citizen	−0.198 (0.422)	0.307 (0.373)	−0.093 (0.483)	0.032 (0.425)
Constant	−1.363 (0.871)	−0.041 (0.749)	−2.616*** (0.838)	−0.769 (0.764)
Observations	377	455	471	456

Source: Detroit Arab American Study 2003.
Note: Parentheses contain standard errors.
*** $p < .001$, ** $p < .01$, * $p < .05$.

Chaldeans with a high commitment to their faith are more likely to write letters to their representatives, but not to engage in other forms of political behavior. For them, strong religious commitment contributes to the strength of their identification as Christians, but piety does not in itself discourage their identification as Arab Americans. Frequent church attendance also has little bearing on their political incorporation, though education and income do. Higher income Chaldeans are more likely to find the media biased against Arab Americans. Chaldeans who have been in the United States longer participate more in the political process, but are less likely to identify as Arab Americans, a point that backs up our earlier assertion that Chaldean distinctiveness from other Arabs is nurtured in Detroit, though not, as we had expected, by participation in Chaldean rite churches.

Table 4.6   Worry, Discrimination, and Bias Among Muslims

	Worry	Fair Trial	Media Bias Against Arab Americans	Media Bias Against Muslims
Mosque	0.024	0.023	−0.236*	−0.181
attendance	(0.131)	(0.107)	(0.103)	(0.116)
Religious	1.017***	−0.375	0.142	0.556**
commitment	(0.270)	(0.219)	(0.208)	(0.234)
Gender	0.553	−0.483	0.041	0.511
	(0.314)	(0.265)	(0.272)	(0.287)
Education	0.466***	−0.328***	0.484***	0.593***
	(0.152)	(0.117)	(0.112)	(0.129)
Income	0.326	−0.564***	0.322**	0.516***
	(0.207)	(0.158)	(0.137)	(0.157)
Immigrant	0.377	−0.512**	−0.307	−0.099
cohort	(0.286)	(0.236)	(0.233)	(0.234)
Citizen	0.319	0.293	−0.293	−0.497
	(0.382)	(0.328)	(0.326)	(0.331)
Constant	−3.773***	3.421***	−0.788	−2.321**
	(1.157)	(0.985)	(0.894)	(0.960)
Observations	287	328	335	338

Source: Detroit Arab American Study 2003.
Note: Parentheses contain standard errors.
*** $p < .001$, ** $p < .01$, * $p < .05$.

Lebanese and Syrian Christians, on the other hand, are more likely to contribute to political campaigns when they have a high commitment to their faith. Those who attend church more frequently vote in higher percentages than others. High religious commitment also encourages strong Christian identification. Church attendance, however, discourages concern about Arabs receiving a fair trial in the United States. Thus we see that, among Lebanese and Syrian Christians, churches can indeed act as a slight wedge between Christian and Muslim concerns, whereas among Palestinian Christians no such effect is present. Palestinian Christians look like Christians as a whole on the question of political incorporation. Education, income, and time in America—

rather than personal religious commitment or church attendance—drive political participation.

Given that Arab Christians are much less likely than Muslims to be immigrants, especially recently arrived immigrants, their churches do not play an active role in inhibiting their political incorporation, as Philip Hitti once feared. Where church attendance does play a role in incorporation, it correlates always to increased activity, especially among Catholics, either in the form of increased political protest for highly committed Catholics, increased voting for Lebanese and Syrians, or increased letter writing among Chaldeans. Frequent church attendance also plays a role in creating solidarity between Christians and Muslims, at least among those moderately committed to their faith and among the Orthodox. This solidarity is expressed in a shared sense of media bias against both the Arab community as a whole and against Muslims and Islam in particular. Moderately pious Christians are also more concerned about the civil liberties of Arab Americans when they attend church frequently than when they do not. Syrian and Lebanese Christians, however, contradict this pattern somewhat. For them, frequent church attendance decreases their perception of media bias against Muslims. Among Chaldeans, concern for media bias against Muslims is low overall.

National origins and sectarian affiliations also influence the impact religious piety and mosque attendance have on the political incorporation of Muslims, their identification as Arab Americans, and their perception of discrimination. Among the Sunni, for example, religious attendance encourages political protest and identification as Arab American. Sunni women and more educated Sunnis are also more likely to identify strongly as Arab American. Those with a high level of religious commitment are more likely to worry about the future, which might explain why, for them, frequent mosque attendance encourages political protesting and petition signing. As further evidence that this particular part of the Muslim community feels distress, mosque attendance also contributes to their sense of bias in the mainstream American media against both Islam and Arab Americans.

Among the Shi'a, a different pattern holds sway. Mosque attendance is linked again to political protest, letter writing, and greater worry about the future. Education also matters for the types of political activity Shi'a engage in, encouraging either political contributions or letter writing. Neither longer residence in the United States nor American birth seems to encourage political activities such as voting or making political contributions, as they do among

Arab Christians, but they do reduce concerns about the future. Although none of these factors contribute significantly to whether Shi'a Americans also identify as Arab Americans, those who do identify as Arabs and are also more pious, attend mosque more frequently, and have higher incomes.

Lebanese and Syrian Muslims, who are majority Shi'a, are also affected by frequent mosque attendance, which encourages their participation in political protests, and by high levels of religious commitment, which encourages greater concern about the future and a stronger sense that the media is biased against Muslims and the Arab American community. Education and income influence the political incorporation of this group far more than either religious commitment or mosque attendance. In this respect, they resemble Arab Christians. The wealthier and better educated they are, the more likely they are to participate across the political spectrum and the more likely they are to be concerned about Arabs receiving fair trials and about media bias against the Arab community and Muslims. For the Lebanese, the longer one has lived in the United States and having been born in the United States both contribute greatly to political participation as well, mirroring patterns found among Arab Christians. Piety and attendance, for this group, also contribute to their identification as Muslims.

The political incorporation of Yemenis, however, who tend to have arrived more recently and are uniformly Sunni, does not appear to be influenced by religious commitment or mosque attendance. High commitment Yemenis worry about the future and are less likely to believe that Muslims and Arabs can obtain a fair trial. High commitment Yemenis and those who attend mosque frequently, like other Muslims, are more likely to both identify as Arab American and have a strong sense of their religious identity. Yemenis with more education vote less, perhaps because fewer well-educated Yemenis are citizens, but education does, as in other populations, encourage other forms of political participation as well as higher concern about media biases against both Arabs and Muslims.[12]

These findings confirm that piety and regular attendance at religious services have consequences for the incorporation of Arab Americans, but these consequences do not encompass the population as a whole, nor do they show Christian or Muslim populations to be consistently unlike each other. In chapter 2, Shryock and Lin describe two zones of identity construction for Arab Detroit: one that is predominately Christian, suburban, and likely to identify as white and a second that is largely Muslim, residing in or near Dearborn or

Detroit, and likely to identify as other. In the first zone, religious attendance and religious commitment contribute occasionally to increased voting, donating money to campaigns, and protesting. Sometimes they instill greater confidence in the future. In the second zone, however, they are much more likely to intensify concern about discrimination and media stereotyping and to encourage political activity that is correspondingly more oppositional in nature, such as protesting and petitioning. Yet our findings also highlight the internal diversity of these zones. In many ways, different Arab ethnonational and sectarian populations are charting their own routes to incorporation. This is especially relevant when we consider how religious commitment and church-mosque attendance augment pan-Christian or pan-Muslim identities, but have different effects on the overarching Arab American identity that transects both of Arab Detroit's dominant identity zones.

CONCLUSION

Detroit's churches and mosques are organized around beliefs and practices that lend a sacred quality to ethnic and national identities. By emphasizing religious traditions linked to a history of immigration, Arab American churches and mosques connect their members to Arab homelands, to believers around the globe, and to other Americans. Religious observances create communities of shared suffering and co-responsibility (Werbner 2001); they enact the grief and joy that fill ritual calendars, strengthening bonds to the living and the dead with an immediacy that secular forms of Arab American ethnicity can seldom reproduce. They also contribute to the identities, sectarian and ethnonational, through which Detroiters engage the political process.

Our findings suggest that for Arabs in greater Detroit, the relationships between piety, ethnic identity, and political incorporation are difficult to reconcile. On the one hand, it appears that Arab Christians are already well along the path to full American citizenship, regardless of whether they identify as Arab Americans, Chaldean Americans, as some other ethnic appellation, or simply as Americans. Their churches play little role in encouraging or discouraging their participation in the American political process; in this respect, they resemble other Detroiters who, on average, attend church with slightly higher frequency than Arab Christians but whose church attendance has limited bearing on their political participation when viewed in the aggregate (Baker and Boudens 2008). Among pious Arab Christians generally, and among Chaldeans in particular, church attendance does little to encourage identification as Arab American, but it also does little to discourage this panethnic identity. Among those with a moderate religious commitment, however, and among the Orthodox in particular, church attendance does lead to greater solidarity with Arab and Muslim Americans.

Arab Muslims, by contrast, are in a very different sociopolitical location. They experience a greater sense of exclusion, a not-quite-us status, whether they identify as Arab Americans or not. Muslims with a higher commitment to the practice of Islam feel a greater sense of discrimination than other Muslims do. Local mosques do not necessarily foster this sense of stigma. Mosque participation does, however, encourage Muslims to express their political dissatisfaction with American policies through demonstrations and petitioning.[13] Overall, levels of political participation are slightly lower among Arab Muslims than among Arab Christians, a tendency we attribute to the more recent arrival of most Muslim immigrants. Yet these findings are somewhat ambiguous given that the DAAS survey was administered just before and during the United States invasion of Iraq in 2003. This event led to heated political activity on the part of Arab Detroiters who expressed strong views for and against the war (see chapter 8). Not surprisingly, Arab Christians were more likely (5.5 percent) and Arab Muslims much more likely (14.8 percent) to participate in demonstrations and political protests in the year before the DAAS survey than residents of the Detroit area generally were (3.8 percent). Our evidence cannot tell us whether the same pattern would emerge in less eventful calendar years.

Our findings suggest that Arab churches today are not the zones of political and ethnic isolation Philip Hitti criticized several generations ago, nor are they sites of accelerated incorporation. In this regard, they resemble other churches in the Detroit area. It is harder to describe mosques in this way. Arab Muslims, despite their commitment to becoming U.S. citizens, find themselves subject to the widespread belief they are not in fact citizens, that their civil liberties can be infringed upon, that their political opinions do not matter, and that they are potentially a threat to other Americans. In short, Muslims do not have the same access to the benefits of citizenship as other Americans, and they are keenly aware of this inequality. Some Muslim populations (Yemenis, for example) are indeed associated with ethnic and religious isolationism, whereas others (Lebanese) are not, but congregations of both frequently play host to politicians who are running for office in local, state, and national elections. Governor Jennifer Granholm and Senator Debbie Stabenow were both on hand in 2005 for the opening of the Islamic Center of America, a predominately Lebanese American mosque that is arguably the largest in North America. The day before, both governor and senator had attended the opening of the American Moslem Society's renovated and expanded facility, where they were welcomed by a congregation that is predominately Yemeni American. Congressmen John Dingell and John Conyers are familiar faces at local mosque dinners, as is Senator Carl Levin. In greater Detroit, mainstream politicians cannot afford to ignore Muslim voters, and they are more likely to attend the fundraising banquets of large mosques than to attend events hosted by Arab or Chaldean churches.

We cannot conclude with certainty that Muslim isolation, when it does exist, is due primarily to the recent arrival of immigrants, to a political climate in which Islam is denigrated and treated with suspicion, to the religious and ideological understandings of Muslim Americans themselves, or even to variable combinations of such factors. The complexity of this situation can be seen, with disturbing regularity, in Detroit's popular media, where numerous stories highlight the difficulty Muslims encounter when they try to engage fully in American electoral politics. In May of 2008, for instance, Ali Jawad, a prominent Lebanese American business leader in Dearborn, was pressured to step down as chairman of the Michigan finance committee for U.S. presidential candidate John McCain after a local blogger accused Jawad of being an agent of Hizbullah. Two months later, Mazen Asbahi, an advisor to the Barack Obama campaign, was forced to resign under even more egregious circumstances because of his past membership on a mainstream Muslim American financial investment board. Christian Arabs are less likely to attract this sort of negative attention, which is one reason Michigan's Christian Arab politicians have been more successful over time.[14] Citing a long history of setbacks like the one Jawad suffered, Muslim activists are sometimes reluctant to go public with their support of candidates lest they (and the candidates they endorse) become targets of slanderous accusations and political blacklisting.

If some Christian Arabs in Detroit are prone to shy away from the public embrace of Arab American identity, it is often because this identity is commonly associated with Islam and Muslims. Whether they are Christian or Muslim, most Arab Americans agree that national media are biased against Islam, and 41 percent of Detroit's general population share this belief. In explaining lower levels of cultural membership among those who identify as Arab Americans (see chapter 6), and especially among those who identify as

Arab Muslims, it would be premature to argue that mosques and churches are somehow to blame, whereas anti-Arab prejudice and U.S. foreign policy in the Middle East are not. Higher education, greater income, and increased time in America actually contribute to a sense of marginalization among Muslims (and among some Christians as well). Religious piety and attendance at Friday prayers or Sunday services play a less important role. The latter trends suggest an ironic truth: as Arab Muslims become more American culturally, their awareness of not being accepted as Americans by their fellow citizens grows more acute. As a result, this sensibility comes to occupy a central place in the American identities that Arab Muslims, and by extension all Arab Americans, can make for themselves.

NOTES

1. For an example of a sincerity challenge, see Andrew Shryock (2002). During his 2008 presidential campaign, volunteers for Senator Barack Obama's campaign in Detroit barred two hijab-wearing Arab Americans from sitting on the podium where they would be visible to television cameras recording the senator's speech.

2. In 2006, for example, a high profile incident of this nature drew national media coverage. Six religious leaders who were returning home from a conference were pulled off a plane, detained, and questioned by Homeland Security personal after a fellow passenger raised concerns about them in response to seeing them pray at the airport (see Jessica Bennet and Matthew Philips, "Flying While Muslim," *Newsweek,* November 22, 2006).

3. In the Ottoman Province of Syria, which was home to Detroit's first Arab Muslims, mosques were supported by religious endowments rather than by local congregations.

4. It can be argued that Chaldean and other more recently arrived Assyrian communities are in the midst of reproducing this process today, opting for an Assyrian identity in order to avoid association with either Arab or Syrian panethnicities. In Detroit these populations have long participated in organizations and activities associated with the empowerment of Arab Americans as a whole, like the Arab World Festival and the American-Arab Anti-Discrimination Committee, while striving to preserve Chaldean (and other forms of) particularity.

5. The national sample of Muslims shows that only 21 percent have not completed high school, compared to Detroit's 34 percent (Pew Forum on Religion and Public Life 2007).

6. Nationally, they constitute 25 percent of the Muslim population (Pew Forum on Religion and Public Life 2007).

7. The Cronbach's alpha for these three variables stands at .8934 for Muslims and .8242 for Christians. These high reliability scales tell us the variables are tapping into similar dimensions of religious piety. Note also that our measure is slightly unusual in that it leaves off attendance at Sunday (for Christian) and Friday (for Muslim) religious services to facilitate comparability between Muslim and Christian attendance patterns. Eighty-three percent of Christians, compared to 46 percent of Muslims, said it is important for them to attend weekly services.

8. Our questions about religious practice were designed to include both Muslim and Christian practices and not to tease apart the nuances of either tradition.

9. Our attendance measure refers to mosque attendance for purposes other than weddings and funerals and is thus not a measure of Friday prayer attendance as other surveys tend to be. On the question of Friday congregational prayer attendance, 46 percent of Muslims believe that it is important to attend Friday prayers, 35 percent of women and 57 percent of men. Eighty-three percent of Christians believe it is important to attend Sunday services.

10. The alpha reliability scale is .7880 for Christians and .7876 for Muslims.

11. The alpha reliability scale is .8769.

12. Because of space limitations only the regression results with the categories of Muslim and Christian are reported here. The regression models for ethnic, national, and sub-religious identities are available upon request.

13. Using a different measure of congregational participation, Ronald Stockton came to a similar conclusion about both Christian and Muslim Arabs for whom "congregational involvement appears to be linked to an 'oppositional' culture and a love-hate relationship with power" (2006, 62).

14. Spencer Abraham, for example, is a former U.S. senator and served as secretary of energy in the George W. Bush administration. Mike Bouchard, Oakland County sheriff, lost his race for the U.S. Senate in 2006 but is now considered a viable gubernatorial candidate for 2010. The state's highest ranking Muslim official, Ismael Ahmed, holds an appointed position, secretary of the Department of Human Services, rather than an elected one. for more information on greater Detroit's Arab politicians, elected and appointed, see chapter 3.

REFERENCES

Abraham, Nabeel. 2000. "Arab Detroit's 'American' Mosque." In *Arab Detroit: From Margin to Mainstream,* edited by Nabeel Abraham and Andrew Shryock. Detroit, Mich.: Wayne State University Press.

Ahdab-Yehia, May. 1983. "The Lebanese Maronites: Patterns of Continuity and Change." In *Arabs in the New World: Studies on Arab-American Communities,* edited by Sameer Abraham and Nabeel Abraham. Detroit, Mich.: Wayne State University Press.

Allhoff, John. 1969. "Analysis of the Role of St. Raymond's Maronite Church as an Agent in the Assimilation of Lebanese Families in St. Louis." Masters thesis, University of Missouri, St. Louis.

Ammerman, Nancy. 1997. "Organized Religion in a Voluntaristic Society." *Sociology of Religion* 58(3): 203–15.

Aossey, Bill Yahya. 1978. "The Role of the Islamic Center and Its Necessity in the Development of Muslim Communities in North America." Unpublished. Naff Collection, National Museum of American History 78:1-k-1-b.

Baker, Wayne, and Connie Boudens. 2008. "Voting Your Values." In *Christian Conservatives and American Democracy.* New York: Russell Sage Foundation.

Bagby, Ihsan. 2004. *A Portrait of Detroit Mosques: Muslim Views on Policy, Politics and Religion.* Clinton Township, Mich.: Institute for Social Policy and Understanding.

Besecker-Kassab, Charlotte Kay. 1992. "Immigrant Use of Political Media in the U.S.: A Case Study of the Maronite Lebanese of South Florida." Ph.D. dissertation, University of Miami.

Bukhari, Zahid, Sulayman Nyang, Mumtaz Ahmad, and John Esposito, eds. 2004. *Muslims' Place in the American Public Square.* New York: AltaMira Press.

Cesari, Jocelyne. 2004. *When Islam and Democracy Meet: Muslims in Europe and the United States.* New York: Palgrave Macmillan.

Detroit Arab American Study (DAAS). 2003. Unpublished dataset. Ann Arbor, Mich.: Institute for Social Research.

Djupe, Paul A., and J. Tobin Grant. 2001. "Religious Institutions and Political Participation in America." *Journal for the Scientific Study of Religion* 40(2): 303–14.

Dudziak, Mary, ed. 2003. *September 11 in History: A Watershed Moment?* Durham, N.C.: Duke University Press.

Elkholy, Abdo A. 1966. *The Arab Moslems in the United States: Religion and Assimilation.* New Haven, Conn.: College and University Press.

Foley, Michael, and Dean Hoge. 2007. *Religion and the New Immigrants: How Faith Communities Form Our Newest Citizen.* New York: Oxford University Press.

Fuligni, Andrew J. 1998. "The Adjustment of Children from Immigrant Families." *Current Directions in Psychological Science* 7(4): 99–103.

Green, John. 2007. "A Response to Tamney." *Newsletter of the Sociology of Religion Section of the American Sociological Association* 8(2): 4–7.

Haddad, Yvonne, and John Esposito, eds. 1998. *Muslims on the Americanization Path?* Atlanta, Ga.: Oxford University Press.

Haddad, Yvonne, and Jane Smith. 1993. *Mission to America.* Gainesville: University Press of Florida.

Harris, Fredrick C. 1994. "Something Within: Religion as a Mobilizer of African American Political Activism." *Journal of Politics* 56(1): 42–68.

Hitti, Phillip. 1924. *The Syrians in America.* New York: George H. Doran Company.

Horowitz, David. 2004. *Unholy Alliance: The Radical Islam and the American Left.* New York: Regnery Publishing.

Howell, Sally. 2000a. "Finding the Straight Path: A Conversation with Mohsen and Lila Amen about Faith, Life, and Family in Dearborn." In *Arab Detroit: From Margin to Mainstream,* edited by Nabeel Abraham and Andrew Shryock. Detroit, Mich.: Wayne State University Press.

———. 2000b. "Politics, Pragmatism and the 'Arab Vote': A Conversation with Maya Berry." *Arab Detroit: From Margin to Mainstream,* edited by Nabeel Abraham and Andrew Shryock. Detroit, Mich.: Wayne State University Press.

———. 2007a. "Mosque History." In *The Encyclopedia of Islam in the United States,* edited by Jocelyne Cesari. Cambridge, Mass.: Harvard University Press.

———. 2007b. "Detroit: History and Development." In *The Encyclopedia of Islam in the United States,* edited by Jocelyne Cesari. Cambridge, Mass.: Harvard University Press.

Jamal, Amaney. 2005. "Mosques, Collective Identity, and Gender Differences Among Arab American Muslims." *Journal of Middle Eastern Women's Studies* 1(1): 53–78.

Joseph, Suad. 1999. "Against the Grain of the Nation." In *Arab in America: Building a New Future,* edited by Michael Suleiman. Philadelphia: Temple University Press.

Jones, Richard. 2000. "Egyptian Copts in Detroit: Ethnic Community and Long-Distance Nationalism." In *Arab Detroit: From Margin to Mainstream,* edited by Nabeel Abraham and Andrew Shryock. Detroit, Mich.: Wayne State University Press.

Jones-Correa, Michael A., and David L. Leal. 2001. "Political Participation: Does Religion Matter?" *Political Research Quarterly* 54(4): 751–71.

Kayal, Philip. 1973. "Religion and Assimilation: Catholic 'Syrians' in America." *International Migration Review* 7(4): 409–25.

———. 2002. "So Who Are We? Who Am I?" In *Community of Many Worlds: Arab Americans in New York City,* edited by Kathleen Benson and Philip Kayal. Syracuse, N.Y.: Syracuse University Press.

Khan, Muqtedar. 2003. "Constructing the American Muslim Community." In *Religion and Immigration,* edited by Yvonne Haddad, Jane Smith, and John Esposito. Walnut Creek, Calif.: AltaMira Press.

Leonard, Karen. 2003. *Muslims in the Untied States: The State of Research.* New York: Russell Sage Foundation.

Levitt, Peggy. 2004. "Redefining the Boundaries of Belonging: The Institutional Character of Transnational Religious Life." *Sociology of Religion* 65(1): 1–18.

———. 2007. *God Needs No Passport: Immigrants and the Changing American Religious Landscape.* New York: New Press.

Majid, Anouar. 2007. *A Call for Heresy: Why Dissent in Vital to Islam and America.* Minneapolis: University of Minnesota Press.

Makdisi, Nadim. 1959. "The Moslems of America." *The Christian Century* 76(34): 969–71.

Mamdani, Mahmood. 2004. *Good Muslims, Bad Muslims: America, the Cold War, and the Roots of Terror.* New York: Doubleday.

Mattson, Ingrid. 2003. "How Muslims Use Islamic Paradigms to Define America." In *Religion and Immigration,* edited by Yvonne Haddad, Jane Smith, and John Esposito. Walnut Creek, Calif.: AltaMira Press.

McAlister, Melani. 2001. *Epic Encounters: Culture, Media, and U.S. Interests in the Middle East, 1945–2000.* Berkeley: University of California Press.

McCloud, Beverly. 2003. "Islam in America: the Mosaic." In *Religion and Immigration,* edited by Yvonne Haddad, Jane Smith, and John Esposito. Walnut Creek, Calif.: AltaMira Press.

Modood, Tariq. 2005. *Multicultural Politics: Racism, Ethnicity, and Muslims in Britain.* Minneapolis: University of Minnesota Press.

Moore, R. Laurence. 1986. *Religious Outsiders and the Making of Americans.* New York: Oxford University Press.

Naber, Nadine. 2005. "Muslim First-Arab Second: A Strategic Politics of Race and Gender." *The Muslim World* 95(4): 479–96.

———. 2008. "Introduction: Arab Americans and U.S. Racial Formations." In *Race and Arab Americans Before and After 9/11,* edited by Amaney Jamal and Nadine Naber. Syracuse, N.Y.: Syracuse University Press.

Naff, Alixa. 1985. *Becoming America: The Early Arab Immigrant Experience.* Carbondale: Southern Illinois University Press.

Pew Forum on Religion and Public Life (PEW). 2007. *Muslim Americans: Middle Class and Mostly Mainstream.* Washington, D.C.: Pew Research Center.

Pew Global Attitudes Project. 2006. *The Great Divide: How Westerners and Muslims View Each Other.* Washington, D.C.: Pew Research Center.

Pipes, Daniel. 2003. *Militant Islam Reaches America.* New York: W. W. Norton.

Portes, Alejandro, and Rubén Rumbaut. 1996. *Immigrant America: A Portrait.* Berkeley: University of California Press.

Prashad, Vijay. 2001. *The Karma of Brown Folk.* Minneapolis: University of Minnesota Press.

Rosenstone, Steven J., and John Mark Hansen. 1993. *Mobilization, Participation and Democracy in America.* New York: Macmillan.

Rutledge, Paul. 1992. *The Vietnamese Experience in America.* Bloomington: Indiana University Press.

Safi, Louay. 2006. "Blaming Islam: Examining the Religion Building Enterprise." Clinton, Mich.: Institute for Social Policy and Understanding.

Said, Edward. 2000. *Reflections on Exile and Other Essays.* Cambridge, Mass.: Harvard University Press.

Sengstock, Mary. 1999. *Chaldean Americans: Changing Conceptions of Ethnic Identity.* New York: Center for Migration Studies.

Shryock, Andrew. 2002. "New Images of Arab Detroit: Seeing Otherness and Identity through the Lens of 9/11." *American Anthropologist* 104(3): 917–22.

Shryock, Andrew, and Nabeel Abraham. 2000. "Introduction: Religion." In *Arab Detroit: From Margin to Mainstream.* Detroit, Mich.: Wayne State University Press.

Stockton, Ronald. 2006. "Arab-American Political Participation: Findings from the Detroit Arab American Study." In *American Arabs and Political Participation.* Washington: Woodrow Wilson International Center for Scholars.

Suleiman, Michael. 1992. "Arab-Americans and the Political Process." In *The Development of Arab-American Identity,* edited by Ernest McCarus. Ann Arbor: University of Michigan Press.

———. 2007. " 'I Come to Bury Caesar, Not to Praise Him': An Assessment of the AAUG as an Example of an Activist Arab-American Organization." *Arab Studies Quarterly* 9(3–4): 75–95.

Tamney, Joseph. 2007. "Methodological Biases in the Study of Religion and Politics." *Newsletter of the Sociology of Religion Section of the American Sociological Association* 8(2): 3–4.

U.S. Bureau of the Census. 2007. "Selected Social Characteristics in the United States: 2005, Dearborn, Michigan." *American Fact Finder.* Washington: U.S. Department of Commerce.

Verba, Sidney, Kay Lehman Schlozman, and Henry Brady. 1995. *Voice and Equality: Civic Voluntarism In American Politics.* Cambridge, Mass.: Harvard University Press.

Walbridge, Linda. 1997. *Without Forgetting the Imam: Lebanese Shi'ism in an American Community.* Detroit, Mich.: Wayne State University Press.

Warner, R. Stephen, and Judith Wittner. 1998. *Gatherings in Diaspora: Religious Communities and the New Immigration.* Philadelphia: Temple University Press.

Wasfi, Atif. 1971. *An Islamic-Lebanese Community in U.S.A.: A Study in Cultural Anthropology.* Beirut: Beirut Arab University.

Werbner, Pnina. 2002. *Imagined Diasporas Among Manchester's Muslims.* Oxford: James Currey.

Wigle, Laura. 1974. "An Arab Muslim Community in Michigan." In *Arabic-Speaking Communities in American Cities,* edited by Barbara Aswad. New York: Center for Migration Studies.

Wilcox, Clyde, and Leopoldo Gomez. 1990. "Religion, Group Identification, and Politics among American Blacks." *Sociological Analysis* (fall): 271–85.

Wolf, C. Umhau. 1960. "Muslims in the Midwest." *The Muslim World* 50: 39–48.

Wuthnow, Robert. 1999. "Mobilizing Civic Engagement: The Changing Impact of Religious Involvement." In *Civic Engagement in American Democracy,* edited by Theda Skocpol and Morris P. Fiorina. Washington: Brookings Institution Press.

CHAPTER 5

Values and Cultural Membership

Wayne Baker and Amaney Jamal

Arabs in Detroit take great pride in their traditions, customs, and values. The region is home to Arabs from across the Arab world, including Lebanon, Syria, Palestine, Yemen, Egypt, the Gulf, and North Africa. Cultural values and traditions are a unifying force for this heterogeneous population. Consider, for example, the Dearborn Arab International Festival. Held each summer, and attracting more than 300,000 visitors, the festival embraces the area's diversity with its Arab traditions. Dance and Dabke troops, art, food from falafel and shawarma to hummus and baked delicacies, Arab music, henna booths, coffee cup readings, and Arab merchandise are a few of the ways in which Arabs share their traditions with one another. Underlying these vibrant cultural traditions are deep-rooted values. But are the values that unite the diverse Arab population also the root of divisiveness between Arab Americans and mainstream American society?

This question has been present explicitly or implicitly in private worries, public debates, and scholarly discourse about the place of Arabs and Muslims in American society, especially since 9/11. For example, as noted in chapter 1, many Americans express concerns about the compatibility of Arab Americans and other Americans, indicating less acceptance of Arab Americans than any other group, including whites, African Americans, Asians, and Hispanics (Farley, Krysan, and Couper 2006). Some scholars draw sharp symbolic boundaries, defining recent immigrants, especially Hispanics and Muslims, as outsiders who threaten the cultural unity of the nation (Schlesinger 1991; Huntington 2004). From a citizenship perspective, these negative views imply that many Americans—and some scholars—feel that Arabs and Muslims may not be cultural citizens of society, that they may not share important values or "moral bonds" (Edgell, Gerteis, and Hartmann 2006) with the general population.

Cultural citizenship, as described in chapter 1, relates to the multicultural-ism theme in citizenship theory, which focuses on how to reconcile diversity and differences in values among citizens with the need for national unity and a conception of belonging. Of course, symbolic boundaries that define Muslims and Arabs as other have implications for the rights theme as well. Defining members of a group as other is often used as moral justification to deny or abridge the rights of members of the group (see, for example, chapters 2 and 3). Thus, the post-9/11 era has had an impact on both the rights and multi-culturalism notions of citizenship, such as the erosion of the protections of legal citizenship in the name of national security, and concerns about the compatibility of Arab as an identity with American as shared values (Lipset 1996; Baker 2005).

In this chapter, we map values and view them in cross-cultural perspective, using a unique combination of data that allows us to compare the values of Arab Americans in the Detroit region with members of the general population living in the same area, with Americans nationwide, with the peoples of four Arab nations, and with a large number of other societies.[1] We define what we mean by values, focusing on two dimensions of values—a continuum of traditional versus secular-rational values and a continuum of survival versus self-expression values—shown to be valid for making comparisons across cultures as well as within American society (see, for example, Inglehart and Baker 2000; Norris and Inglehart 2004; Baker 2005; Baker and Forbes 2006). As we elaborate, the first dimension taps a constellation of values about God, country, and family. Consistent with usage in previous research, we use the label *traditional* because these values are more than just strong religious values. Similarly, we use the label *secular-rational* because these values are more than the absence of strong religious beliefs; *rational* is used in the Weberian sense to indicate the "use of reason, logic, science, and means-ends calculations rather than religion or long-established customs to govern social, political, and economic life" (Baker 2005, 7). In this chapter, we use *secular* as a shorthand but always mean secular-rational. The second dimension represents a constellation of values about security and safety, trust, tolerance, and well-being. Survival values, as we define, are at one end of this dimension. Self-expression values are at the other. We use the labels *survival* and *self-expression* to retain consistency with usage in previous research. Of course, values other than traditional–secular-rational values and survival–self-expression values are important and could be examined, but other values have not been examined as systematically around the world as these two dimensions.

After producing a cultural map showing the positions of various popula-tions, we analyze how and why values vary along each dimension, considering the influences of U.S. citizenship, immigrant status, experiences related to 9/11, language, religion, country of origin or ancestry, education, household income, and other demographic variables. We interpret our findings by con-sidering the unique role of values as the cultural foundation of American soci-ety (Baker 2005) and highlight some of the unique cultural tensions in American society that are intensified when crisis situations—like 9/11—are perceived to threaten the moral and political boundaries of the national com-munity. We conclude by returning to the opening questions of this chapter, arguing that judging whether the values of Arab Americans and other Americans are close enough or too far apart depends on frame of reference—the perspec-tive one takes (local, national, or global) and the theory of citizenship one uses (narrow assimilation or broad cultural citizenship).

MAPPING VALUES IN CROSS-CULTURAL PERSPECTIVE

What are values? Values are emotionally held beliefs about desirable goals; val-ues transcend specific situations and are used as principles or standards to guide actions, to make decisions, and to evaluate people, actions, policies, and events (Schwartz 1994; Schwartz and Bardi 2001). There are, of course, many values that could be considered. Because our focus is cross-cultural, however, we study values that have been shown to be "reasonably comprehensive and universally applicable" in cross-cultural research (Rokeach 1973, 89). Only two systematic approaches to the cross-cultural study of values meet Rokeach's criterion, and only one—the World Values Surveys—includes surveys of Arab nations.[2] The World Values Surveys were designed by an international team of scholars, including some from Arab or predominately Muslim countries (such as Bangladesh, Iran, Jordan, Nigeria, and Turkey), with cross-cultural comparisons in mind: "building on extensive previous cross-national survey research and extensive pilot testing . . . it was developed to ask questions that *do* have shared meaning across many cultures" (Inglehart 1997, 91). The World Values Surveys now cover more than eighty nations, including four that are Arab—Jordan, Egypt, Morocco, and Algeria (for details on the design, methodologies, and coverage of the World Values Surveys, see www.worldvaluessurvey.org.)

Early researchers analyzed data from World Values Surveys to determine the best way to compare and contrast the basic values of the peoples of diverse cultures around the globe. Their goal was to identify a valid and parsimonious set of dimensions that would reveal important similarities and differences in values across cultures. Teams of investigators in disparate regions, such as Africa, Latin America, the Nordic region, and eastern Europe, worked independently and without knowledge of one another's findings. And yet each team discovered and replicated the same dimensions (see discussion in Inglehart 1997, 91–92). These dimensions have proved to be robust, reproduced each time a new wave of the World Values Surveys is conducted (for the latest findings, see www.worldvaluessurvey.org). These dimensions are important because they reveal a coherent and comprehensive cultural geography of the world. We have therefore adopted the same dimensional framework for our analysis of the values of Arab Americans in cross-cultural perspective.

The first of two dimensions is a continuum of what are called traditional values versus secular values (see, for example, Inglehart 1997; Inglehart and Baker 2000; Inglehart and Norris 2003; Baker 2005).[3] There is debate about the meaning and indicators of traditional and secular values (see Gorski 2000; Hout and Fischer 2003; Marwell and Demerath 2003). In general, the traditional-secular dimension represents a constellation of values about God, country, and family. Traditional values are indicated, for example, by strong beliefs in the importance of God, the importance of religion, frequent attendance at religious services, and a great deal of confidence in the country's religious leaders and institutions; those who hold traditional values get comfort and strength from religion, and describe themselves as religious persons. Those with traditional values tend to have absolute rather than relative standards of morality. They believe that divorce, suicide, and euthanasia are not justifiable. Those with traditional values believe that it is more important for children to learn obedience and religious faith than independence and determination, and that one of the main goals in life is to make one's parents proud. Those with traditional values favor more respect for authority, take protectionist attitudes toward foreign trade, emphasize social conformity rather than individualism, and report high levels of national pride. Secular values emphasize the opposite positions on all these topics. This chapter uses a broad definition of secular, based on a set of values about religion, country, and family, whereas chapter 4 uses a narrow definition of secular that focuses on religious practices and religious identification. These definitions are different but compatible.

The second dimension is a continuum of survival values versus self-expression values—security and safety, quality of life, well-being, trust, and tolerance. Survival values are indicated, for example, by an emphasis on physical and economic safety and security above all other goals. Those with survival values tend to distrust other people in general. They feel threatened by foreigners, by ethnic diversity, and by cultural change; they are intolerant of members of outgroups. Those with survival values are not involved in politics or political participation—for example, they rarely, if ever, sign a petition. They are favorable to authoritarian government. Survival values are indicated by support of traditional gender roles and the Strict Father family model (Lakoff 1996). Those with survival values emphasize materialist values; a strong economy is more important than protecting the environment. Self-expression values emphasize the opposite positions on these topics. For example, self-expression values relate to what Fogel calls spiritual or immaterial needs, such as "the struggle for self-realization, the desire to find a deeper meaning in life than the endless accumulation of consumer durables and the pursuit of pleasure, access to the miracles of modern medicine, education not only for careers but for spiritual values, methods of financing an early, fruitful, and long-lasting retirement, and increasing the amount of quality time available for family activities" (2000, 176–77).

By putting these two dimensions together, we can draw a cultural map of the world. One such map is presented in figure 5.1. The location of each society is based on the typical values of the population on each dimension. (We use the word *typical* in the statistical sense to mean the average for all respondents in a specific population. The average indicates the central tendency in a population.) As shown, similar nations tend to cluster. For example, historically Protestant nations tend to be located in the upper-right quadrant of the map. These are among the most secular and self-expression oriented nations of all. The United States is also one of the most self-expression oriented nations, but it has unusually traditional values, more traditional than the values of the peoples of most of western Europe. The Muslim world (the Middle

Figure 5.1   Two Dimensions of Values, Arab Americans and Other Americans

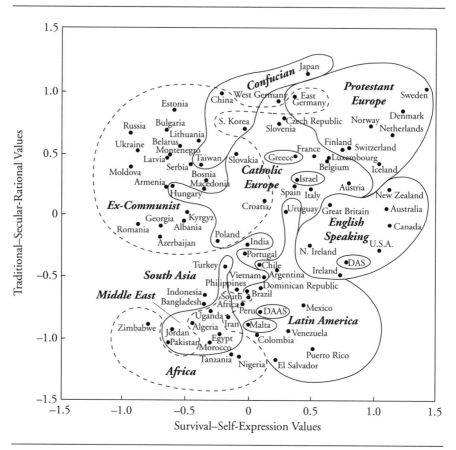

Source: Authors' compilation.

East, North Africa, Central Asia, Pakistan, Bangladesh, Indonesia, Malaysia, parts of India) tends to be in the lower-left quadrant. The four Arab nations (Jordan, Egypt, Morocco, and Algeria) are a tight group inside the Middle East cluster. Turkey is the most secular nation in the Middle East cluster, almost at the same position on the traditional-secular dimension as the United States. This location makes sense, given that Turkey is an officially secular society with a republican parliamentary democracy.

Other analysts have demonstrated that nations cluster in patterns based, in part, on similar levels of economic development (Inglehart and Baker 2000;

Inglehart and Norris 2003; Baker 2005). For example, the two-value dimensions are highly correlated with the United Nations Development Programme's (UNDP) Human Development Index, as well as with other indictors of existential conditions, such as real GDP per capita, population growth, political governance, and human rights (see, for example, Inglehart and Baker 2000; Inglehart and Norris 2003; Norris and Inglehart 2004). The UNDP Human Development Index is a composite measure based on life expectancy, educational attainment, and adjusted real income. The fact that it is closely correlated with traditional-secular values and survival–self-expression values supports the argument that existential conditions influence values. For example, the nations of western Europe rate high on the Human Development Index, and those of the Middle East rate at considerably lower levels (table 5.1). Correspondingly, we see many western nations in the upper-right quadrant of the cultural map, and Middle Eastern in the lower-left quadrant (figure 5.1). This pattern suggests that differences in existential conditions are one reason why the values of the peoples of western and Middle Eastern nations are different (see also Inglehart 2007).

Of course, many other factors influence values as well, such as political relations, political power, histories of colonial domination, class inequalities, and so on. The values held by a people represent their entire historical heritage (Inglehart and Baker 2000, 31). For example, the same analyses that demonstrate the effect of level of human development on values also report that the religious and cultural heritage of a nation exerts an independent effect on values (Inglehart and Baker 2000). Pippa Norris and Ronald Inglehart used the term *cultural traditions axiom* to help explain the link. According to this axiom, "the distinctive worldviews that were originally linked with religious traditions have shaped the cultures of each nation in an enduring fashion; today, these distinctive values are transmitted to the citizens even if they never set foot in a church, temple, or mosque" (Norris and Inglehart 2004, 17–18). They argue that the media and educational institutions are the main agents of socialization, but we add that in nations where the large majority of people profess strong religious values—such as those of the Middle East and America (Baker 2005)—religious institutions continue to act as influential agents of socialization. Religious values are reinforced and transmitted by a nation's culture by the policies of its religious organizations and its government, and by social networks—for example, in nations where most people are religious, the "pool of potential friends, teachers, work colleagues, and marriage-partners" are similarly religious (Kelley and De Graaf 1997).

Table 5.1   Human Development Index for Selected Nations, 2003

Western Nations	Middle Eastern Nations
1 Norway	44 Qatar
2 Iceland	46 Kuwait
3 Sweden	48 United Arab Emirates
4 Australia	73 Saudi Arabia
5 Netherlands	79 Oman
6 Belgium	83 Lebanon
7 United States	90 Jordan
8 Canada	96 Turkey
10 Switzerland	98 Occupied Palestinian Territories
11 Denmark	106 Iran
12 Ireland	107 Algeria
13 United Kingdom	110 Syria
14 Finland	120 Egypt
15 Luxembourg	126 Morocco
16 Austria	148 Yemen
17 France	
18 Germany	
19 Spain	
20 New Zealand	
21 Italy	
23 Portugal	
Average Human Development Rank = 11.7	Average Human Development Rank = 91.6

Source: United Nations Development Programme 2003.

The effect of religious-cultural heritage is evident in the global map (figure 5.1). Nations with similar heritages tend to cluster together: historically Protestant Europe, Catholic Europe, English speaking nations, Confucian, ex-Communist, Orthodox, South Asia, Middle East (including the four Arab nations), Latin America, and Africa. Of course, various other historical factors matter and compose the religious-cultural heritage of a nation (for example, see Moaddel 2005). Together, religious-cultural heritage and level of human development make up the formative experiences of peoples around the world, explaining a considerable amount of cross-cultural variation in values (Inglehart and Baker 2000).

Where are Arab Americans? As shown in figure 5.1, Arab Americans in the Detroit region (marked DAAS on the map) are located closer to the Arab world than to the general population in the Detroit region (marked DAS) or to the United States as a whole. Arab Americans have stronger traditional values than the values of black Americans and Hispanic Americans, according to our analyses (not shown here). The values of black and Hispanic Americans are considerably less traditional than the values of Arab Americans, but are more so than those of white Americans. At the other end of the traditional-secular dimension, Asian Americans have values that are considerably more secular than those of white Americans. Arab Americans also have more survival-oriented values than black Americans or Hispanic Americans, whose values in turn are more survival oriented than those of white Americans. Asian Americans are about as self-expression oriented as Americans generally.

Given that almost three-quarters of Arab Americans are immigrants, we expected that their typical values would be closer to those of their region of birth than to the general population in the Detroit region (most of whom are U.S.-born).[4] A large body of research shows that basic values are established in one's formative years and tend to remain stable over time, even when experiences and circumstances in later life are different. Experiences in adolescence and early adulthood make an indelible imprint on one's values, an impression that persists throughout the life course (Mannheim [1928]1952; Schuman and Scott 1989; Inglehart 1997; Inglehart and Baker 2000; Norris and Inglehart 2004; Tessler, Konold, and Reif 2004). People who come of age in times and places when and where they cannot take their safety and survival for granted—because, for example, of poverty, economic depression, political turmoil, repression, natural disasters, war, or terrorism—will have fundamentally different values from those who could take safety and survival for granted. Accordingly, the typical values of Arab Americans should be expected to be more traditional and more survival oriented than those of other Americans.

VARIATIONS IN VALUES

So far we have considered the central tendencies of a nation or population. Of course, not everyone in the same population has the same values; there is always some variation. We now shift to analyze this variation within a population, examining how and why Arab Americans vary along each of the two dimensions of values. For purposes of comparison, we conduct a similar analysis for members of the general population. Our use of the cultural maps allowed us to make comparisons considering the two dimensions together, but we now analyze each dimension separately.

We consider three groups of characteristics or experiences that may be related to variations in values. The first group includes markers or indicators of cultural membership—legal citizenship, place of birth (United States versus other), language (English or Arabic), religion (Christian or Muslim), and residence (inside or outside the Dearborn and Dearborn Heights enclave). The second group includes experiences after 9/11, positive and negative, and harassment or discrimination experienced by a person or a person's family during the two years after 9/11. The third group includes various sociodemographic variables, such as age, education, household income, race, gender, marital status, and country of birth or ancestry. Table 5.2 provides statistical results comparing Arab Americans and the general population; table 5.3 presents statistical results for immigrant Arab Americans.

Table 5.2   Statistical Results, Arab Americans and General Public

Independent Variables	Arab Americans (DAAS)		General Population (DAS)	
	Traditional-Secular Values	Survival–Self-Expression Values	Traditional-Secular Values	Survival–Self-Expression Values
Cultural membership				
U.S. citizenship	−.060	.171*	—	—
	(.066)	(.079)		
U.S.-born	.067	.444***	.334*	.446**
	(.067)	(.126)	(.127)	(.122)
Language (English)	−.010	.206**	—	—
	(.063)	(.075)		
Religion (Christian)	−.023	.132*	−.306**	−.020
	(.080)	(.067)	(.095)	(.083)
Residence (outside enclave, DAAS; outside Detroit, DAS)	.061	−.120	.062	.255*
	(.072)	(.068)	(.099)	(.075)

Table 5.2 *(continued)*

Independent Variables	Arab Americans (DAAS)		General Population (DAS)	
	Traditional-Secular Values	Survival–Self-Expression Values	Traditional-Secular Values	Survival–Self-Expression Values
Experiences related to 9/11			—	—
Bad experience	−.021	−.157*	—	—
	(.069)	(.064)		
Received support	−.034	.253***	—	—
	(.044)	(.057)		
Harassment in last two years				
Type 1 (verbal insults, threatening gestures)	.097	−.195**	.008	−.005
	(.069)	(.065)	(.085)	(.092)
Type 2 (vandalism, loss of employment, physical attack).	.211*	.050	−.242	−.179
	(.096)	(.090)	(.118)	(.120)
Sociodemographics				
Education	.084***	.042	.117***	−.004
	(.023)	(.023)	(.031)	(.037)
Household income	.003	.104***	.013	.165**
	(.031)	(.032)	(.048)	(.048)
Working now	−.018	.101	.141	.160
	(.050)	(.071)	(.098)	(.074)
Youth (18 to 25)	−.027	−.052	.362*	−.256
	(.083)	(.089)	(.144)	(.116)
Middle age (26 to 54)	.176**	−.133	.084	−.066
	(.061)	(.095)	(.080)	(.087)
Gender (male)	−.022	−.003	.200*	−.199*
	(.042)	(.053)	(.077)	(.074)
Race (white)	−.142**	.052	.187	.275*
	(.048)	(.063)	(.131)	(.098)

(*Table continues on p. 146.*)

Table 5.2   (continued)

Independent Variables	Arab Americans (DAAS)		General Population (DAS)	
	Traditional-Secular Values	Survival–Self-Expression Values	Traditional-Secular Values	Survival–Self-Expression Values
Marital status	−.184*	.058	−.090	.143
(married)	(.075)	(.081)	(.082)	(.084)
Birth or ancestry				
Lebanon-Syria	.048	.130*	—	—
	(.075)	(.085)		
Palestine-Jordan	.013	.144	—	—
	(.080)	(.089)		
Other country	−.019	.203*	—	—
	(.092)	(.082)		
Constant	−.898**	−.536***	−1.095***	.082
	(.174)	(.155)	(.210)	(.167)
Adjusted R^2	.090	.301	.168	.209
N of observations	1016	1016	508	508

Source: Authors' compilation.

Notes: U.S. citizenship is a dummy variable, 1 = U.S. citizen, 0 = not citizen (DAAS only). Because 96 percent of the general population are U.S. citizens, this variable is not included in the analysis for the DAS.

Language is a dummy variable, indicating the language of the interview, 1 = English, 0 = Arabic. This variable is not applicable to the DAS because all interviews were in English. Gender is a dummy variable, 1 = male, 0 = female.

Religion is a dummy variable. For DAS, Christian = 1, 0 = other. For DAAS, 1 = Christian, 0 = Muslim.

Residence is a dummy variable. For DAS, 1 = other, 0 = Detroit. For DAAS, 1 = outside enclave, 0 = Dearborn–Dearborn Heights (enclave).

Omitted category for country of birth-ancestry is Iraq. Comparable questions were not asked in the DAS.

Race is a dummy variable. For DAS, 1 = non-black, 0 = black. For DAAS, 1 = white, 0 = non-white.

Total sample size for 2003 Detroit Area Study = 508. Total sample size of DAAS = 1016.

These results reflect adjustments for complex design features, sampling weights, and imputation of missing data.

Parentheses contain standard errors.

*** $p < .001$, ** $p < .01$, * $p < .05$.

Table 5.3   Statistical Results, Immigrant Arab Americans

Independent Variables	Immigrant Arab Americans		Immigrant Arab Americans (with Length of Stay Included)	
	Traditional-Secular Values	Survival–Self-Expression Values	Traditional-Secular Values	Survival–Self-Expression Values
Cultural Membership				
U.S. citizenship	−.063	.201*	−.089	.145
	(.065)	(.088)	(.108)	(.141)
Language (English)	−.007	.212**	−.015	.192*
	(.068)	(.075)	(.079)	(.096)
Religion (Christian)	−.040	.085	−.047	.070
	(.067)	(.079)	(.072)	(.070)
Residence (outside enclave, DAAS; outside Detroit, DAS)	.077 (.079)	.082 (.080)	.075 (.078)	.078 (.079)
Experiences related to 9/11				
Bad experience	.005	−.262**	.006	−.261**
	(.081)	(.064)	(.081)	(.083)
Received support	−.065	.249***	−.068	.242***
	(.058)	(.074)	(.056)	(.072)
Harassment in last two years				
Type 1 (verbal insults, threatening gestures)	.103 (.077)	−.115 (.078)	.103 (.077)	−.115 (.078)
Type 2 (vandalism, loss of employment, physical attack).	.170 (.101)	.001 (.090)	.169 (.101)	−.002 (.090)

(*Table continues on p. 148.*)

Table 5.3   (continued)

Independent Variables	Immigrant Arab Americans		Immigrant Arab Americans (with Length of Stay Included)	
	Traditional-Secular Values	Survival–Self-Expression Values	Traditional-Secular Values	Survival–Self-Expression Values
Sociodemographics				
Education	.085***	.033	.087***	.037
	(.024)	(.027)	(.025)	(.027)
Household income	−.003	.110***	−.005	.104**
	(.031)	(.034)	(.033)	(.038)
Working now	−.052	.112	−.052	.112
	(.050)	(.081)	(.049)	(.080)
Youth	−.004	.030	.021	.085
	(.100)	(.140)	(.092)	(.168)
Middle age	.150**	−.111	.161*	−.086
	(.055)	(.108)	(.073)	(.136)
Gender (male)	−.026	−.017	−.026	−.010
	(.047)	(.055)	(.047)	(.057)
Race (white)	−.099	.058	.100	.053
	(.056)	(.064)	(.057)	(.067)
Marital status (married)	−.195**	.047	−.192**	.056
	(.076)	(.112)	(.068)	(.103)
Lebanon-Syria birth	.063	.095	.059	.086
	(.080)	(.086)	(.083)	(.081)
Palestine-Jordan birth	−.041	.173	−.050	.153
	(.084)	(.092)	(.087)	(.079)
Other country birth	−.141*	.269***	−.147*	.257***
	(.066)	(.080)	(.071)	(.073)
Length of stay in United States	—	—	.018	.042
			(.048)	(.071)
Constant	−.840***	−.596***	−.887***	−.704***
	(.139)	(.155)	(.130)	(.181)

Table 5.3   (continued)

Independent Variables	Immigrant Arab Americans		Immigrant Arab Americans (with Length of Stay Included)	
	Traditional-Secular Values	Survival–Self-Expression Values	Traditional-Secular Values	Survival–Self-Expression Values
Adjusted R²	.092	.212	.093	.214
N of observations	737	737	737	737

Source: Authors' compilation.
Notes: U.S. citizenship is a dummy variable, 1 = U.S. citizen, 0 = not citizen.
Language is a dummy variable, indicating the language of the interview, 1 = English, 0 = Arabic.
Gender is a dummy variable, 1 = male, 0 = female.
Religion is a dummy variable, 1 = Christian, 0 = Muslim.
Residence is a dummy variable, 1 = outside enclave, 0 = Dearborn–Dearborn Heights (enclave).
Length of stay is a single discrete variable representing five cohorts of immigration. No alternative measure of length of stay is significantly associated with the dependent variables.
Omitted category for country of birth-ancestry is Iraq.
Race is a dummy variable, 1 = white, 0 = nonwhite.
Total sample size for size of DAAS = 1016, 73 percent of which are immigrants.
These results reflect adjustments for complex design features, sampling weights, and imputation of missing data.
Parentheses contain standard errors.
*** $p < .001$, ** $p < .01$, * $p < .05$.

Cultural Membership

Legal citizenship provides certain rights and protections. Legal citizenship is also a symbol of commitment to American values—an indicator that the citizen considers herself or himself to be inside the moral boundaries of the nation. However, the rights of Arab Americans as U.S. citizens are under assault in the post-9/11 era, and their cultural membership has been called into question. Nonetheless, we would expect that Arab Americans who are U.S. citizens feel safer and more secure than those who are not. If they do, we should see a difference between the survival–self-expression values of Arab Americans who are U.S. citizens and those who are not. We do. The values of Arab Americans who are U.S. citizens are more self-expression oriented (less survival oriented) than the values of those who are not citizens, controlling for other factors. The effect of U.S. citizenship remains significant even when we restrict our analysis to immigrant Arab Americans. However, when we add length of stay to the analysis for immigrants, the effect becomes insignificant. It appears, therefore, that citizenship in the narrow, legal sense makes Arab Americans feel safer and more secure, even though the legal rights of Arab Americans as U.S. citizens are under assault in the post-9/11 era. But once we control for length of stay, U.S. citizenship does not make immigrants feel safer or more secure than those who are not citizens. U.S. citizenship does not have a significant effect on traditional-secular values for Arab Americans: those who are U.S. citizens and those who are not have equally strong traditional values.

Place of birth—United States versus elsewhere—should have an effect on values similar to the effect of U.S. citizenship. Generally, U.S.-born Arabs experience greater economic prosperity and security; their educational experiences, facility in English, and contact with other Americans expose them to the nation's dominant religious-cultural heritage (Ajrouch 2004; Suleiman 1999). Therefore, we expect that the values of U.S.-born and foreign-born Arabs to be different, controlling for other factors. We find that Arab Americans born in the United States are significantly more self-expression oriented (less survival oriented) than those born in the Middle East. Place of birth has the same effect in the general population: those born outside the United States are more survival oriented. However, the values of U.S.-born Arab Americans are as traditional as those of the foreign-born. In contrast, in the general population, those born in the United States are more secular than immigrants. The different effects of place of birth on the values of these two populations are shown graphically in figure 5.2.[5]

Surprisingly, length of stay—how long an immigrant has been in the United States—does not influence values. We tried four formulations of length of stay to make sure this finding was correct. First, we included a simple count of the number of years. Second, we used a set of variables corresponding to three cohorts of immigration: before 1970, capturing two waves of immigration that began in the late 1800s; from 1970 to 1989, a period of continued immigration from the Arab world, with a significant percentage from Lebanon due to the Lebanese civil war; and from 1990 to 2003, immigrants from across the Middle East, including significant numbers of Iraqi Shi'a displaced after the 1991 Gulf War. Third, we used a series of variables representing five cohorts of immigration: 1996 to 2003, 1990 to 1995, 1980 to 1989, 1970 to 1979, and before 1970. Fourth, we used a simple variable represent-

Figure 5.2   Effects of Place of Birth

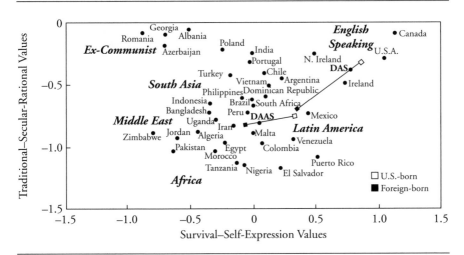

Source: Authors' compilation.

ing five cohorts of immigration. None of these had a significant effect on traditional-secular values or survival–self-expression values.

Language is both a marker of cultural membership and a tool for negotiating the social, economic, and political environment. Arab Americans whose preferred or only language is Arabic (Arabic speakers) may be stigmatized by the general population, compared to those whose preferred or only language is English (English speakers). Arabic speakers would be shielded from the cultural influence of mainstream American society and less able to negotiate the wider environment, which, in the post-9/11 era, would be a source of insecurity. Accordingly, we find Arab Americans who speak Arabic as their only or preferred language are more survival oriented and less self-expression oriented than those who speak English as their only or preferred language. This significant effect is virtually the same for all Arab Americans and for Arab immigrants. However, language is not associated with traditional-secular values: English and Arabic speakers have similar traditional values.

A common stereotype is that the values of Muslims and Christians are somehow different. We find, however, that Arab Muslims and Arab Christians have similar traditional values. This similarity holds for all Arab Americans and for Arab immigrants. In contrast, the values of Christians in the general

Figure 5.3   Effects on Religion

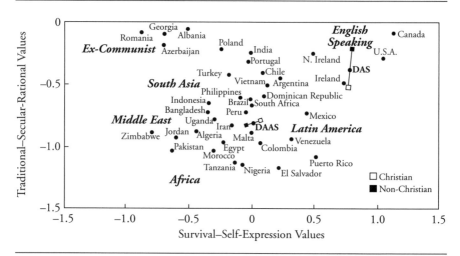

Source: Authors' compilation.
Note: Line for DAAS shows Arab Christians versus Arab Muslims.

population are considerably more traditional than the values of non-Christians. This means that the traditional values of Christians in the general population are closer to the traditional values of Arab Muslims and Arab Christians than they are to non-Christians in the general population. This similarity is shown in figure 5.3. However, religious differences in the Arab American population are associated with differences on the survival–self-expression values dimension: Arab Christians are somewhat more self-expression oriented and less survival oriented than Arab Muslims. This difference makes sense, given that Muslims are the focus of suspicion, surveillance, and investigation (see, for example, chapter 2, this volume). Surprisingly, this difference between Muslims and Christians disappears when we restrict our analysis to Arab immigrants. The values of immigrant Arab Muslims and Christians do not differ on the survival–self-expression dimension; nor do they differ on the traditional-secular dimension.

We expected that those living in the Dearborn–Dearborn Heights enclave would have different values than those living outside of it. This enclave is both an immigrant enclave and an ethnic community, according to John Logan, Richard Alba, and Wenquan Zhang's typology of segregated neighborhoods (2002). As an immigrant enclave, it is a destination for relatively poor Muslim immigrants whose values and social capital are closely bound to their ethnic-religious immigrant community (see also chapter 6, this volume, on social capital). As an ethnic community, it "is grounded in motives associated more with taste and preference than with economic necessity, or even with ambitions to create neighborhoods that will symbolize and sustain ethnic identity" (Logan, Alba, and Zhang 2002, 300). However, we found that place of residence is not associated with differences in the values of Arab Americans on either dimension. The values of those who live outside the enclave are as traditional and as survival oriented as the values of those who live inside it. In the general population, place of residence does make a difference: the values of those who live outside the city of Detroit are less survival oriented (more self-expression oriented) than those of city residents.

In sum, four of five indicators of cultural membership—U.S. citizenship, place of birth, language, and religion—are significantly related to survival–self-expression values for all Arab Americans. U.S. citizenship and language are significantly related to this dimension for Arab immigrants. The Arab Americans who are closest to other Americans on this dimension—that is, more self-expression oriented—have characteristics that match those of mainstream American society: U.S. citizens, born in the United States, who speak English and are Christian. Those who are furthest from mainstream society on this dimension are not U.S. citizens, are foreign-born, are Arabic speakers, and are Muslim. Of all the indicators, place of birth and language have the biggest effects on survival–self-expression values. Not one of the indicators of cultural membership has an effect on traditional-secular values.

Experiences After 9/11

Once formed, values tend to be stable over time. For example, a large body of research shows that values are more stable and less subject to occasional events than attitudes, such as prejudice, or emotions or moods, such as depression. Nonetheless, major historical events can impact values, even if they tend to be stable. One of these is 9/11. The 9/11 backlash was less severe in the Detroit area than elsewhere (see chapter 2, this volume), but 15 percent of Arab Americans reported having a bad personal experience after 9/11. These experiences involved negative interactions with members of the general population, such as verbal threats, public rudeness, insults, refusal of service, workplace intimidation or discrimination, assault, and so on. About 25 percent reported that, in the two years after 9/11, they or someone in their household had experienced one or more acts of harassment and discrimination due to race, religion, or ethnicity. What we call Type 1 harassment includes verbal insults or abuse and threatening words or gestures. Type 2 harassment includes physical attack, vandalism or destruction of property, or loss of employment. We also asked in our survey about positive experiences between Arab Americans and the general population after 9/11. We found that a third of Arab Americans reported receiving expressions of support and solidarity from people who were not from Middle Eastern descent.

Negative experiences shake one's perception of security and safety; positive experiences strengthen it. Therefore, we expect that Arab Americans who personally had a bad experience after 9/11, or whose families suffered harassment or discrimination, would exhibit more survival oriented values than those of Arab Americans who did not have similar experiences. In contrast, Arab Americans who received expressions of solidarity and support should report more self-expression-oriented values. Our findings are consistent with these expectations.[6] The values of Arab Americans who had a negative experience after 9/11 are more survival oriented and less self-expression oriented than those who did not. The values of Arab Americans are even more survival oriented if they or anyone in their households experienced Type 1 harassment or discrimination during the past two years. Among Arab immigrants, a negative experience after 9/11 also yields values that are more survival oriented, though Type 1 harassment does not affect survival–self-expression values. Type 2 harassment is not associated with differences in survival–self-expression values for all Arab Americans or Arab immigrants. Neither Type 1 nor Type 2 affects values in the general population. The values of Arab Americans who had a positive interaction with the general population—an expression of solidarity and support after 9/11—are more self-expression oriented and less survival oriented than the values of those who did not. The same is true for Arab immigrants.

The sizable effect of experiences after 9/11 on the values of Arab Americans indicates the magnitude of this event and its aftermath. The general population's reactions to this event were transmitted through positive and negative interactions with Arab Americans, making measurable impressions on their values. Positive experiences shifted orientations toward self-expression values, an indication that these contacts made Arab Americans feel safer, more secure, more trusting, and more tolerant; negative experiences shifted orientations in the opposite direction.

Sociodemographic Factors

Socioeconomic status can influence values because it reflects existential security (Inglehart 1997; Inglehart and Baker 2000; Norris and Inglehart 2004). Education, for example, reflects experiences during the formative years (more economically secure families provide more formal education for their children) as well as current prosperity (more education often translates into better, higher paying jobs) (Inglehart 1997, 151–56). We therefore expect that higher socio-economic status, indicated by level of formal education, household income, and employment, is associated with secular values and self-expression values. As expected, higher levels of education are related to secular values and lower levels to traditional values for all Arab Americans, for Arab immigrants, and for the general population. However, education is not associated with survival–self-expression values. As expected, household income is positively associated with survival–self-expression values for all Arab Americans, Arab immigrants, and the general population but it is not associated with traditional-secular values. Working now is not associated with either dimension of values.

These findings suggest a simple pattern: higher education tends to produce secular values, and higher household income tends to produce self-expression values. This pattern is the same in both populations, but still there are notable differences between Arab Americans and the general population. For example, our analyses show that higher education is associated with secular values in both populations, but the values of Arab Americans with the most education (graduate or professional degree) are about as traditional as those of the general population with the least education (less than high school). Higher income is associated with self-expression values in both populations, but the values of Arab Americans with the highest household incomes ($100,000 or more) are still more survival oriented than those of the general population with the lowest household incomes (less than $20,000).

Values vary by age when the formative experiences of the young are different than those of the old (Inglehart and Baker 2000). For example, 9/11 and its aftermath are notable formative experiences for all young Americans, but these experiences may have been especially traumatic for young Arab Americans, those who were between eighteen and twenty-five years old at the time of our survey in 2003. These events were traumatic experiences for older Americans, too, but would have been assimilated into a mental framework that was already well established in earlier years. Of course it is possible that 9/11 and its aftermath were so traumatic that these events had a similar impact on people of all ages. Surprisingly, the values of the youngest age cohort of Arab Americans—those who experienced the events of 9/11 in their formative period—are not significantly different from the values of the oldest cohort (age fifty-five and older).[7] We do find, however, that the values of the middle cohort (age twenty-six to fifty-four) are significantly more secular than the values of the oldest cohort; this is true for all Arab Americans as well as for Arab immigrants. One reason may be that the middle cohort has had substantial contact with mainstream society in ways that secularize their values. Further, the middle-age cohort is most likely the cohort to have been influenced by the wave of national secularism in the Arab world from the 1960s to the 1970s. Age, however, does not influence survival–self-expression values.

Gender does not have a significant effect on values in the Arab American population. In the general population, however, the values of men are more secular and more survival oriented than those of women. Arab Americans who classify their race as white have more secular values than those who do not, though race does not influence survival–self-expression values. We see a different pattern in the general population: those who classify their race as white are more self-expression oriented, though race does not influence traditional-secular values. Married Arab Americans have more traditional values than those who are not married. Marital status does not influence values in the general population.

Finally, we consider how values may be influenced by the formative experiences of national origin and ancestry. We analyzed the effects of the three largest groups living in the Detroit region, plus a residual category: Lebanon-Syria, Palestine-Jordan, Iraq, and other nations. We used Iraq as the comparison group. The values of Lebanese and Syrian Arab Americans are more self-expression oriented than those of Iraqis, though this is true only when we consider U.S.-born and foreign-born Arab Americans together. Iraqi immigrants are more survival oriented and more secular than Arab immigrants from nations not included in our largest groups. The values of Palestinian and Jordanian Arab Americans are not significantly different from those of Iraqi Arab Americans.

INTERPRETING VALUES IN THE AMERICAN CONTEXT

The preceding analysis yields statistical facts about the values of Arab Americans. What do the facts mean? Facts do not speak for themselves; they must be interpreted. This is so even in the physical realm. For example, astronomers can agree on the facts of celestial observations but disagree about what they mean and why they occur (Kuhn 1957; Baker 2005, 125). In the cultural realm, there is even more room for interpretation. To interpret the statistical facts about the values of Arab Americans, we need to consider the role of values in American society and some of the cultural tensions that are intensified when crisis situations—such as 9/11—threaten the moral and political boundaries of the national community.

The contemporary focus on Arab Americans is only a recent instance of debates about values and cultural citizenship that have persisted throughout American history. Even before the nation's founding, the peoples who migrated to what became America debated questions of cultural membership, erected and contested symbolic boundaries between groups, and on occasion clashed violently because of differences in values, among other reasons (Fischer 1989). Since then, American history has been punctuated repeatedly by clashes of values (Baker 2005). The specific events, conditions, or social problems that trigger these clashes are too many and too diverse to revisit here (but see Baker 2005, 112–30). The point is that concerns about the compatibility of Arab American values with mainstream values are a contemporary case of concerns that echo throughout American history about the compatibility of different groups and American society.

Why is this so? The source of clashes of values is rooted deep in American society. Many observers have noted that America is unusual, deviant, exceptional—qualitatively different from other Western societies (de Tocqueville 1988; Kingdon 1999). These qualitative differences are sometimes called American exceptionalism. The location of the United States on the cultural map (figure 5.1) vividly illustrates American exceptionalism. For example, the nation has unusually traditional values, compared to other economically developed democracies. Americans are more religious, moralistic, absolutist, and patriotic than the peoples of virtually all other economically advanced democracies. These traditional values are widely shared and stable over time (Baker 2005). However, America has strong self-expression values that have become even stronger over time. Over time, America is moving horizontally across the cultural map (figure 5.1) and most other economically advanced democracies are moving upward and to the right, becoming more secular and more self-expression oriented (Baker 2005; Inglehart and Baker 2000). The combination of stable traditional values and increasingly strong self-expression values means that America is a "mixed system" of values (Baker 2005, 161). This mixed system "contains cultural contradictions because its prevailing principles provide contrary guides to conduct" (Baker 2005, 161). On the one hand, traditional values demand obedience to an absolute and external moral authority—God, country, and family—and strict conformity to mainstream traditional American values. On the other hand, self-expression values demand obedience to oneself as the source of moral authority and promote tolerance, understanding, and acceptance of difference. Differences in values are accepted and even celebrated.

Real or perceived differences in values can be viewed as threats to the cultural integrity of the nation (Baker 2005). This is one reason that strict assimilation has been the traditional American response to difference—immigrants who bring different values to America are not threats if they melt into the dominant American culture (see chapter 1, this volume). America's mixed system means that strict assimilation (conformity to American values) and broad cultural citizenship (acceptance of diversity) are jostling strands in American culture. One may have prominence over the other, but both are always present. When crisis situations threaten the imagined community, America's traditional values gain prominence and responses to difference swing toward strict assimilation. This reaction was prominent after 9/11, for example, and continues today. When crisis situations subside, America's self-expression values gain prominence and responses to difference swing toward broad cultural citizenship. The events of 9/11 crossed America's physical boundaries and threatened its ideology. Responses included the backlash against Arab and Muslim Americans and foreign military actions that took on the character of moral crusades. Tolerance, understanding, and acceptance of difference were not lost, which is one reason why the backlash in the Detroit region was less severe than elsewhere (see chapter 2, this volume). But the dominant, lasting reaction to 9/11 has been concern about the compatibility of Arab Americans and American society.

CONCLUSION

We have documented that the typical values of Arab Americans living in the Detroit region are closer to the Arab world—strong traditional values coupled with strong survival values—than to those of the general population in the Detroit region or of Americans nationwide. Arab Americans have stronger traditional values, and more survival oriented values, than black Americans and Hispanic Americans. Moreover, the traditional values of Arab Americans do not vary by legal citizenship, place of birth, language, religion, or residence. Taken together, these findings indicate that Arab Americans maintain a distinctive traditional culture—one that is different from mainstream American culture.

An irony is that the traditional values of Arab Americans are not that far from the traditional values of other Americans, once we view values in global perspective. Consider, for example, that the values of almost all European nations (another major destination for Arabs and Muslims) are quite secular, and the gap between their secular values and the traditional values of Arabs and Muslims is wider there than it is in the United States. These differences can be seen in the global map (figure 5.1) and are particularly striking when we compare the locations of various European nations, Middle Eastern nations, Arab Americans, and the American general population on two components of the traditional-secular scale—importance of God and justifiability of abortion (figure 5.4). Not only are Arab Americans closer to other Americans than to most European nations, Americans in general are closer to Arab Americans and the Middle East than they are to the peoples of all historically Protestant European nations.

Judging whether the values of Arab Americans and other Americans are close enough or too far apart is an exercise of interpretation. It depends on frame of reference—the perspective one takes and the theory of citizenship one uses. From the local perspective of the Detroit region or from the national American perspective, the values of Arab Americans and other Americans appear to be far apart; in global perspective, however, their values are closer to one another than to many economically affluent democracies. From a strict assimilationist theory of citizenship, the gap between the values of Arab Americans and other Americans may be too wide to consider Arab Americans as cultural members of mainstream society. Using a broad theory of cultural citizenship, however, Arab Americans foreshadow a possible future of citizenship in the postnation era, where shared collective identity is formed through accommodation rather than suppression of ethnic identities (Kymlicka 1995), where a minority group believes in and participates in democratic institutions, yet exercises the universal right to one's own culture (Soysal 1997) and preserves its own social space in mainstream society (Rosaldo 1997). Because 9/11 and its aftermath continue to threaten the moral and political boundaries of the national community, it is more likely that the differences between Arab Americans and other Americans will continue to be interpreted from a strict assimilationist frame of reference.

Figure 5.4   Comparisons on Justifiability of Abortion and Importance of God

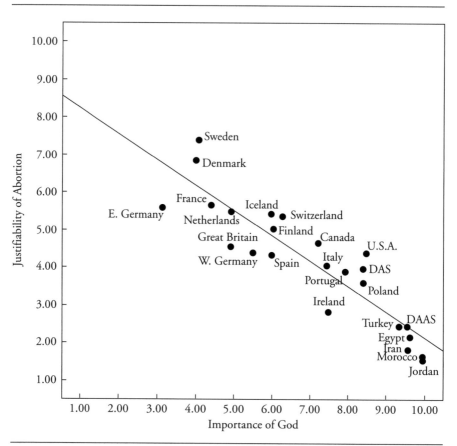

Source: Authors' compilation.
Notes: Ten-point response scale for justifiability of abortion, where 1 = can never be justified and 10 = can always be justified. Ten-point response scale for importance of God, where 1 = not at all important and 10 = very important.
Each dot represents the average scores for a given population.
Diagonal line represents best linear fit between two items (correlation = .900).

NOTES

1.   Specifically, we combine data from the 2003 Detroit Arab American Study (DAAS); the 2003 Detroit Area Study (DAS), a survey of the general population living in the same region; and the World Values Surveys (WVS), the largest systematic attempts ever made to document values, attitudes, and beliefs around the world.

2. The other approach, developed mainly by a psychologist, examines ten values: universalism, benevolence, tradition, conformity, security, power, achievement, hedonism, stimulation, and self-direction (Schwartz 1994; Schwartz and Bardi 2001). These have been applied in surveys in more than fifty nations, but mostly the samples have been of specific categories of people (such as teachers or students), not representative national surveys. More important, the values have not been surveyed in Arab nations.

3. These two dimensions are the first and second factors, respectively, from a factor analysis of ten items. The following five items load primarily on the first factor: the importance of God in the respondent's life, justifiability of abortion, autonomy index (qualities that children should learn at home—obedience and religious faith versus independence and determination), respect for authority, and national pride (patriotism). The following five items load primarily on the second dimension: subjective well-being (self-reported happiness), interpersonal trust, justifiability of homosexuality, priority of economic and physical security versus self-expression and quality of life (called the Materialism Index), and political participation (signing a petition). These ten items are correlated in sensible ways with dozens of other survey items (for further details on these dimensions and their statistical underpinnings, see Inglehart and Baker 2000; Baker 2005; factor loadings are available at www.detroitarabamerican study.org).

4. The values of Arab Americans and the general population are statistically different on both value dimensions, as well as on eight of the ten items that make up the traditional-secular and survival–self-expression dimensions. The largest differences, where Arab Americans have stronger traditional values than the general population, are justifiability of abortion, justifiability of homosexuality, and the belief that religious faith and obedience are more important for children to learn than independence and self-determination. The largest differences on the other scale, where Arab Americans have stronger survival values, are trust and political participation (signing a petition). This analysis, not shown here, is available at www.detroitarabamericanstudy.org.

5. Figure 5.2 and related figures show the predicted values on the traditional–secular-rational scale and survival–self-expression scale, using the regression equations in table 5.2, when the independent variable under consideration, such as place of birth, is at its minimum and maximum. For place of birth, the minimum value = 0 (born outside the United States) and the maximum value = 1 (born in the United States). The average values of all other independent variables in the

equations are used. Each figure displays the results (predicted values) of eight regression equations (minimum and maximum values of the independent variable under consideration X two values scales X two populations). To conserve space, only the bottom half of the map is shown.

6. We did not expect experiences after 9/11 to be related to traditional-secular values. To our surprise, Type 2 harassment is significantly associated with traditional-secular values for all Arab Americans; those who experienced Type 2 have more secular values than those who did not (table 5.2). Because this effect is not significant for Arab immigrants (table 5.3), we suggest a reverse explanation. Instead of Type 2 experiences "causing" more secular values, those with more secular values—who would be more assimilated in the larger society—are more likely to live and work with non-Arabs and thus more likely to have Type 2 experiences.

7. The values of the youngest age cohort in the general population are significantly more secular than the oldest age cohort (table 5.2), suggesting that factors other than 9/11 had more influence on the values of the young.

REFERENCES

Ajrouch, Kristine J. 2004. "Gender, Race and Symbolic Boundaries: Contested Spaces of Identity Among Arab-American Adolescents." *Sociological Perspectives* 47(4): 371–91.

Baker, Wayne E. 2005. *America's Crisis of Values: Reality and Perception.* Princeton, N.J.: Princeton University Press.

Baker, Wayne E., and Melissa Forbes. 2006. "Moral Values and Market Attitudes." *Society* (January–February):23–26.

de Tocqueville, Alexis. 1988. *Democracy in America,* translated by George Lawrence, edited by J. P. Mayer. New York: HarperCollins.

Edgell, Penny, Joseph Gerteis, and Douglas Hartmann. 2006. "Atheists as 'Other': Moral Boundaries and Cultural Membership in American Society." *American Sociological Review* 71(April): 211–34.

Farley, Reynolds, Maria Krysan, and Mick Couper. 2006. "Attitudes about Arab-Americans: Detroiters' Views." Paper presented at the 61st Annual Conference of the American Association for Public Opinion Research. Montreal, Canada (May 18–21).

Fischer, David Hackett. 1989. *Albion's Seed: Four British Folkways in America.* New York: Oxford University Press.

Fogel, Robert William. 2000. *The Fourth Great Awakening and the Future of Egalitarianism.* Chicago: University of Chicago Press.

Gorski, Phillip S. 2000. "Historicizing the Secularization Debate: Church, State, and Society in Late Medieval and Early Modern Europe, ca. 1300 to 1700." *American Sociological Review* 65(1): 138–16.

Hout, Michael, and Claude S. Fischer. 2003. "O Be Some Other Name." *American Sociological Review* 68(2): 316–18.

Huntington, Samuel P. 2004. *Who Are We?* New York: Simon and Schuster.

Inglehart, Ronald. 1997. *Modernization and Postmodernization: Cultural, Economic and Political Change in 43 Societies.* Princeton, N.J.: Princeton University Press.

———. 2007. "The Worldviews of Islamic Publics in Global Perspective." In *Values and Perceptions of the Islamic and Middle Eastern Publics,* edited by Mansoor Moaddel. New York: Palgrave Macmillan.

Inglehart, Ronald, and Wayne E. Baker. 2000. "Modernization, Cultural Change, and the Persistence of Traditional Values." *American Sociological Review* 65(1): 19–51.

Inglehart, Ronald, and Pippa Norris. 2003. *Rising Tide: Gender Equality and Cultural Change Around the World.* Cambridge: Cambridge University Press.

Kelley, Jonathan, and Nan Dirk De Graaf. 1997. "National Context, Parental Socialization, and Religious Beliefs: Results from 15 Nations." *American Sociological Review* 62(3): 639–59.

Kingdon, John W. 1999. *America the Unusual.* New York: Worth Publishers.

Kuhn, Thomas S. 1957. *The Copernican Revolution: Planetary Astronomy in the Development of Western Thought.* Cambridge, Mass.: Harvard University Press.

Kymlicka, Will. 1995. *Multicultural Citizenship: A Liberal Theory of Minority Rights.* Oxford: Oxford University Press.

Lakoff, George. 1996. *Moral Politics.* Chicago: University of Chicago Press.

Lipset, Seymour Martin. 1996. *American Exceptionalism.* New York: W. W. Norton.

Logan, John R., Richard D. Alba, and Wenquan Zhang. 2002. "Immigrant Enclaves and Ethnic Communities in New York and Los Angeles." *American Sociological Review* 67(2): 299–322.

Mannheim, Karl. [1928]1952. "The Problem of Generations." In *Essays on the Sociology of Knowledge,* by Karl Mannheim. London: Routledge and Kegan Paul.

Marwell, Gerald, and N. J. Demerath III. 2003. " 'Secularization' by Any Other Name." *American Sociological Review* 68(2): 314–16.

Moaddel, Mansoor. 2005. *Islamic Modernism, Nationalism, and Fundamentalism.* Chicago: University of Chicago Press.

Norris, Pippa, and Ronald Inglehart. 2004. *Sacred and Secular-Rational: Religion and Politics Worldwide.* New York: Cambridge University Press.

Rokeach, Milton. 1973. *The Nature of Human Values.* New York: Free Press.

Rosaldo, Renato. 1997. "Cultural Citizenship, Inequality, and Multiculturalism." In *Latino Cultural Citizenship: Claiming Identity, Space, and Rights,* edited by William V. Flores and Rina Benmayor. Boston, Mass.: Beacon Press.

Schlesinger, Arthur A. Jr. 1991. *The Disuniting of America: Reflections on a Multicultural Society.* New York: W. W. Norton.

Schuman, Howard, and Jacqueline Scott. 1989. "Generations and Collective Memories." *American Sociological Review* 54(3): 359–81.

Schwartz, Shalom. 1994. "Are There Universal Aspects to the Structure and Content of Human Values?" *Journal of Social Issues* 50(4): 19–45.

Schwartz, Shalom, and Anat Bardi. 2001. "Values Hierarchies Across Cultures." *Journal of Cross-Cultural Psychology* 32(3): 268–90.

Soysal, Yasemin. 1997. "Changing Parameters of Citizenship and Claim Making: Organized Islam in European Public Spheres." *Theory and Society* 26(4): 509–27.

Suleiman, Michael. 1999. "Introduction: The Arab American Experience." In *Arabs in America,* edited by Michael Suleiman. Philadelphia: Temple University Press.

Tessler, Mark, Carrie Konold, and Megan Reif. 2004. "Political Generations in Developing Countries: Evidence and Insights from Algeria." *Public Opinion Quarterly* 68(2): 184–216.

United Nations Development Programme. 2003. Human Development Report. New York: Oxford University Press.

CHAPTER 6

Local and Global Social Capital

Wayne Baker, Amaney Jamal, and Mark Tessler

The aspirations of many Arab Americans in the post-9/11 era reflect the tensions inherent in the meaning of citizenship in a diverse society (chapter 1, this volume). Consider, for example, a common theme that emerged from answers to an open-ended question in our survey about the most pressing needs facing the community: to keep Arab culture alive in America and to strengthen Arab cultural institutions. But another common theme was the call for more unity between Arabs and non-Arabs in the Detroit region and an urging for Arab Americans to accept American culture, assimilate, or at least to be open to life in mainstream American society (Baker et al. 2004, 22). Each side of this tension has different implications for *social capital,* "social networks and the norms of reciprocity and trustworthiness that arise from them" (Putnam 2000, 19; see also Coleman 1988, 1990). On one side, maintaining distinct identities and cultural institutions calls for *bonding* social capital—exclusive networks that reinforce identity and maintain homogenous groups (Putnam 2000, 22). On the other, more unity between Arabs and non-Arabs and integration in mainstream society calls for *bridging* social capital—inclusive networks that are "outward looking and encompass people across diverse social cleavages" (Putnam 2000, 22).

Bonding and bridging social capital are not mutually exclusive (Putnam 2007). Usually, there is a mix of both forms and the mix itself can change over time (Hagan 1998). For example, the traditional assimilationist view of citizenship (see chapter 1, this volume) assumes a certain temporal sequence. First, immigrants settle in areas populated by coethnics. Strong bonding social capital among coethnics provides short-term benefits, such as financial aid and assistance, initial housing, information about local job opportunities, and emotional and cultural support (Hagan 1998, 55; Massey 1985). Second, within-group bonding social capital weakens as the migrants (or their children) enter into new social relationships and networks with members of the general population, developing bridging social capital.

Although the traditional model assumes cultural assimilation (adopting mainstream beliefs) and structural assimilation (developing mainstream social bonds), the expansive vision of cultural citizenship (chapter 1, this volume) recognizes the value of well-established minority communities in which minorities feel safe and at home, "while still situating themselves in the broad context of continental American society" (Flores and Benmayor 1998, 16). These communities are not marginalized (Pakulski 1997) but rather are integral parts of the social structure of society. These communities, and the ethnic, religious, and racial identities they support, are confluences of the mainstream. However, the post-9/11 crisis context heightens the traditional expectation of the two-stage, bonding-to-bridging transition for Arab Americans as they are pressured to prove their status as Americans. At the same time, however, the strong preference among members of the general population for social distance from Arab Americans is a barrier to the creation of bridging social capital (Farley, Krysan, and Couper 2006). The post-9/11 state of social capital among Arab Americans is, at least in part, the resultant of these conflicting forces.

In this chapter, we assess the state of local and global social capital for Arab Americans and for the general population, using data from the Detroit Arab American Study (DAAS) and the companion Detroit Area Study (DAS). We assessed local social capital—social capital bound to the Detroit region—by including in both the DAAS and DAS the short form of the Social Capital Benchmark Survey created and sponsored by the Saguaro Seminar: Civic Engagement in America Project at the John F. Kennedy School of Government at Harvard University (Social Capital Community Benchmark Survey Short Form 2002). The short form is a subset of social capital questions from the original survey and includes the questions determined to be the most effective measures of social capital.[1] We report findings for various dimensions of local social capital, based on measures from the short form (see table 6.1):

- informal social ties—the extent of informal socializing with friends, between people of different racial groups, and between people from different neighborhoods
- formal ties—membership and involvement in voluntary organizations and associations
- civic participation—voting, signing a petition, contacting government officials, and protesting
- trust—perceptions of the trustworthiness of others in general and of people of different races

We also document the extent of global social capital, examining variations in transnational ties and communication, based on questions we added to the short form for Arab Americans and for the general population. As Roger Waldinger and Greta Gilbertson noted, "in the context of immigrant adaptation, transnational networks are a source of 'social capital' (Coleman 1988), facilitating the search for jobs and housing and the organization of informal mechanisms of upward mobility" (1994, 433). Transnational ties are also social capital for the maintenance of identity and family and community solidarity. Though transnational ties may span the globe, they are forms of bonding social capital—ties that connect people of similar ethnicity, religion, and places of origin. In particular, we asked about ties to family, friends, and business contacts outside the United States and, for the Arab population only, about the consumption of Arabic programs originating in the Arab world. We did not ask about sending funds or traveling to the Middle East, though these are important components of global social (and financial) capital. We avoided these questions because of concerns by Arab American leaders that, especially after the attacks of September 11 and the subsequent war on terror, any data collected about funds or travel might attract the interest of government agencies and jeopardize the confidentiality of subjects. The University of Michigan's Behavioral Sciences Institutional Review Board expressed similar concerns.

WHY IS SOCIAL CAPITAL IMPORTANT?

A large body of research on social capital, conducted by scholars in a variety of social science disciplines, documents the benefits of social capital for people,

Table 6.1   Comparison of Local Social Capital Dimensions

Dimensions	Arab Americans (DAAS)	General Population (DAS)
Generalized trust (1 = people can be trusted; 0 = you can't be too careful or it depends.)	.22 (.01)	.38 (.02)
Racial trust (average trust of Arab Americans, whites, blacks, Hispanics, 1 = trusts all races; 0 = distrusts all races.)	.63 (.02)	.78 (.02)
Civic participation (4-point scale, 0 = does not sign petition, vote, contact government official, or protest; 4 = does all four.)	.88 (.04)	1.71 (.04)
Faith-based engagement (frequency of attendance at religious services, excluding weddings and funerals.)	27.35 (1.41)	33.9 (1.92)
Associational involvement (count of membership in secular organizations: sports/recreation, art/ music/cultural, labor union, parents' association, professional/business. Excludes religious organizations.)	2.04 (.13)	1.90 (.10)
Attended club or organizational meeting (number of times in the past twelve months, excludes meetings for work.)	3.40 (.65)	7.76 (1.20)
Interracial socializing (number of times in the past twelve months that you have been in the home of a friend of a *different race* or had them in your home.)	11.05 (1.29)	14.80 (2.44)
Interneighborhood socializing (number of times in the past twelve months that you have been in the home of a friend of a *different neighborhood* or had them in your home.)	16.98 (1.63)	30.05 (3.08)
Have friends over to home (number of times in the past twelve months.)	29.57 (2.12)	48.22 (4.68)

Source: Authors' compilation.
Notes: Values are mean score on each indicator. Standard errors are in parentheses. These indicators are based on the Social Capital Benchmark Survey short form (2002).

communities, organizations, and nations. For example, governmental institutions function better and economies grow faster in communities with
higher social capital than in those with lower social capital; communities
with higher social capital produce greater levels of education attainment
and suffer less violence and crime (Putnam 2000, 18–25). Democracy itself
is strong when social capital is high (Putnam 1993, 2000). For individuals,
social capital contributes to career success and achievements (Baker 2000,
9–15; Lin 2001) and it improves quality of life—better health, more happiness, and even longer lives (see reviews in Baker 2000, 15–19; Putnam
2000, 18–25).[2]

Social capital and citizenship go hand in hand. For example, volunteering, active political involvement, and good citizenship are mutually reinforcing: "Volunteers are *more* interested in politics and *less* cynical about
political leaders than non-volunteers are. Volunteering is a sign of positive
engagement with politics. . . . [In contrast,] political cynics, even young
cynics, are less likely than other people to volunteer" (Putnam 2000, 132).
Similarly, trust and good citizenship go together: "Other things being equal,
people who trust their fellow citizens volunteer more often, contribute more
to charity, participate more often in politics and community organizations,
serve more readily on juries, give blood more frequently, comply more fully
with tax obligations, are more tolerant of minority views, and display many
other forms of civic virtue" (Putnam 2000, 136–37). In general, there is
a positive correlation between the level of social capital in a community
and its degree of political integration in American democracy (Jacobs and
Tillie 2004).

Social capital is important for the effective exercise of civic and political
rights and duties. Citizens with more social capital are more likely to be cog-
nizant of their rights and the rights of others. They are more likely to care
about what happens in their local communities and use their rights to improve
their surrounding conditions. In effect, higher levels of social capital, like volunteerism, trust, and civic participation, allow citizens to exercise their rights
in ways that contribute to collective benefits to society as a whole. In this process,
citizens become aware of their citizenship privileges and obligations. Through
volunteerism, informal social ties, participation in formal organizations and
associations, civic engagement, and trust, citizens learn to appreciate and respect
others while simultaneously working with others for collective benefits. This

cooperation entails a better appreciation of the rights and obligations linked to citizenship more broadly.

Local bridging social capital reduces the probability of tension and conflict between majority and minority groups. Indeed, a large body of empirical research demonstrates that more interpersonal contact between groups lowers prejudice and raises acceptance and mutual understanding (Pettigrew 1998; Pettigrew and Tropp 2006). Citizens who interact with one another are more likely to develop an appreciation for and tolerance of differences in ways that reinforce multicultural successes. Through active civic involvement, citizens are more likely to learn about others and value the similarities that unite people rather than focus on the differences that divide communities. When citizens from different backgrounds engage and aid one another through an active spirit of volunteerism, they are more likely to feel part of a larger common entity. This sense of belonging is vital for a flourishing model of multiculturalism, where people of different backgrounds maintain their identities while becoming part of the larger community. In contrast, the absence of bridging social capital creates the potential for cultural misunderstanding and conflict, even without a volatile crisis context like 9/11. As Robert Putnam, Lewis Feldstein, and Donald Cohen put it, "a society that has only bonding social capital risks looking like Bosnia and Belfast" (2003, 279). For example, the Asian and black communities in the Lozells area of Birmingham, England, developed strong within-group networks but failed to build bridging ties across the racial divide. The absence of between-group ties led to repeated misunderstandings and episodes of violent racial conflict (Easton 2006; Baker and Faulkner forthcoming).

For immigrants, social capital plays important roles in many areas, such as the decision to immigrate, where to go, how to get there, settlement patterns, and incorporation (Grasmuck and Pessar 1991; Massey et al. 1987; Hagan 1994, 1998; Wierzbicki 2004). For example, existing contacts influence choice of destination. Sometimes, it is even possible to trace a chain of immigrants to the original immigrant, as Jacqueline Hagan did for the Guatemalan (Mayan) community in Houston, Texas (1998, 57). Social capital may enable immigrants to adapt to their new location and find housing, jobs, health care, places of worship, and supportive ethnic associations; it may also provide emotional, cultural, and financial support to aid the settlement and incorporation of immigrants (see chapter 2, this volume, for a description of support structures for Arabs in the Detroit region).

Despite these benefits, previous research on immigrants and social capital reveals that, across the board, immigrant communities generally have less local social capital than native born or white citizens do.[3] These differences occur for many reasons. The local networks of new immigrants may be limited to a small circle of kin and coethnics (Wierzbicki 2004). Language barriers, cultural differences, religious divides, and other factors can inhibit the growth and diversification of networks over time. For example, an immigrant parent may not be able to take an active role in her child's education because language barriers and differing social customs make it difficult for the parent to interact with the parents of her child's friends, their teachers, and school organizations (Pong, Hao, and Gardner 2005). Type of employment can prevent the growth and diversification of networks. For example, Hagan found that Mayan women in Houston had tighter within-group ties than Mayan men because they were employed in private-household domestic work and lacked opportunities to build bridging ties with non-Mayans (1998). Over time, these closed networks became even smaller and more inward-looking. In contrast, the men were engaged in work that put them in contact with long-term immigrants and the native-born outside the community. Mayan men were more likely than Mayan women to legalize, in part because their growing network of weak ties (bridging social capital) provided information about the legalization process and the affidavits they needed to legalize.

Pressure from inside the minority community itself may depress the level of social capital that a member of an immigrant or ethnic population enjoys. For example, ethnic insiders might "attempt to monopolize job opportunities for members of their core networks and restrict outsiders," reproducing networks that are closed and exclusionary (Waldinger 1999, 230). And, as Alejandro Portes argued, groups whose solidarity depends on an identity as outsiders, whose "solidarity is cemented by a common experience of adversity and opposition to mainstream society," become obstacles for members who wish to build networks and succeed outside their ethnic community (1998, 17).

Like inequalities in education or wealth, there is inequality in social capital—"the extent to which social capital is unequally distributed across social groups in a community or population" (Lin 2001, 99). Research on immigrants reveals that they typically begin with less local social capital than the general population and, due to a variety of factors, may fail to develop social capital, especially bridging social capital, over time. When social capital does develop, it often does so unevenly, producing inequalities linked to gender, age, place of birth, language, place of residence, citizenship status, and so on. Our assessment of the social capital of Arab Americans considers how their social capital varies by such factors, after first making basic comparisons between the social capital of Arab Americans and the general population.

LOCAL SOCIAL CAPITAL

Arab Americans score lower, on average, than members of the general population on almost every dimension of local social capital we examined, consistent with the experiences of other largely immigrant groups in America. This pattern is shown in table 6.1, which presents basic comparisons of the social capital of Arab Americans and of the general population. For example, members of the general population have friends over to their homes on average forty-eight days a year, versus thirty days a year for Arab Americans. Those in the general population have been in the homes of people from different neighborhoods, or have had them in their homes, on average thirty days a year, versus seventeen days for Arab Americans. The frequency of informal socializing with friends of different races is also different. On average, members of the general population have been in the homes of people of different races, or have invited them to their homes, fifteen days a year, versus eleven days a year for Arab Americans. These differences are illustrated in figure 6.1.

Members of the general population attend religious services more frequently—about forty days a year, on average, compared with twenty-seven days a year for Arab Americans. However, Arab Americans and the general population have similar levels of involvement with other types of voluntary organizations and associations (table 6.1). On average, Arab American and other Americans are formal members of about two nonreligious organizations or associations.[4] Members of the general population, however, are more active participants, attending club or organizational meetings an average of almost eight days a year, versus about three and a half days a year for Arab Americans.

Levels of civic participation—indicated by voting, contacting a government official, signing a petition, or participating in a demonstration or protest—also differ between the two populations (table 6.1). On average, members of the general population engage in twice as many civic activities as Arab Americans.

Figure 6.1   Average Number of Days Per Year for Socializing

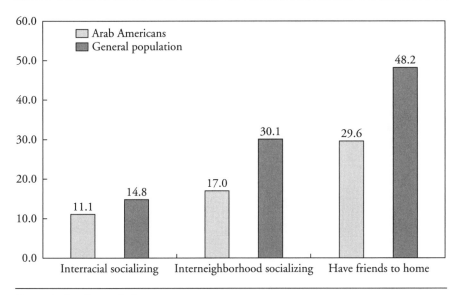

Source: Authors' compilation.
Note: DAS sample size = 508; DAAS sample size = 1016.

Majorities of both populations say that one cannot be too careful or that it depends when it comes to trusting others, but a higher proportion of the general population (38 percent) than of Arab Americans (22 percent) says that most people can be trusted. This type of trust is called social or generalized trust, which "can be viewed as a 'standing decision' to give most people—even those who one does not know from direct experience—the benefit of the doubt" (Rahn and Transue 1998, 545). When asked about trusting members of four specific racial or ethnic groups—whites, blacks, Hispanics, and Arab Americans[5]—members of both populations reported higher levels of this group-specific form of trust than generalized trust, though there still is a difference between the two, with Arab Americans slightly less trusting.[6] These differences in levels and types of trust are presented in figure 6.2.

Overall, these basic comparisons reveal a fundamental inequality. Arab Americans have, on average, less local social capital than members of the general population. They are less likely to socialize across racial or neighborhood

Figure 6.2 Levels of Generalized and Racial Trust

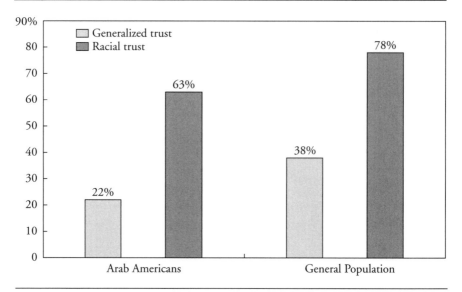

Source: Authors' compilation.

Notes: Generalized trust is the percentage of a population who say that most people can be trusted versus those who say that one can't be too careful or it depends. Racial trust is the average of how much a person trusts whites, blacks, Hispanics, and Arab Americans, where trust for a specified group equals 1 when a persons trusts members of the group "a lot" or "some," and trust for the group equals 0 when a person reports "only a little" or " not at all." DAS sample size = 508; DAAS sample size = 1016.

lines, less active in secular organizations and attend religious services less frequently, less involved civically, and less trusting of other people, either in general or as specific ethnoracial groups. However, these inequalities vary within the Arab American population and within the general population. Whereas table 6.1 presented simple comparisons of the two populations, tables 6.2 and 6.3 show the effects of several factors—education, age, gender, household income, citizenship, language, religion, and place of residence—on various dimensions of local social capital for Arab Americans and for members of the general population. As expected, based on the experiences of other immigrant groups in the United States, Arab immigrants have less local social capital than those born in the United States. Arab immigrants have less bridging social capital, for example, and are involved in fewer voluntary organizations and are less active in those in which they are involved. Arab immigrants exhibit less civic

Table 6.2 Civic Participation and Informal Networks

Independent Variables	Civic Participation		Have Friends to Home		Interneighborhood Socializing		Interracial Socializing	
	Arab Americans (DAAS)	General Population (DAS)	Arab Americans (DAAS)	General Population (DAS)	Arab Americans (DAAS)	General Population (DAS)	Arab Americans (DAAS)	General Population (DAS)
Education	.200***	.220***	.946	−11.02**	−1.42	−5.85**	−1.56	−6.51
	(.025)	(.036)	(1.62)	(4.00)	(1.03)	(2.43)	(.959)	(3.93)
Age	.172**	.287***	−9.42**	−33.61***	−9.85***	−10.11*	−10.49***	−18.52*
	(.048)	(.067)	(3.68)	(8.33)	(2.67)	(4.66)	(2.56)	(7.74)
Gender	.027	−.161*	4.04	9.47	1.69	7.73	−3.30	6.89
	(.059)	(.079)	(3.92)	(7.36)	(2.96)	(5.22)	(2.57)	(5.40)
Income	.151***	.101*	3.86	−3.28	3.09	−.457	1.22	.971
	(.031)	(.047)	(2.48)	(4.51)	(1.70)	(3.38)	(1.10)	(3.16)
U.S. citizen	.442***	.832***	6.53	33.84	2.82	19.16*	5.45*	21.91
	(.058)	(.227)	(4.35)	(18.33)	(3.53)	(8.85)	(2.43)	(10.64)
U.S.-born	.630***	.488**	3.23	3.49	9.60*	4.46	8.79*	−*1.33
	(.092)	(.188)	(6.65)	(10.22)	(4.89)	(7.32)	(3.85)	(6.99)
Language	.218**	—	15.30**	—	3.68	—	5.04	—
	(.075)		(4.91)		(3.21)		(2.57)	

(Table continues on p. 176.)

Table 6.2 (continued)

Independent Variables	Civic Participation		Have Friends to Home		Interneighborhood Socializing		Interracial Socializing	
	Arab Americans (DAAS)	General Population (DAS)	Arab Americans (DAAS)	General Population (DAS)	Arab Americans (DAAS)	General Population (DAS)	Arab Americans (DAAS)	General Population (DAS)
Religion	.228**	−.152	−8.27	9.03	−2.65	6.33	−3.00	−1.25
	(.088)	(.086)	(5.01)	(8.74)	(4.56)	(5.23)	(3.74)	(6.41)
Residence	.008	−.015	5.49	−13.05	−6.54	−11.37	−3.93	.818
	(.088)	(.104)	(4.98)	(11.49)	(3.98)	(7.09)	(3.55)	(6.70)
Constant	−1.32***	−1.21***	3.07	129.28***	26.94**	50.32***	26.60***	48.25**
	(.1799)	(.223)	(13.39)	(26.92)	(9.59)	(13.29)	(7.60)	(17.04)
R^2	.362	.306	.076	.118	.082	.046	.101	.090
N	1016	503	1006	500	1015	500	1010	499

Source: Authors' compilation.

Notes: U.S. citizenship is a dummy variable, 1 = U.S. citizen, 0 = not citizen.

Language is a dummy variable, indicating the language of the interview, 1 = Arabic; 0 = English. This variable is not applicable to the DAS because all interviews were in English.

Gender is a dummy variable, 1 = male, 0 = female.

Religion is a dummy variable. For DAS, Non-Christian = 1, Christian = other. For DAAS = 1 Muslim, 0 = Christian.

Residence is a dummy variable. For DAS, 1 = Detroit, 0 = other. For DAAS, 1 = Dearborn–Dearborn Heights (enclave), 0 = outside enclave.

Total sample size for 2003 Detroit Area Study = 508. Total sample size of DAAS = 1016.

These results reflect adjustments for complex design features, sampling weights, and imputation of missing data.

R^2 for OLS models is adjusted R^2. For logistic models (generalized trust), it is estimated Nagelkerke pseudo R^2.

Parentheses contain standard errors.

*** $p < .001$, ** $p < .01$, * $p < .05$.

Table 6.3 Trust, Faith-Based Engagement, Associational Involvement, and Attendance at Club or Organizational Meetings

Independent Variables	Generalized Trust		Racial Trust		Associational Involvement		Attend Club or Organizational Meetings		Faith-Based Engagement	
	Arab Americans (DAAS)	General Population (DAS)	Arab Americans (DAAS)	General Population (DAS)	Arab Americans (DAAS)	General Population (DAS)	Arab Americans (DAAS)	General Population (DAS)	Arab Americans (DAAS)	General Population (DAS)
Education	.334***	.282**	-.023*	.063***	.225***	.321***	1.08**	-1.11	-.106	.207
	(.079)	(.111)	(.011)	(.017)	(.057)	(.077)	(.346)	(1.66)	(.627)	(1.02)
Age	.312*	.561**	-.079***	.046	.124	.037	.738	.747	3.045**	4.83**
	(.156)	(.209)	(.022)	(.030)	(.110)	(.132)	(.661)	(2.81)	(1.194)	(1.60)
Gender	.146	-.122	-.043	-.015	.114	.276	-.270	2.82	-.674	-3.67
	(.181)	(.235)	(.027)	(.034)	(.134)	(.157)	(.931)	(2.84)	(1.421)	(2.12)
Income	.158	.441**	-.022	.053*	.058	.267**	.681	.227	.462	.062
	(.095)	(.141)	(.013)	(.022)	(.070)	(.101)	(.539)	(1.49)	(.787)	(1.42)
Citizenship	-.425	-1.25	-.001	.122	.629***	-.261	.290	1.22	.694	-6.71
	(.272)	(.887)	(.037)	(.125)	(.174)	(.480)	(.800)	(3.92)	(1.885)	(8.47)
Place of birth	.515*	.631	-.053	-.024	.456**	.744*	3.18*	4.24	1.51	-8.20
	(.222)	(.585)	(.034)	(.070)	(.180)	(.333)	(1.56)	(2.39)	(1.949)	(5.14)
Language	.261	—	-.031	—	.364*	—	1.28	—	.531	—
	(.242)		(.037)		(.173)		(1.07)		(1.863)	
Religion	.248	-.107	.012	-.118**	-.180	-.157	.790	3.69	-10.44***	-7.58***
	(.248)	(.256)	(.038)	(.038)	(.180)	(.171)	(1.55)	(3.09)	(2.02)	(2.21)

(Table continues on p. 178.)

Table 6.3 (continued)

Independent Variables	Generalized Trust		Racial Trust		Associational Involvement		Attend Club or Organizational Meetings		Faith-Based Engagement	
	Arab Americans (DAAS)	General Population (DAS)	Arab Americans (DAAS)	General Population (DAS)	Arab Americans (DAAS)	General Population (DAS)	Arab Americans (DAAS)	General Population (DAS)	Arab Americans (DAAS)	General Population (DAS)
Residence	-.659**	-.861*	.057	-.183**	-.537**	1.31***	1.30	-6.15	-4.62*	8.05**
	(.262)	(.398)	(.039)	(.060)	(.179)	(.257)	(1.718)	(3.29)	(2.05)	(3.12)
Constant	-3.62***	-2.87**	.714***	.218	-.035	-.731	-5.95**	5.84	18.53***	17.35*
	(.698)	(.941)	(.087)	(.145)	(.429)	(.512)	(2.45)	(10.16)	(4.76)	(8.47)
R^2	.118	.134	.057	.176	.157	.142	.040	.016	.134	.095
N	1008	471	996	492	1014	503	1014	500	1010	503

Source: Authors' compilation.

Notes: U.S. citizenship is a dummy variable, 1 = U.S. citizen, 0 = not citizen.

Language is a dummy variable, indicating the language of the interview, 1 = Arabic, 0 = English. This variable is not applicable to the DAS because all interviews were in English.

Gender is a dummy variable, 1 = male, 0 = female.

Religion is a dummy variable. For DAS, Non-Christian = 1, Christian = other. For DAAS, 1 = Muslim, 0 = Christian.

Residence is a dummy variable. For DAS, 1 = Detroit, 0 = other. For DAAS, 1 = Dearborn–Dearborn Heights (enclave), 0 = outside enclave.

Total sample size for 2003 Detroit Area Study = 508. Total sample size of DAAS = 1016.

These results reflect adjustments for complex design features, sampling weights, and imputation of missing data.

R^2 for OLS models is adjusted R^2. For logistic models (generalized trust), it is estimated Nagelkerke pseudo R^2.

Parentheses contain standard errors.

*** $p < .001$, ** $p < .01$, * $p < .05$.

participation and are less trusting of people in general than those born in the United States.

Similarly, Arabs who are not U.S. citizens are less likely than citizens to socialize with people of different races. In both populations, those who are not U.S. citizens are less engaged civically than citizens. Arab Americans whose only or preferred language is Arabic are less likely to have friends visit their homes than those who prefer English. Arabs living in the Dearborn–Dearborn Heights enclave are less trusting of people in general than Arab Americans elsewhere, but they have similar levels of racial trust. Members of the general population living in Detroit—many of whom are African Americans—are less trusting in general and also have lower levels of racial trust, compared to members of the general population who live outside the city. Arab Americans who live in the enclave, however, are just as engaged civically as those who live outside it; they socialize at similar rates and exhibit similar levels of bridging social capital.

Religious differences have little effect on most indicators of local social capital. Arab Christians and Arab Muslims socialize at the same rate, have similar levels of bridging social capital, are similarly trusting of others in general, and are involved in the same number of voluntary organizations and attend meetings with the same frequency. The only significant differences are rates of civic participation (Arab Muslims are less involved civically than Arab Christians) and faith-based engagement (Arab Muslims attend religious services less frequently than Arab Christians). Similar patterns emerge in the general population—religious differences generally do not influence social capital. The only differences are racial trust (non-Christians are less trusting than Christians) and faith-based engagement (non-Christians attend religious services less frequently than Christians).

Education is associated with higher levels of social capital in both populations—those with more education are more engaged civically, more trusting, and involved in more voluntary associations. Education depresses rates of socializing for the general population, but has no effect for Arab Americans. Higher household income is associated with more civic participation in both populations, but income differences have no effect on rates of socializing or the level of bridging social capital in either population. Among the general population, those with more household income are more trusting and involved in more voluntary associations than those with less. Among Arab Americans, however, differences in household income are not associated with differences in trust or associational involvement.

Age has similar effects on social capital for Arab Americans and the general population. Younger people engage in more bridging social capital than older people do. Arab or not, younger Americans socialize more often across neighborhoods and across racial groups than older Americans. They also invite friends to their homes more often. Younger and older Americans have similar levels of involvement with secular voluntary organizations and associations, but older Americans attend religious services more frequently. Similarly, older Americans, Arab or not, are also more engaged in civic activities and are more trusting of people in general. In fact, the only difference in the effects of age on social capital for Arabs and other Americans is racial trust—older Arab Americans are less trusting of various racial groups, but there is no difference in racial trust by age in the general population. Gender has virtually no effect on social capital in either population. Men and women in both populations exhibit similar levels of social capital. The only significant effect is the level of civic participation in the general population: men participate less than women.

In these ways, the experiences of Arab Americans are much like the experiences of other largely immigrant groups—Arabs who are immigrants, who are not U.S. citizens, and who do not speak English have lower local social capital than those who are U.S.-born, citizens, and who speak English. Once we control for these factors, the sources of inequality for Arabs and the general population are similar. Differences in education and income, differences in place of residence, and especially differences in age account for much of the variation in the local social capital of both populations.

GLOBAL SOCIAL CAPITAL

Although Arab Americans in the Detroit region have less local social capital, they have more global social networks than the general population (illustrated in figure 6.3). For example, 56 percent of Arab Americans, versus only 15 percent of the general population, have family outside the United States with whom they are in monthly contact. Similarly, 26 percent of Arab Americans, versus only 12 percent of the general population, have friends outside the United States with whom they are in monthly contact. Only 11 percent of Arab Americans do not have family or friends outside the United States. The only measure of global networks in which the general population surpasses Arab Americans is business contacts outside the United States. However, the proportion in each population is quite low: only 4.7 percent of Arab Americans

Figure 6.3   Frequent Contact Outside the United States

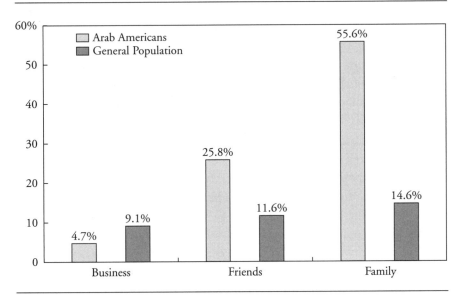

Source: Authors' compilation.

Notes: Business is the percentage of a population that has business contacts outside the United States and has monthly communication with them; friends is the percentage of a population that has friends outside the United States and has monthly communication with them; family is the percentage of a population that has family outside the United States and has monthly communication with them. DAS sample size = 508; DAAS sample size = 1016.

and 9.1 percent of the general population have business contacts outside the United States with whom they are in frequent contact.

Media consumption reveals sharp differences between the two populations. Only 6 percent of the general population reported watching television programs in a language other than English regardless of where the programs originate. By contrast, more than 50 percent of Arab Americans watch satellite television programs originating in the Arab world, most watching on a weekly basis. The most popular network is Arab Radio and Television, which is headquartered in Saudi Arabia and Jordan and operating multiple channels with a wide variety of entertainment and cultural programming, closely followed by al-Jazeera and Dubai TV. Media consumption appears to support or reinforce the traditional values of the Arab world (see chapter 5, this volume). For example, in analyses not shown here but available on request, we find—controlling for education, income, percentage of time lived in the United States, and other factors—that Arab Americans who watch television programs originating in the Arab world tend to disapprove of divorce, women with young children working outside the home, consumption of alcohol, premarital sex, homosexuality, and abortion.

Just as there are inequalities in local social capital, there are inequalities in global social capital. This is demonstrated in table 6.4, which shows the effects of various factors on indicators of global social capital for Arab Americans. Given the low incidence of global ties in the general population and a sample size of 508, there is too little variation to conduct a similar analysis for them. Similarly, the low incidence of business ties outside the United States in the Arab American population means there is too little variation to conduct a multivariate analysis. Not surprisingly, Arab immigrants have more global ties than Arabs born in the United States do. U.S.-born Arab Americans are considerably less likely to have family or friends outside the United States and to have frequent contact with them. This difference also appears when we examine the effect of immigrant status (and other factors) on a scale that combined information about ties to family and friends outside the United States. This scale ranges from 1 to 5, where a score of 1 is assigned to those who have and talk at least monthly to both family and friends (about 22 percent of Arab Americans) and a score of 5 to those who have neither family nor friends outside the United States (about 11 percent). As shown in table 6.4, U.S.-born Arab Americans are less likely to have both family and friends outside the United States with whom they are in monthly contact, and more likely to have neither.

U.S. citizenship and language have similar effects on the extent of global social capital. Arab Americans who are U.S. citizens and those whose only or preferred language is English are less likely to have family ties outside the United States and to have monthly contact with them. Religious differences do not influence local social capital but do affect global social capital: Arab Muslims are more likely to have family ties outside the United States and to have frequent contact with them than Arab Christians. Age plays a major role in local social capital, but does not have a significant effect on the extent of transnational ties. Differences in education and household income influence both local and global social capital—Arab Americans who are more educated and enjoy higher incomes have more transactional ties than those who are less educated and have lower incomes.

Several factors—immigrant status, language, place of residence, religion, age, income, and education—influence the consumption of Arabic programs

Table 6.4 Global Social Capital

Independent Variables	Has Satellite TV and Watches Arabic Programs	Extent of Contact with Transnational Ties	Monthly Contact with Friends Outside the United States	Monthly Contact with Family Outside the United States
Education	−.221**	.142***	.152*	.127
	(.074)	(.036)	(.075)	(.075)
Age	−.570***	−.045	.098	−.255
	(.143)	(.069)	(.159)	(.145)
Gender	−.315	.006	.208	−.176
	(.167)	(.081)	(.176)	(.168)
Income	.275**	.140***	.339***	.258**
	(.092)	(.043)	(.094)	(.093)
U.S. citizen	.323	−.241*	.074	−.593*
	(.235)	(.111)	(.233)	(.242)
U.S.-born	−1.509***	−.839***	−1.103***	−1.522***
	(.229)	(.113)	(.276)	(.233)
Language	.917***	.426***	.396	1.138***
	(.214)	(.107)	(.227)	(.218)
Religion	.889***	.422***	.249	.749**
	(.229)	(.113)	(.238)	(.239)
Residence	.683**	.068	.367	−.310
	(.253)	(.116)	(.244)	(.255)
Constant	.922*	3.392***	−2.919***	−.038
	(.459)	(.231)	(.162)	(.473)
R^2	.327	.200	.105	.290
N	828	808	764	762

Source: Authors' compilation.
Notes: U.S. citizenship is a dummy variable, 1 = U.S. citizen, 0 = not citizen.
Language is a dummy variable, indicating the language of the interview, 1 = Arabic, 0 = English.
Gender is a dummy variable, 1 = male, 0 = female.
Religion is a dummy variable, 1 = Muslim, 0 = Christian.
Residence is a dummy variable, 1 = Dearborn–Dearborn Heights (enclave), 0 = outside enclave.
Coefficients are from logistic regression for Arabic TV, monthly contact with friends, and monthly contact with family; OLS regression for extent of contact with transnational ties.
R^2 for logistic models is Nagelkerke pseudo R^2.
Total sample size for DAAS = 1016.
Parentheses contain standard errors.
*** $p < .001$, ** $p < .01$, * $p < .05$.

Table 6.5   Summary of Main Effects of Sociodemographics

Characteristic	Local Social Capital	Global Social Capital
Immigrant	−	+
Not a U.S. citizen	−	+
Arabic speaker	−	+
Residence in enclave	−	+
Muslim	−/+	+
Education (higher)	+	−/+
Income (higher)	+	+
Age (older)	+	−

Source: Authors' compilation.
Notes: A minus sign (−) indicates an inverse relationship between a characteristic and all or most indicators of local (or global) social capital; a plus sign (+) indicates a positive relationship for all or most indicators. A mixed sign (−/+) indicates that a characteristic has an inverse relationship with some indicators of local (or global) social capital and a positive relationship with other indicators of local (or global) social capital.
Signs represent significant coefficients in the multivariate analyses (tables 6.2, 6.3, and 6.4).

originating in the Arab world. Arab immigrants who speak Arabic, live in the Dearborn–Dearborn Heights enclave, and are younger and Muslim are more likely to watch satellite Arabic programs than U.S.-born Arabs who speak English, live outside the enclave, and are older and Christian. Income and education have opposite effects on media consumption, unlike their similar (and positive) effects on local social capital. Arab Americans who have more household income are more likely to watch Arabic programs from the Arab world than those who have less. Arab Americans who are more highly educated, however, are less likely to watch Arabic programs, and those who are less educated are more likely to do so.

Once we compare local and global social capital, we see that many of the characteristics associated with more global social capital are also associated with less local social capital, as summarized in table 6.5. For example, Arabic-speaking immigrants who are not U.S. citizens and who live in the enclave have more global but less local social capital; conversely, Arabs born in the United States who speak English and live outside the enclave have less global but more local social capital. Higher education and higher household income are associated with more of both local and global social capital, except for the negative association of education and consumption of Arabic television programs. Although these comparisons are based on a cross-sectional picture of social capital, they do suggest that the temporal sequence assumed by the traditional assimilationist view of citizenship is accurate. That is, the mix shifts from the high global–low local social capital of Arab immigrants to the low global–high local social capital of those born in the United States.

CONCLUSION

Our analysis demonstrates that, like other largely immigrant groups in America, Arab Americans have lower local social capital than the general population. This difference applies to both bonding and bridging local social capital. Compared to the general population, Arab Americans on average are less trusting, less involved civically, less involved in either religious or secular voluntary organizations, less likely to have friends to their homes, and less likely to socialize with people from other neighborhoods or of other races. Arab Americans do have, on average, more global social capital than the general population—a type of bonding social capital because it connects people who are similar. However, once we control for immigrant status, as well as immigrant markers such as Arabic language use and enclave residence, the differences shrink and the factors that elevate local social capital are largely the same.

Like other immigrants, the level and mix of social capital for Arab Americans have a lot to do with assimilation success. Arab Americans with more financial resources and education are more likely to have more local social capital, both bridging and bonding. These factors are also crucial for connecting local social capital to global transnational linkages. One of the characteristics commonly assumed to inhibit Arab American social capital—inherent Islamic traits—is not significantly associated with most indicators. Arab Muslims are not more marginalized than Arab Christians. The factors that depress Arab American social capital have more to do with the immigrant experience generally. Thus it is not surprising that those immigrants who lack English skills and U.S. citizenship status also tend to have less local social capital.

Our findings, extrapolated from a cross-sectional analysis to a temporal sequence, support the traditional two-stage model of assimilation. The results indicate that the lower local social capital and higher global social capital of immigrants are reversed over time. Within-group bonding social capital may weaken as the U.S.-born enter into new social relationships and networks with members of the general population, developing more local bridging and less global bonding. This sequence does not preclude the maintenance of well-established minority communities. The results suggest that such communities are not marginalized but instead integrated parts of society.

Our analysis underscores the importance of assimilation in building social capital. That education and income are consistently significant in shaping the content and form of social capital indicates that social capital and upward mobility go hand in hand. As other research shows, social capital enables the development of human capital, and human capital supports the development of social capital (Coleman 1988; Putnam 2000; Lin 2001). Thus, one way to enhance the social capital of local immigrant communities is to ensure that the pathways to economic and educational success remain open. Provided that the immigrant community fosters an ethos of assimilation, mainstream society has an important role to play in ensuring that immigrants enjoy equal access to educational and economic opportunities. The task also falls on the immigrant groups to enhance their social capital in ways that enable rather than impede economic and educational success.

NOTES

1.   The original Social Capital Community Benchmark Survey was devoted entirely to measuring social capital (2002). This twenty-five-minute telephone survey was administered in 2000 to about 30,000 Americans (27,000 in forty communities plus a nationally representative sample of 3,000 Americans). The original survey included many competing questions about social capital to determine those that were the most effective measures. One reason the short form was developed was to enable survey researchers to add a subset of proven social capital questions to a survey that was designed to cover a number of different topics. According to the authors of the short form, the suitability of items was evaluated with four criteria in mind: "a question's centrality to a dimension of social capital" (using factor analysis to identify items that had the highest loadings on a dimension of social capital); "intrinsic interest in the answer to question itself"; "the stability (over time) of responses to a question" (test-retest reliability); and "economy of time" (questions that were quick to ask and answer, or fit a battery of items with a similar form). The results of the original Social Capital Benchmark Survey are available at the Saguaro Seminar website at Harvard's Kennedy School (www.ksg.harvard.edu/saguaro/communitysurvey) and the Benchmark data are available at the Roper Center (www.ropercenter.uconn.edu/scc_bench.html).

2.   Of course, there is a dark side to social capital. It can, for example, enable successful economic crimes (Baker and Faulkner 1993, 2004).

3.   For example, data from the original Social Capital Benchmark Survey, fielded in 2000, revealed that Latino immigrants had lower social capital compared with the general population (Robert Putnam, personal communication 2007; see also Putnam 2007).

4.   As presented in table 6.1, we asked about formal membership in five types of secular voluntary organizations and associations: sports-recreation, art-music-cultural, labor union, parents' association, and professional-business.

5.   Called racial trust in table 6.1, this indicator of social capital is the average of how much a person trusts whites, trusts blacks, trusts Hispanics, and trusts Arab Americans, where trust for a specified group equals 1 when a person trusts members of the group "a lot" or "some," and trust for the group equals 0 when a person reports "only a little" or "not at all." The measure of racial trust was calculated this way to make direct comparisons with the measure of generalized trust.

6.   Not surprisingly, members of a racial group trust themselves more than they trust members of any other group. For example, 74.8 percent of Arab Americans trust themselves a lot or some, with their trust of white members of the general population a close second (70.1 percent). Eighty percent of members of the general population trust themselves a lot or some, with their trust of blacks a close second. Members of the general population (white or black) trust Arab Americans the least, but only by small margins. For both subpopulations, white or black, there is less than a 10 percentage point difference between trusting themselves and trusting Arab Americans.

REFERENCES

Baker, Wayne E. 2000. *Achieving Success Through Social Capital: Tapping the Hidden Resources in Your Personal and Business Networks.* San Francisco, Calif.: Jossey-Bass.

Baker, Wayne E., and Robert Faulkner. 1993. "The Social Organization of Conspiracy: Illegal Networks in the Heavy Electrical Equipment Industry." *American Sociological Review* 58(6): 837–60.

———. 2004. "Social Networks and Loss of Capital." *Social Networks* 26(3): 91–111.

———. Forthcoming. "Social Capital, Double Embeddedness, and Mechanisms of Stability and Change." *American Behavioral Scientist.*

Baker, Wayne, Sally Howell, Amaney Jamal, Ann Chih Lin, Andrew Shryock, Ron Stockton, and Mark Tessler. 2004. "Preliminary Findings from the Detroit Arab

American Study." Ann Arbor: University of Michigan Institute for Social Research and University of Michigan–Dearborn Center for Arab American Studies.

Coleman, James S. 1988. "Social Capital in the Creation of Human Capital." *The American Journal of Sociology* 94(supplement): S95–S120.

———. 1990. *Foundations of Social Theory.* Cambridge, Mass.: Belknap Press of Harvard University.

Easton, Mark. 2006. "Does Diversity Make Us Unhappy?" *BBC News,* May 30. Available at: http://news.bbc.co.uk/go/pr/fr//2/hi/programmes/happiness_formula/5012478.stm (accessed May 30, 2006).

Farley, Reynolds, Maria Krysan, and Mick Couper. 2006. "Attitudes About Arab-Americans: Detroiters' Views." Paper presented at the 61st Annual Conference of the American Association for Public Opinion Research. Montreal, Canada (May 16–18).

Flores, William V., and Rina Benmayor, eds. 1998. "Constructing Cultural Citizenship." In *Latino Cultural Citizenship: Claiming Identity, Space, and Rights.* Boston, Mass.: Beacon Press.

Grasmuck, Sherri, and Patricia Pessar. 1991. *Between Two Islands: Dominican International Migration.* Berkeley: University of California Press.

Hagan, Jacqueline. 1994. *Deciding To Be Legal.* Philadelphia: Temple University Press.

———. 1998. "Social Networks, Gender, and Immigrant Incorporation: Resources and Constraints." *American Sociological Review* 63(1): 55–67.

Jacobs, Dirk, and Jean Tillie. 2004. "Introduction: Social Capital and Political Integration of Migrants." *Journal of Ethnic and Migration Studies* 30(3): 419–27.

Lin, Nan. 2001. *Social Capital: A Theory of Social Structure and Action.* Cambridge: Cambridge University Press.

Massey, Douglas. 1985. "Ethnic Residential Segregation: A Theoretical Synthesis and Empirical Review." *Sociology and Social Research* 69(3): 315–50.

Massey, Douglas, Rafael Alcaron, Jorge Durand, and Humberto Gonzalez. 1987. *Return to Aztlan: The Social Process of Migration from Western Mexico.* Berkeley: University of California Press.

Pakulski, Jan. 1997. "Cultural Citizenship." *Citizenship Studies* 1(1): 73–84.

Pettigrew, Thomas F. 1998. "Intergroup Contact Theory." *Annual Review of Psychology* 49(1): 65–85.

Pettigrew, Thomas F., and Linda R. Tropp. 2006. "A Meta-Analytic Test of Intergroup Contact Theory." *Journal of Personality & Social Psychology* 90(5): 751–83.

Pong, Suet-ling, Lingxin Hao, and Erica Gardner. 2005. "The Roles of Parenting Styles and Social Capital in the School Performance of Immigrant Asian and Hispanic Adolescents." *Social Science Quarterly* 86(4): 928–50.

Portes, Alejandro. 1998. "Social Capital: Its Origins and Applications in Modern Sociology." *Annual Review of Sociology* 24(1): 1–27.

Putnam, Robert D. 1993. *Making Democracy Work.* Princeton, N.J.: Princeton University Press.

———. 2000. *Bowling Alone: Collapse and Revival of the American Community.* New York: Simon and Schuster.

———. 2007. "*E Pluribus Unum:* Diversity and Community in the Twenty-First Century/The 2006 Johan Skytte Prize Lecture." *Scandinavian Political Studies* 30(2): 136–74.

Putnam, Robert D., Lewis Feldstein, and Donald J. Cohen. 2003. *Better Together: Restoring the American Community.* New York: Simon and Schuster.

Rahn, Wendy M., and John E. Transue. 1998. "Social Trust and Value Change: The Decline of Social Capital in American Youth, 1976–1998." *Political Psychology* 19(3): 545–65.

Social Capital Community Benchmark Survey Short Form. 2002. Saguaro Seminar: Civic Engagement in America Project, John F. Kennedy School of Government, Harvard University (July 2002 version).

Waldinger, Roger. 1999. "Networks, Bureaucracy, and Exclusion: Recruitment and Selection in an Immigrant Metropolis." In *Immigration and Opportunity,* edited by Frank D. Bean and Stephanie Bell-Rose. New York: Russell Sage Foundation.

Waldinger, Roger, and Greta Gilbertson. 1994. "Immigrants' Progress: Ethnic and Gender Differences Among U.S. Immigrants in the 1980s." *Sociological Perspectives* 37(3): 431–44.

Wierzbicki, Susan. 2004. *Beyond the Immigrant Enclave: Network Change and Assimilation.* New York: LFB Scholarly Publishing.

PART III

Political Ideology

CHAPTER 7

Civil Liberties

Ronald R. Stockton

To the founding fathers, civil liberties were central to the way they understood their republic. They wanted to create a restrained government that guaranteed citizens the rights to privacy, individual discretion, and protection from abuse by authority. Not only did the Bill of Rights enshrine due process for those accused of an offense, it also contained an inherent protection of group rights. Because most religious groups at the time were also ethnic groups (Fischer 1989), the guarantee of religious freedom was implicitly an accommodation to religioethnic pluralism. In the other direction, they also believed that citizenship placed a responsibility on citizens to be aware of how unique it was to live in a republic, and to be appreciative of that fact. In some states, people who lived overseas for a season were barred from voting for that length of time to re-acclimatize them to republican values (Kettner 1978, 218).

For reasons of history or culture or politics, most Americans have enjoyed more than the average number of freedoms. We look back into history to those occasions when rights were seriously violated and view them as aberrations. The Alien and Sedition Acts of 1798 were never fully implemented and were in fact rejected once the next presidential election occurred; the suspension of habeas corpus during the Civil War was in Lincoln's mind necessary to save the republic (for the Lincoln rationale, see Rehnquist 1998). The detention of Japanese Americans during World War II was so unusual that Congress subsequently apologized and paid reparations to the victims; and the harassment of the Left in the 1920s and the 1950s is attributed to individuals, the Palmer Raids, and McCarthyism, and was challenged and pushed back.

Likewise, few Americans are fully aware of the systematic monitoring and harassment of black leaders, including Marcus Garvey, Malcolm X, Martin Luther King, and Louis Farrakhan (O'Reilly 1994). Few know of Operation Boulder, a program to monitor and harass not only aliens but also Arab Americans and their organizations (Fischman 1985) or the proposal of the Immigration and Naturalization Service to hold Arabs from unfriendly states in a detention camp in Louisiana (U.S. INS 1986).[1] Larger issues of slavery and the dispossession of Native Americans, or the denial of the franchise to women or African Americans, are such extreme violations of group rights, so at odds with the American principles of liberty and justice for all, that they are routinely treated as historic anachronisms or as original sins, not entirely relevant to contemporary situations.

Americans today are proud of their freedoms, but they also feel that those freedoms are sometimes misused. The attacks of September 11 were not carried out by a foreign army but by individuals who used the openness of American society as a weapon against it. This was a shocking realization for many Americans and raised complex issues involving the tension between individual rights and security. Seldom would they suspend their own rights, but the rights of perceived abusers are a different matter.

This chapter examines the terms under which different elements of the Arab American population—the probable target of any security crackdown—support civil liberties, or their restriction, within the context of one of the major traumas in American history.[2] On most abstract civil liberties issues, Arab Americans and the general public have fairly similar views, but when Arab Americans are considered an enemy element or are put collectively at risk, they are far less likely than other Americans to sanction harsh treatment or the loss of liberty. We will show how Arab Americans and non-Arabs reacted differently to these issues, but also that there were elements in each population that took opposing positions. Civil liberties and equal treatment before the law are fundamental issues of citizenship. What Arab Americans discovered in the aftermath of September 11 was that for them both dimensions of these guarantees—due process and group rights—were challenged. Most Arab Americans were willing to make sacrifices for the protection of the country, but most also felt that they had been singled out or called on to make disproportionate sacrifices. It is in the interaction between this willingness to share sacrifice and the fear of being singled out that we find the most revealing and interesting patterns.

SUPPORT AND BACKLASH

In the aftermath of the attacks of September 11, there was an explosion of patriotism in the country. Even Arabs and Muslims benefited from this mood. President Bush went to the Islamic Mosque and Cultural Center in Washington and proclaimed Islam to be a religion of peace. Surrounded by mosque leaders, he said that those who attacked America were extremists who did not represent Islam, and in fact had betrayed it (Bush 2003, 9–10). Governors, mayors, senators and other officials across the country made similar visits and expressions of good will. In the Detroit area, interfaith groups accelerated their activities. Pulpit exchanges and visitations involved Muslims, Christians, and Jews. There were group meetings, newspaper editorials, invited speakers. Bookstores reported increased sales of items relating to Islam and the Arab world, and mosques reported increased requests for copies of the Qur'an. The Pew Research Center found that positive perceptions of Islam and Muslims actually increased from the previous year, from 45 percent to 59 percent (2001). Most Americans saw the attacks as political (49 percent) rather than religious (30 percent).[3]

But not everything was positive. Passengers refused to board airplanes with Arabs and innocent individuals had to disembark; mosques were vandalized and hate crimes increased (Council of American-Islamic Relations 2004). From March 2002 to July 2003, the percentage of Americans who believed that Islam encouraged violence increased from 25 percent to 44 percent; 31 percent said they would not vote for a Muslim. Comparable figures for Jews were 14 percent, Catholics 15 percent, and Evangelicals 20 percent (Pew 2003).

The backlash took two forms: a security backlash (discussed in chapter 3) and an ideological one. The ideological backlash was led by a powerful center of public opinion formation—the media. It constituted a major assault on Arabs and Muslims, dehumanizing them and portraying them in a most unfriendly way. To be sure, the depiction was not new. For decades, Hollywood had produced film after film with Arab villains. Jack Shaheen reviewed more than 900 films with Arab characters and found just over fifty with positive Arab images (2001). Hollywood Arabs were portrayed as "brute murderers, sleazy rapists, religious fanatics, oil-rich dimwits, and abusers of women" (Shaheen 2001, 2). Most of these negative images appeared in films released in the last third of the twentieth century, when the film industry was systematically reducing hostile images of other ethnic groups. Overall, Shaheen argued, there was a "systematic, pervasive, and unapologetic degradation and dehumanization of a people" (2001, 1).

After the 9/11 attacks, certain media personalities, many from the right wings of the evangelical Christian and Jewish communities, became notorious for their hostility toward Arabs and Muslims. The typical assault suggested that pathology and violence were at the heart of Islamic and Arabic culture. A guest on Pat Robertson's *700 Club* television show spoke of Islam as a "false and corrupt doctrine" that "commands Muslims to wipe Christians and Jews out to the last" (Craig Winn, "The Origins of Islam," *700 Club,* February 5, 2003). Islam has a legacy of "bloodshed and terror" and "September 11 happened because the Muhammad depicted in the Islamic Hadith was a terrorist." Winn said that "Muhammad's life mirrored Hitler's" in that he practiced genocide and was "a polygamist, into incest, a rapist, a pedophile, a sadist, a sexist, a womanizer, a liar, a scheming politician, an assassin, and a terrorist." Another example was Daniel Pipes, who wrote in 2006 that individual "Islamists may appear lawabiding and reasonable, but they are part of a totalitarian movement, and as such, all must be considered potential killers" ("Fighting Sudden Jihad Syndrome," *Washington Jewish Week,* March 23, 2006, 16). What Pipes called the sudden jihad syndrome occurred when "normal-appearing Muslims abruptly become violent. It has the awful but legitimate consequence of casting suspicion on all Muslims. Who knows whence the next *jihadi?* How can one be confident a law-abiding Muslim will not suddenly erupt in a homicidal rage?" (16). It is hard to imagine any other group being subjected to such vilification.

Public opinion does not drive policy but sets parameters within which authorities can operate. To be sure, the authorities are not passive recipients of public input. They can expand the range of opinion by working with media allies to shape and modify public perceptions of reality. In a democracy, where policy legitimacy is measured by whether the public supports what authorities are doing, collusion between governmental and media interests is a critical element of policy making. If fear can expand the range of acceptable actions against targeted groups, then an electronic medium that uses threat almost as an advertisement for its news coverage is not just a neutral source of information but is a source of anti–civil liberties activism. Hollywood's undeclared war on Arabs and Muslims, or CNN's inflammatory news slogans after September 1— "America Under Attack" and "America Strikes Back"—become, to borrow from Jacques Ellul, active efforts at propaganda on behalf of powerful, dangerous forces (1969).

WHAT AND HOW THE PUBLIC THOUGHT
ABOUT SECURITY ISSUES

In the aftermath of September 11, Americans were afraid. Their fear took two forms: a personal fear of harm to themselves or their loved ones, and a sociotropic fear of harm to "society or cherished values and norms" (Davis and Silver 2004a, 30; see also Davis 2006, 60–69). Studies showed that both types of fear were extensive. Most Americans (83 to 90 percent) believed there could be a second attack (Davis and Silver 2004b, 15; Nisbet and Shanahan 2006); 34 percent believed they or a family member could be a victim, and 35 percent gathered information on how to handle a bioterrorism attack during the anthrax scare of late 2001 (Huddy, Khatib, and Capelos 2002, 442).

Americans were committed to security but divided about whether to compromise civil liberties. Asked in a January 2002 poll if the government "should take all steps necessary to prevent additional acts of terrorism in the United States even if it means basic civil liberties would be violated," 47 percent said yes (Tabrizi 2004). The alternate choice, that the government "should take steps to prevent additional acts of terrorism but not if those would violate basic civil liberties," won 49 percent support. This divide created inconsistencies in public thinking: "The American people were unsure about their civil liberties after September 11 and remained unsure one year later. They . . . anticipated restrictions, but they were unwilling to tread on privacy or free speech in cases that did not involve suspected terrorists or their supporters. They were concerned about the rights of citizens but unwilling to completely protect non-citizens in the same manner. They saw profiling of religious groups as distasteful but were willing to consider race and ethnicity as factors in targeting suspected terrorists" (Tabrizi 2004, 195). For most Americans, the debate was not abstract because most "believed they would have to give up some freedoms or civil liberties in order to combat terrorism" (Huddy, Khatib, and Capelos 2002, 420). The percentage anticipating personal sacrifice of rights was 55 percent after September 11, but fell to 44 percent in August 2003 and 38 percent in August, 2004 (Pew 2004). Part of the decline was because most Americans were "wary from the onset" about what the government had in mind (Huddy, Khatib, and Capelos 2002, 419). They supported restrictions in principle but balked on specifics. Abstract surveillance received 59 percent support but more specific surveillance—of telephone or email communications, for example—received only 26 percent support. Initially, support for strong security policies was high in almost all demographic and political groups but fell over time. By 2004, the only bastions of support were among Republicans, conservatives, those forty and older, and upper-income groups (Pew 2004).

Response patterns were sensitive to question wording. Allowing the government to "question 5,000 Middle Eastern immigrants on the basis of their religion or nationality" even though "some local officials have refused to perform the questioning, suggesting the government needs to show more cause to question the visitors," garnered 67 percent support. When the question was framed differently, the outcome changed. Asked if the United States, "in response to the terrorist attacks," should "put Arabs and Arab-Americans in this country under special surveillance" or whether it would be a mistake "to target a nationality group as was done with the Japanese-Americans after Pearl Harbor," 62 percent said such policies would be a mistake. Asked if the government should "be allowed to investigate religious groups that gather at mosques, churches or synagogues without evidence that someone in the group has broken the law," 75 percent said no (Tabrizi 2004, 193–94).

Data from the Detroit Area Study (DAS) and the Detroit Arab American Study (DAAS) allow us to compare and contrast the two populations with regards to civil liberties. This dual-sample approach has a significant advantage over studies that survey the general public, few of whom would be the objects of restrictions. Respondents in both studies were asked seven questions about civil liberties. All focused on due process rights. The first asked about personal sacrifice: "Would you be willing to give up some civil liberties if that were necessary to curb terrorism in this country?" Then came three restrictions that would apply to everyone "as a way to reduce terrorist acts:" "increasing surveillance of U.S. citizens by the government;" "giving the police powers to stop and search anyone at random;" and "detaining some suspicious individuals even if there is not sufficient evidence to prosecute them in the courts." Finally, these questions were repeated with Arab Americans as the targets: "increasing surveillance of Arab Americans by the government;" "giving the police powers to stop and search anyone who appears to be Arab or Muslim, at random;" and "detaining some suspicious Arabs or Muslims even if there is not sufficient evidence to prosecute them in the courts."

Figure 7.1 shows that similar proportions of Arab Americans and the general public would give up some civil liberties, increase surveillance of U.S. citizens, and support random stops and searches. However, wide differences open up on the question of detention without sufficient evidence to prose-

Figure 7.1   Perspectives on Civil Liberties

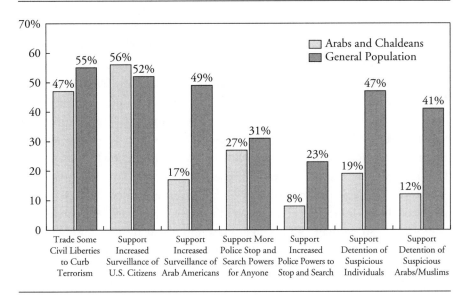

Source: Baker et al. 2004.

cute and on all questions targeting Arabs and Muslims. The general public is 15 percentage points more likely to support stops and searches of people who appear to be Arab or Muslim, and around 30 percent more likely to support detention without prosecution and increased surveillance of Arab Americans. The general population expressed greater reservations at these more restrictive options, but the big shift was among Arab Americans, where exceptional levels of doubt emerged about restrictions targeted at their community. Still, an element among Arab Americans was willing to accept such restrictions. Understanding the dynamics of these opinions can lead to a better understanding of how civil liberties attitudes are formed in a time of national crisis, especially in a population likely to be the object of the restrictions.

EXISTING RESEARCH PATTERNS

Decades of research have produced a common conclusion about civil liberties attitudes. Paul Sniderman and his colleagues summarized it nicely: "every large systematic study of the views of political elites and of ordinary citizens" found elites more supportive of civil liberties than the general public (1996, 24). Herbert McCloskey and Alida Brill argued that leaders are different by virtue of "their social location, their greater education, their more frequent involvement in community activities, their participation in the public colloquy on questions of the day, and their affiliation with social networks whose members often discuss and hold informed views on vital public issues" (1983, 29). They are more likely to accept "the ideas and principles which constitute the society's creed," including support for civil liberties (McCloskey and Brill, 1983, 29). This parallels what Samuel Stouffer found during the cold war: "without exception" the leaders of community organizations were more willing to respect the rights of leftists than rank-and-file individuals (1966, 57). Tolerance was low among the religiously active or those who saw a threat to religion (Stouffer 1966, 155, 186). Overall, support for civil liberties was associated with higher levels of education, organizational involvement, and men versus women (because women are generally less informed). This was traditionally called the liberal model.

However, Sniderman and his colleagues noted that support for civil liberties is inevitably a claim for rights by a specific group that would be affected by restrictions. A "politics of rights" means that "claims to rights are not merely act-sensitive—that is, contingent on what one wishes to do or how one wants to be treated—but also agent-sensitive, that is, contingent on who is to receive a public entitlement or benefit" (1996, 19). Most surveys ask a general population if they would tolerate rights for controversial groups. But if respondents are not in the Ku Klux Klan or of Japanese descent or political activists, then restricting the rights of such people involves no personal costs to respondents. Dennis Chong conducted in-depth interviews on civil liberties attitudes and concluded that "most issues are sufficiently complex that they bring forth multiple considerations if respondents are given enough time to reflect upon them" so that "the key to understanding the survey response lies in how people frame the issues they are asked about" (1993, 868–69). He found "two major classes of considerations on civil liberties issues: consideration of principles and rights and considerations about the people or groups that are involved in the issue, including considerations about how the issue might affect oneself" (868–69). Respondents "commonly give responses based on how they are personally affected by the issue or how they feel about the group that wishes to exercise its rights" (885–86).

Mulligan constructed a four-cell framework to test the impact of personal interest on support for civil liberties (2006, 21–25). His two variables were whether policies would threaten the rights of everyone or only the rights of specific groups (terrorist suspects or dissenters); and, when restrictions target the general population, were they mild (metal detectors in buildings) or extreme (random search or wiretapping). He found that those who fear another attack are supportive of all four dimensions of restrictions, that those who take measures to protect themselves from terrorism are more supportive of all restrictions except those targeting dissenters, and that dissent is more tolerated by the educated but less tolerated by those who display an American flag, are conservative, pay attention to politics, and are elderly. Another study by Kip Viscusi and Richard Zeckhauser asked Harvard law students about the trade-off between airport profiling that would allow passengers to move through security checkpoints quickly, versus time they would wait in line with random screening (2003). When respondents would not be profiled, support for profiling was 45 percent if they saved 10 minutes in line, 74 percent if they saved an hour. However, if respondents are themselves to be profiled and searched, support for profiling was insensitive to time: about half support profiling and half do not.[4] Clearly, personal interest is a factor in how people decide whether to yield up rights. We call this the But Not Us model of civil liberties restrictions.

Arab American Perspectives on Civil Liberties

When presenting our preliminary findings to the public, audiences often expressed skepticism about the high level of support for certain security measures among Arab Americans. Skeptics outside the community believed that Arab Americans were pretending to support security but did not truly feel that way. Skeptics within the community said that respondents had been afraid of the interview process and gave answers they believed would satisfy researchers or the security forces. The analysis in this chapter will address these concerns. To start, let us begin with some simple numbers showing how different elements of the Arab American population answered questions.[5]

- Among conservatives, 50 percent would sacrifice some rights of their own to fight terrorism. Among liberals, only 23 percent would.
- Among those with bachelor's degrees, 38 percent would sacrifice rights. Among those with high school diplomas or less, 50 percent would.
- Among citizens, 21 percent support surveillance of Arab Americans. Among non-citizens, 9 percent do.
- Among those who felt September 11 was an attack on American values, 40 percent would detain suspects without sufficient evidence. Among those who did not feel that way, 12 percent would. Among those who felt

at home in America, 20 percent would detain. Among those who did not feel at home, 9 percent would.

- Those who had a bad experience after September 11 were consistently less tolerant of any restrictions. They were 10 percent less willing to sacrifice civil liberties (38 percent to 48 percent) and on three questions restricting the rights of everyone, they averaged 12 percent less likely than those who had no bad experience.

- Among those who felt that the media are biased against Arabs and Chaldeans, 15 percent would allow the authorities to stop and search a suspicious person. Of those who felt the media favor Arabs and Chaldeans, 54 percent would.

- Among Muslims, 42 percent believed an Arab or Muslim accused of terrorism could receive a fair trial. Among Christians, 57 percent did.

In these snippets of data, we see some of the thoughts and fears of Arab Americans. In many cases, the patterns follow previous public opinion research. In showing how Arab Americans are similar to other Americans in certain ways, we can also see how their experience as an exposed community made them different. Several factors shape their attitudes toward civil liberties. Vulnerability, identity, and fear are three. Two population subgroups are particularly vulnerable to civil rights violations, noncitizens and Muslims. But Arab Americans as a group are also suspect. Our data show that they are aware of this threat.

BORN IN THE UNITED STATES   Because 75 percent of Arab Americans were born overseas, many of them in authoritarian states, could they have a cultural predisposition towards security over civil rights? In some ways the idea that being American-born would increase support for civil liberties seems illogical given that the general population is less supportive of such rights than Arab Americans. Correlations (not displayed) show that on six of the seven questions under analysis, there was no difference in attitude between those born in the United States and those born overseas. The only item with a statistically significant difference involved surveillance of citizens, where the foreign-born were less likely than the American-born to agree, 59 percent to 47 percent. Taking the inquiry a step further, to whether one is currently a citizen, the four nontargeted issues showed no differences, but on the three issues targeted at Arab Americans or Muslims, noncitizens were significantly more likely to resist restrictions (figure 7.2).

Figure 7.2   Citizenship and Restrictions on Civil Liberties

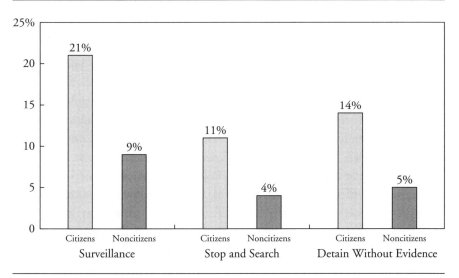

Source: Authors' compilation.
Notes: Surveillance significance = .002; stop and search significance = .02; detain without evidence significance = .005.

What do we make of this? Place of birth does not shape how individuals view civil liberties issues, but being a citizen (or, more important, *not* being a citizen) does. Given that the first and second waves of the much-feared Federal Bureau of Investigation (FBI) interviews were entirely with noncitizens, and that deportations and detentions almost entirely affected noncitizens, such persons could reasonably anticipate that they would be targets of any actions.[6] Some observers have compared the post-September 11 security clampdown to the roundup of West Coast Japanese during World War II, but most of those affected in the 1940s were citizens, whereas the primary targets after September 11 were noncitizens. This point, however, seemed to make little difference in attitude formation. That 75 percent of respondents were immigrants generated a high empathy level for noncitizens. The local media frequently referred to FBI interviews with Arab Americans, not drawing a distinction between those on temporary student, work, or tourist visas and those with citizenship. Many Arab Americans agreed: the citizen-noncitizen distinction was inadequate because it was the community as a whole that was being targeted. The fact that some foreign-born citizens might have been in this country for decades, or had arrived as small children and now had only vague memories of their place of birth, complicated the issue of what shaped their values. On the other hand, noncitizens were all born overseas, and most likely arrived recently. The data show that if anything, they were more resistant to a civil liberties crackdown than others, a reversal of the hypothesis.

MUSLIMS AS AN EXPOSED CATEGORY   If noncitizens were of special interest to the security forces, so were Muslims. In spite of official reassurances about no targeting, many people felt that Arabs and Muslims had become a suspect category and were being subjected to scrutiny in everything from telephone calls to charitable donations or tax returns.[7] The position of the FBI and of airport security officials was that they were monitoring persons with high-risk traits but were not profiling (for a detailed discussion of profiling, see Swiney 2006).[8] That such traits were not specified generated widespread skepticism. Civil liberties attorneys complained that tax violations that would ordinarily receive a fine were treated as terrorism-related criminal offenses and prosecuted. Justice Department records show that those held without charges after September 11 were almost all Muslims (Adam Liptak, "Threats and Responses: The Detainees; for Post-9/11 Material Witness, It Is a Terror of a Different Kind," *The New York Times,* August 19, 2004). This was widely known among Arab Americans.

When we compare Muslims and Christians on these issues, every item shows statistically significant differences. Over the seven items under analysis, the average percentage difference supporting the various restrictions is 15.4. On the three issues where the rights of Arab Americans are concerned, Muslims showed nearly nonexistent support for restrictions (1 percent accepting stop and search, 2 percent supporting detention, 6 percent accepting surveillance). Although support among Christians is also very low (below 20 percent), Christians are more than six times more likely to accept restrictions than Muslims. Further analysis suggests that although these differences manifest themselves through religious categories, they are primarily reflections of vulnerability. Table 7.1 presents the point (adapted from Lin 2004). Iraqi and Lebanese Christians are much more likely than Muslims from the same countries to support increased surveillance and detention of suspicious Arabs and Muslims. The pattern holds for stop and search, but the level of support falls by half, perhaps because people realize it is not always easy to distinguish Christians from Muslims by appearance alone. The patterns disappear into

Table 7.1   Religion, National Origin, and Accepting Restrictions on Arab American Civil Liberties

	Increased Surveillance	Stop and Search	Detain Suspicious
Iraqi Christians	32%**	18%**	23%**
Iraqi Muslims	10	3	5
Lebanese Christians	18**	6**	15**
Lebanese Muslims	5	1	2
Palestinian Christians	9	5	13
Palestinian Muslims	10	0	9

Source: Author's compilation.
Totals: Iraqi Christians by column: 301, 304, 300; Iraqi Muslims by column: 39, 39, 37. Lebanese Christians by column: 121, 125, 125; Lebanese Muslims by column: 231, 235, 231. Palestinian Christians by column: 98, 99, 98; Palestinian Muslims by column: 20, 22, 22.
*** $p < .001$, ** $p < .01$, * $p < .05$.

statistical insignificance among Palestinians, a people who have collectively experienced targeting, profiling, street stops, and surveillance in their home-land and react strongly against such policies. Clearly, vulnerability is shaping how individuals see these issues.[9]

IDENTITY ISSUES: BEING ARAB, BEING AMERICAN

Lloyd Rudolph and Susanne Rudolph, in their classic study of caste politics in India, discussed how traditional identities are transformed in new political and social settings (1967). The authors noted a process of fragmentation whereby some groups break away from others they see as holding them back. This typically occurs when a large caste with lower status is internally differentiated by "education, income, occupation, and cultural style" and a subgroup no longer wants to be associated with the "polluted" aspects of its identity (Rudolph and Rudolph 1967, 27). Because existing labels inhibit this process, it is necessary to create a "radically revisionist history" with "new identities and statuses" based on "the re-examination of the past and the reconstruction of myth and history" (50).

This model is relevant to Arab Americans. From a political perspective, unity is an asset. A host of fragmented and divided groupings would leave Arab pop-

Table 7.2 Views on Restricted Rights

Scale/Item	Feel at Home in America		Proud to Be American			Identify as Arab American	
	Yes	No or Neutral	Not Proud	Proud	Very Proud	Yes	No
Willing to yield your rights	48%	40%	28%	41%	51%***	43%	55%***
Surveillance of all citizens	51	45**	31	47	63***	54	59
Stop and search any person	30	11***	8	19	34***	22	37***
Detain suspects	20	9***	5	12	24***	13	31***
Surveillance of Arab Americans	19	4***	8	9	22***	11	30***
Stop and search Arab Americans	9	2**	1	4	11**	3	18***
Detain Arab Americans and Muslims	13	4**	3	7	15***	5	28***
Is a fair trial possible?	56	20***	24	36	62***	46	60***
Totals	864	142	60	294	624	705	306

Source: Author's compilation.
*** $p < .001$, ** $p < .01$, * $p < .05$.

ulations weak and devoid of influence. Arab American is the label most have chosen as their mobilizing term of choice. As such it is charged with identity, assertions of shared interest, and even destiny (see chapters 2 and 8, this volume). At the same time, however, the term has negative connotations and is not always an asset. The association of Arab with Muslim in the mind of the general public, and the association of both labels with terrorism, add complications for those from the Arab world who are Christian.[10] Table 7.2 illustrates how powerful these differences are in terms of civil liberties issues. Except for the question about surveillance of citizens, those who considered themselves Arab American are consistently more resistant to restrictions on civil liberties than those who did not. The difference is never less than 12 percent and rises to 23 percent when the issue is the possible detention of Arabs or Muslims. As the issues become more serious, the magnitude of difference between the two groups increases. Stop and search, for example, has a magnitude difference of 1.7 when it applied to citizens (22 percent to 37 percent) but rises to 6.0 (3 percent to 18 percent) when it specifies Arabs and Muslims. The difference is in the dramatic falloff of support among those who consider themselves Arab Americans when the community is targeted.

If identification as an Arab American affects civil liberties positions, so does identification as an American. We had two relevant measures: whether individuals felt at home in America (85 percent did) and whether respondents were proud to be American (more than 90 percent were). The pride question sounds a bit odd, perhaps even hackneyed, a strange question to ask an immigrant population, many of whom were being monitored by security forces at the time. But when used cautiously, it produces interesting findings. It is part of the shared symbolic vocabulary of identity that enables Americans, in their exceptional diversity, to debate issues on which they disagree.[11] It also has a strong impact on civil liberties thinking, producing an increased willingness to tolerate restrictions on every single issue. One interpretation might be that there is an authoritarian tendency inherent in American identity, but this assumption overlooks the fact that even the strongest American identifiers remain overwhelmingly resistant to harsh restrictions. Moreover, although the patriotic elements more closely resemble the general public, as the harshness of the restrictions increases, so does the Arab American separation from that same general population, going from single digits of separation into double digits. Their sense of identification with the country may increase acceptance of what they consider tolerable restrictions but it does not extend to the abdication of constitutional rights. More patriotic individuals are also noticeably more willing to yield up their own rights in the interests of security. Again, this is self-sacrifice, not authoritarian control. In a very noteworthy pattern, patriot individuals are also more trusting that an Arab American or Muslim accused of terrorism can receive a fair trial, an affirmation of belief that justice can be found in the American system. These are the only categories where majorities express such confidence (56 percent of the very proud versus 21 percent of the not proud, 56 percent of the at home versus 20 percent of the not at home). In an environment of suspicion and the pursuit of Arab and Muslim suspects, this was an exceptional indication of trust.

The Dimensions of Fear

Darren Davis and Brian Silver found after September 11 that support for civil liberties in the general population was not just a matter of principle but was "highly contingent on other concerns" such that "a large-scale threat to national or personal security can induce a substantial willingness to give up rights" (2004a, 28). Within that context, those who trusted the authorities to do the right thing were more willing to compromise. Conversely, the "lower people's trust in government, the less willing they are to trade off civil liberties for security, regardless of their level of threat" (Davis and Silver 2004a, 28).[12] Sociotropic fear (that society was at risk) is usually more significant but "when threat is personalized the response may become overwhelmingly intolerant toward perceived out groups or threatening groups" (30). Our data show that this dual-threat model worked differently among Arab Americans. For them, the sociotropic threat had two dimensions, not one. It was not just their country at risk but also their community, including perhaps people they knew. The existence of this third type of threat modifies earlier research. Combining personal fear and sociotropic fear, it produces a powerful sense of vulnerability.

We have two measures of personal threat: whether one's sense of security was shaken by September 11 and whether respondents had a bad experience after September 11. The data show that the Davis and Silver expectations were confirmed in the general population but reversed among Arab Americans. In this reversal lies an important insight into the nature of fear and why an exposed minority may not follow mainstream patterns of thinking. In the general public, those who had a bad experience after September 11 are not different on any civil liberties issue. But if September 11 shook their sense of security, there are strong increases in willingness to restrict rights on two items. They are more likely to favor increased surveillance of Arab Americans (60 percent to 47 percent) and to stop and search Arab Americans (29 percent to 17 percent). These policies represent crackdowns on a suspect population, not themselves, and hence are more palatable. For Arab Americans, those with a bad experience were significantly less likely to favor restrictions on each and every item (table 7.3).

This leads to yet another sense of fear, namely that there is a systematic assault upon the community by the media. To scholars, this is often framed as stereotyping (Stockton 1994) but among Arab Americans it is seen as a pervasive threat. We asked two questions: how respondents saw coverage of Arab Americans and Chaldeans and how they saw coverage of Islam and Muslims.

Table 7.3   Enhanced Fear and Views on Restricted Rights

Item/Scale	Bad Experience		9/11 Shook Safety			Media and Arabs		
	Yes	No	Yes	Some	No	+	0	−
Willing to yield your rights	38%	48%**	48%	46%	42%	44%	51%	38%*
Surveillance of all citizens	44	58**	58	55	51	74	64	40**
Stop and search any person	17	29**	26	29	27	54	33	15**
Detain suspects	10	21***	19	18	19	37	22	11**
Surveillance of Arab Americans	8	18**	16	15	21	42	20	9**
Stop and search Arab Americans	4	8*	7	8	11	18	11	2**
Detain Arab Americans and Muslims	7	13*	9	12	20***	18	16	4**
Is a fair trial possible?	43	52*	47	50	62*	69	56	34**
Totals	156	854	484	342	179	35	565	374

Source: Author's compilation.

*** $p < .001$, ** $p < .01$, * $p < .05$.

On every one of the seven civil rights questions, and on the question of whether an Arab or Muslim accused of terrorism could receive a fair trial, those who thought coverage favored those groups (a minority) were much more willing to restrict rights; those who felt it was hostile (the majority) were more resistant.[13] In other words, if there is trust in the fairness of the media, then fear is reduced and respondents feel more confident in permitting security forces to act against harmful elements. This is the other side of the vulnerability thesis—that those who sense hostility take a defensive position.

At this point, we can offer a modified fear hypothesis: for a vulnerable population, the dangers are not only external. The fear of another attack is there, but the more immediate fear lies in an ominous sense that things could go very badly for the community if the security forces overreact in the interests of protecting the country. Combining sociotrophic fear with personal fear (for themselves, their families, or persons they know) produces a powerful effect. It is the danger within more than the danger without that drives frightened Arab Americans in their thinking on civil liberties issues, and it leads them to be staunch defenders of their rights.

A Different Perspective

To seek deeper insight into how Arab Americans view civil liberties issues, we created two additive indices measuring how willing individuals are to compromise rights. The General Rights Index contains the three restrictions directed at the general public. Forty-one percent supported no restrictions, 33 percent accepted one, and 27 percent accepted two or three. The Arab American Rights Index produced even higher resistance: 80 percent would accept no restrictions, 11 percent accepted one restriction, and 9 percent accepted two or three, evenly divided. We also looked closely at the two surveillance questions, which are particularly revealing of how individuals think about civil liberties.

Table 7.4 shows that willingness to support strong security measures by restricting civil liberties—of either Arab Americans or the general population—is disproportionately found in certain parts of the Arab American population. Specifically, such people share five traits. They are very proud of being American. They believe an accused person can receive a fair trial. They believe that the attacks of September 11 were directed at American values. They are more likely to be Christian. They tend to be older. Two beliefs inhibit any willingness to restrict rights: identification as an Arab American and a belief that the media are hostile to Arab Americans and Muslims. Three variables produced no independent impact and are not reported: follow war news, believe in a clash of civilizations, and trust the government in Washington.[14]

There is some divergence, however, in those who resist or accept restrictions on the general public, and those who resist or accept those targeted at Arab Americans. The more highly educated are less willing to tolerate restrictions on general rights but show no difference on attitudes toward Arab American rights. Those with more memberships appear more willing to restrict general rights but, again, are no different regarding Arab American rights. Finally, trusting other people increases support for restrictions on citizens in general but has no impact on Arab American rights. General restrictions appear to follow traditional patterns found in the research literature, but accepting restrictions on Arab Americans, or resisting them, has a different dynamic.

Table 7.4   Acceptance of Civil Liberties Restrictions

Scale/Item	General Rights Index	Arab Rights Index	Surveillance None	Surveillance Both	Surveillance, But Not Us
Education (1 < HS; 2 = HS; 3 = HS+; 4 = BA; 5 = BA+)					
2 versus 1	1.291	0.785	0.996	1.105	1.080*
3 versus 1	0.714	0.941	1.210	1.143	0.946
4 versus 1	0.882	0.998	1.448	1.925	0.684
5 versus 1	0.335*	0.936	2.193*	1.101	0.459*
Age (1 = 18 to 25; 2 = 26 to 54; 3 = 55+)					
2 versus 1	1.515	2.411*	0.669	1.768	0.946
3 versus 1	1.306	2.643*	0.734	3.130*	0.706
Male	0.920	0.887	0.071	0.831	1.016
Christian	2.03**	2.206*	0.912	2.516*	0.853
Conservative	1.230	0.894	0.779	0.869	1.289
Republican	1.328	1.760*	0.618	1.510	1.225
Arab American?	0.666*	0.283***	1.011	0.378****	2.144***
Proud to be American	3.387*	3.514*	0.860	6.130*	0.922
Arabs do all	0.857	1.485	1.261	1.861*	0.545**
Fair trial possible?	2.019**	1.666*	0.525***	2.047**	1.356*
Memberships					
1 versus 1	1.521	1.481	0.880	1.907	0.772
2 versus 1	1.592	1.878	0.527*	2.333	1.243
3 versus 1	1.934	1.853	0.468**	2.498	1.237
4 versus 1	4.382*	2.223	0.171***	1.816	2.941**
5 versus 1	1.407	0.983	0.703	0.863	1.369
Active in congregation	0.996	1.560	0.968	0.860	0.962
Information Index					
1 versus 0	0.843	0.905	1.110	0.935	0.916
2 versus 0	0.660	0.505*	1.540	0.590	0.949
Conflict of values	2.309***	2.339*	0.616*	1.861*	0.913
Extremists	0.633*	2.053*	0.967	1.377	0.939

(*Table continues on p. 212.*)

Table 7.4   (continued)

Scale/Item	General Rights Index	Arab Rights Index	Surveillance None	Surveillance Both	Surveillance, But Not Us
Media hostile					
1 versus 0	0.592*	0.483**	1.386	0.447*	1.211
2 versus 0	0.335***	0.441*	2.672****	0.468	0.559**
Bad experience?	0.672	0.493*	1.384	0.545	1.037
Trust people					
2 versus 1	1.374**	1.256	0.922	0.545	0.948
3 versus 1	0.644	0.889	0.813	0.637	1.363
Hostile to immigrants					
None or some	1.161	2.055*	0.862	1.827	1.048

Source: Author's compilation.

Notes: Reporting logistic coefficients from regression of five indices on Education, Age, Memberships, Information, Media hostile, Trust people, Hostile to immigrants. Dummy variables (1 = yes, 0 = no) are Male, Christian, Conservative, Republican, Consider self Arab American, Feel at home in America, Arabs doing all to stop terrorism, Fair trial possible, Active in congregation, American values attacked on 9/11, Extremists behind attacks, Bad experience after September 11.

Arab American Rights Index accepts restrictions on H14d, H14E, H14f. Categories are 1 = none and 2 = 1 or more.

General rights index accepts restrictions on H14a, b, c. Categories are 1 = none, 2 = 1, and 3 = 2 or 3.

Media hostility index: C36b (3) + C36c (b), none = 0, 1 or 2 = 1.

Immigrant hostility index: F7 (4 or 5) + F8 (1 or 2), none = 0, some = 1 or 2.

Memberships report total affiliations on C 16, 17, 18, 19, 20.

Results based on 857 valid responses.

**** $p < .0001$, *** $p < .001$, ** $p < .01$, * $p < .05$.

Those willing to restrict Arab American rights, definitely the minority position, stand out in several ways. They are less likely to have had a bad experience after September 11, are less friendly to immigrants, are more likely to be Republicans, tend to be older, and tend to be less politically informed. It is no surprise that Republicans would be more supportive of strong security measures, given that at the time a Republican president was pushing a strong war-on-terror agenda. Being less informed is also common among those less supportive of civil liberties. The Immigrant Hostility Index (immigrants are not good for the economy, and immigrants increase crime rates, see table 7.4, footnote 6 for details) produced only one meaningful result but it is right here where we might expect it. At times established populations are unsettled by the influx of immigrants who bring in different views and customs. Arab Americans have a derogatory term for an unacculturated immigrant—a boater. Though often used with a twinkle in the eye, it makes a point of separation (Ajrouch 2004). Among Arab Americans with doubts about immigrants, support for restrictions on Arab American rights doubles.

One belief inhibits a willingness to restrict Arab American rights: those who feel that the media are hostile to Arab Americans and Muslims are far less willing to compromise any rights for anyone. This is an important finding, which we will discuss more fully. Finally, in one interesting reversal, a belief that the attacks of September 11 were by extremist terrorists has the opposite impact on the two indices, reducing willingness to restrict the rights of the general public but increasing it for restrictions on Arab Americans. The very term *extremists* implies individuals not typical of the norm. From this point of view, it would be illogical to put the whole nation under suspicion but it might be logical to focus on those elements perceived to be the source of threat.

In addition to the two rights indices, we also examined the two surveillance questions in more detail. These two items show the biggest drop of any pair of questions in support for civil liberties restrictions, from 56 percent to 17 percent as we move from surveillance of citizens in general to surveillance of Arab Americans. Ironically, surveillance was easier to accept than stop and search, which probably seemed more intrusive and confrontational. In reality, surveillance is a more serious threat because of the hidden implications of the word. Comparing response patterns to the two questions, 46 percent would not surveil anyone, 40 percent would be willing to surveil the public but not target Arab Americans, and 14 percent would surveil both groups. In one sense, these three categories are a progression, from those most supportive of civil liberties to the least supportive. But this leaves out the significant fact that Arab Americans, especially Muslims, are the most likely targets of any surveillance policy regardless of how it is presented. Rather than a continuum, perhaps the categories represent three distinct ways of thinking.

- *Surveil no one.* Those who would surveil no one may be acting on principle. Some might also be thinking of impersonal crowd surveillance, such as street cameras, but with FBI interviews and prosecutions, this is unlikely. Most probably, respondents suspected that any surveillance program, even one aimed at abstract citizens, would target their community.
- *Surveil everyone.* Those who would surveil everyone, including Arab Americans, appear to be security conscious even to the extent of having their own population singled out. If the liberal model holds, they should be less educated, less informed, less involved, and younger. They might also be ideological conservatives, who traditionally support security over civil liberties.[15] They might also suppose that they or their subgroup would be exempted from scrutiny.
- *But not us.* Those who would surveil everyone but not single out Arab Americans could be security conscious individuals with a sense of liberal fairness and insistence on enforcement neutrality. They would be civil liberties advocates but security realists. Alternately, some may lack a civil liberties impulse unless it is in their own interests. On the face of it, we cannot tell.

Table 7.4 shows that these are three distinctive ways of thinking. For example, there are no traits that cut across the three positions, as was the case with the two rights indices. In fact, many traits reverse in their impact as we move from one way of thinking to another. Compare, for example, resistance to any surveillance whatsoever (None) and willingness to target Arab Americans as a part of an overall surveillance policy (Both). Those who reject any surveillance doubt that a person accused of terrorism could receive a fair trial, do not see September 11 as an attack on American values, and see the media as hostile. They also tend to be better educated and less involved organizationally. Some of these patterns reverse or disappear when we look at those who accept surveillance. Such people are more likely to believe that the September 11 attacks were rooted in rejection of American values, do not sense a hostile media, and believe that a person could receive a fair trial. They are more proud of being American, doubt that Arab Americans are doing all they can to fight terrorism, and are less likely to consider themselves Arab American. Christians are more likely to support this position; Muslims less likely.

Regarding the third pattern, generalized surveillance but rejection of targeting (But Not Us), those less tolerant of surveillance are more likely to identify as Arab American, have higher levels of organizational involvement, and a greater sense that the media are hostile. Those who believe an accused person can get a fair trial are more tolerant of surveillance and those who believe that Arabs are doing all they can to fight terrorism resist it.

What can we make of these patterns? First, trust in the legal system is a fail-safe mechanism that increases support for security policies. If authorities ensnare innocent people, they will be checked by the courts.[16] We know trust is linked to a willingness to restrict rights, but this often means trust of other people (that is, of human nature) or trust in the government in Washington. Trust in other people affected only one item, the Arab American Rights Index. Trust in the government in Washington had no impact and was not included in the table. Trust in the legal system is clearly more powerful.

Second, there is grave concern about the role of the media. To many Arab Americans the media is not a neutral information body but a center of power hostile to their community. The greater their fear, the greater their resistance to limits on rights. This is an often overlooked form of political trust. In a sense, it is the opposite of belief in the possibility of fair trials, which appears to free people to trust the government. When social scientists look at whether individuals trust the major institutions of society, they often think of the formal structures of government and the political process. But to many Arab Americans, the media are an independent part of the power structure. They are the fourth estate, not a balance to power but a part of it. They are beyond the control of the electoral process, constitutional restraints, or public accountability. This view of mass media is a key aspect in how people think.

Third, American identity is important. Those proud to be American or who believe September 11 challenged core American beliefs are more likely to support restrictions, often by a factor of two or more. This is a deeply felt defense of American values. It suggests that solidarity with the nation includes a commitment to security and trust in its legal processes. In a sense, trust is a subset of national identity.[17]

Fourth, religious identity is important. Muslims are afraid, with good reason. They have been compromised against their will by violent extremists acting in the name of Islam. Arab Americans, especially Muslims, are entangled in geopolitical conflicts largely beyond their control but that have made them appear to be an alien element. Muslims also tend to be more in confrontation with American foreign policy than Christians.[18] They see the danger lurking within the effort to protect the country from enemies who, in many ways, are thought to resemble them. No matter how patriotic they might be, Muslim Arabs are far more likely to be singled out for surveillance. They are suspect and they know it.

Finally, many conventional findings did not produce significant patterns and were not included in this model. For instance, whether people followed the news from Iraq or the war on terror mattered little. Being a liberal or conservative, Democrat or Republican, male or female, religiously active or not, had no impact on how Arab Americans view civil liberties. Education was much less important than many observers would have guessed. It is clear from these nonfindings (or weak associations) that Arab American perspectives on civil liberties often do not follow the patterns found in the general population. Distinctive considerations shape their thinking, rooted in the fact that Arab Americans are both an engaged community and an exposed community. For them, civil liberties are not abstract matters of principle but vital issues of personal and community interest.

CONCLUSION

In July 2005, London experienced four brutal acts of violence when suicide bombers blew up three subway trains and a bus. Fifty-two people died. What was striking about these incidents when compared with the attacks of September 11 was that though all assailants in both cases were Muslims, in London the four bombers were British—not an alien cell that had infiltrated the country to commit violent deeds. They spoke Midlands-accented English, went to British schools, ate fish and chips, and led lives largely indistinguishable from those of millions of other young Britons.

When those London attacks occurred, the eyes of the nation were on the Muslim community. But the reaction of the national leadership was not to say that Islam was a peaceful religion and that violent extremists had betrayed the faith. It was to say that the Muslim community had to look within to see why these incidents had happened. Prime Minister Tony Blair said it was time to stop talking about multiculturalism and start talking about British values. The four Muslim members of parliament, while noting the danger of an overreaction, nevertheless were blunt in stating that they had long fought extremism and that now Muslim community leaders had to join the battle ("Deep Rooted Problems," *The Guardian,* July 14, 2005). Muslims were told to stop thinking of themselves as foreigners in a corrupt land. The tone was dramatically different from how the American elite had responded. In both cases the security forces began accelerated surveillance of Muslims, but the rhetoric in Britain was often harsh.

This example may help us grapple with one of the most perplexing aspects of this analysis: namely, that some persons who might theoretically be subject to targeted restrictions of their rights are willing to support such restrictions. One explanation is that it is primarily Christians who take this position, but that is inadequate. As we have shown, Muslims are in some ways the statistical outliers on civil liberties issues, showing the most deviation from the general population because of their vulnerability and exposure. Moreover, as is clear from table 7.1, not only are Christians overwhelmingly resistant to restrictions on rights, but at times Christians and Muslims are also very similar in their views. The religious difference is there, but it is not enough to explain the larger patterns. That explanation also includes fear, bad experiences (personal and collective), and identification.

At the heart of this chapter is a debate over the nature of civil liberties and how those liberties relate to the concept of citizenship. Most people understand civil liberties as legal conventions that guarantee individual rights to expression (in speech and in practice) and due process (for those accused of an offense). This is the Bill of Rights approach. It assumes that the American tradition (at least in its best practice and aspiration) is rooted in an exceptional range of individual discretion and personal freedom, and a restrained authority structure that operates within strict limits. This approach is complicated, however, by the fact that there can never be just one right involved in a dispute. All disputes involve a clash of rights. The issue is not whether rights should be honored but which rights take precedence.

Jennifer Hochschild addressed these issues in her critique of the liberal model (1986). Let us consider an example that follows her logic. Suppose we ask in a local survey whether a person caught running a drug house in a neighborhood should be kept in jail without bail until the trial or allowed bail as any other accused person would be. We might find that better educated citizens are more supportive of granting bail. How would we account for this? One explanation is that education introduces individuals to the complexity of life and to the values and traditions of the society, including the right to be assumed innocent until proven guilty. But there is another possibility. What if we ask a follow-up question about why people answered as they did and discover that well-educated people tend not to have drug houses in their neighborhoods. For them, the issue is a matter of principle. In contrast, the less educated are more likely to be familiar with the phenomenon of the crack house because they have friends or relatives whose lives have been negatively affected by them. Given this insight, we might conclude that the person resisting bail is a champion of child safety and the rights of good citizens to live in peace, free from drug-related violence. So which is the true advocate of citizen rights? Both are, but in different ways.

In the aftermath of the London bombings, I met with a group of Arab American students and told them of the attacks and the danger they caused for Muslims in Britain. I asked a hypothetical question: What if one of the airplanes on September 11 had been flown entirely by students from this university? They were stunned at the thought. Of the few cases of alleged terrorism in Michigan, none involved violence. Most involved fundraising for organizations with charitable wings and were arguably benign (Ann Mullen, "Haddad Breaks his Silence," *Metro Times Detroit,* March 17, 2004). The idea that homegrown terrorists might actually kill people in the United States was a frightening thought. One student, known for his outspoken defense of the Muslim community's rights, put his head in his hands and said, "Don't even think that." He could see the danger immediately.

It is obvious that Arab Americans, especially Muslims, are in a vulnerable situation. Not only are they a minority population, they are largely an immigrant population. Some from their homelands or their faith tradition are hostile to the United States. As the DAAS interviews were ongoing, American soldiers were fighting and dying in two Muslim countries, and the United States was actively supporting governments elsewhere in their campaigns against Muslim forces. More than once, Arab organizations in Michigan sent out advisory messages telling people to secure their buildings, be cautious in their public movements, ask for help if approached by the security forces, and support responsible charities. Surely this sense of vulnerability explains a great deal about why Arab Americans are so resistant to restrictions on rights that target them and their communities. But how do we explain those willing to accept restrictions?

Let us return to the Arab American willing to accept increased surveillance of Arab Americans. What does this statement really mean? The liberal model assumes that individuals with this view are probably less educated, not civil libertarians, less trusting, and not politically active. But none of these expectations work with Arab Americans. Far more significant are pride in being an American, trust in the legal system to protect the innocent, and trust in the media to be fair. There is no doubt that Christians find it easier to be comfortable in this country than do Muslims (see chapter 8, this volume). It is also true that the assailants of September 11 were Muslims rather than Christians. There is also the lurking fear, often not even voiced because of the serious implications, that a second attack, especially one conducted British-style from within, could produce an even more extreme reaction against Muslim Americans. Perhaps some Arab Americans, especially Christians, and especially those who identify more overtly with the country, sense a greater danger in new attacks than in the political costs that would come with enhanced and perhaps unfair security policies.

Elevated from the mundane to the philosophical level, this scenario expresses the logic of classical conservatism, which emphasizes that although individuals have rights, societies also have rights, and in the event of a clash, the rights of society outrank the rights of individuals (Kirk 1953). The great debate over liberty is based on these issues. But our task is less to engage that debate than to understand the logic of those we interviewed. It is clear that there are strong sentiments among Arab Americans on behalf of their rights. Community leaders have expressed grave concerns about legal harassment. Their organizations have challenged administrative and prosecutorial actions against members of the community but also have met with security officials to discuss how to cooperate in protecting society without sacrificing freedom (see chapter 3, this volume). Even those who are steadfast champions of civil liberties recognize the need for society to protect itself. These sometimes contradictory views manifest themselves in different ways, but they share a fundamental concern. If this reasoning is correct—and it will have to remain in the realm of hypothesis because we cannot know for certain from the data—then those who resist and those who would tolerate the civil liberties limitations outlined in this chapter are both acting to protect the Arab American community from bad outcomes.

Three conversations about the aftermath of September 11 illustrate the range of sentiments within the community. In one, a Yemeni immigrant who lived in Dearborn expressed distress at the attacks and what they meant for people such as himself: "I came to America to escape these people, and now they are following me." The second conversation involved an Iraqi Chaldean who was a successful businessman. Asked if his community, which was concentrated in the suburbs, had experienced discrimination or harassment he said, "No. We are doing well. It is our Muslim brothers and sisters who are having difficulties." The third conversation was with an outspoken advocate of Arab community rights. "If you and I are getting onto an airplane and they say that everyone has to have a full search, I will accept that in the interests of security. But if they say that you get the normal security check and I get the full search, I will not accept that."

These three people share an acknowledgement of external threat, a willingness to accept certain security restrictions, and a concern for the welfare of their communities. Some focus more upon government excess, some focus more upon checking threats. However, these are not dichotomous positions. They are points on a continuum that blur into each other and overlap and double back. The key to understanding the response is to understand how the person framed the larger issues. These three individuals reflect the complexity, fear, and confusion Americans experienced in an exceptionally dangerous and difficult time.

NOTES

1. The "preliminary decisions" of the INS focused on "alien terrorists and undesirables," from Libya but also from Algeria, Tunisia, Iran, Jordan, Syria, Morocco, and Lebanon. The government would "distinguish and isolate those members of the nationality group whose presence is inimical to national security interests." There would be "close cooperation and an exchange of information" with the CIA and FBI and other "agencies with national intelligence and security functions." There would be a "General Registry" of all such individuals, hearings *in camera,* use of classified information, denial of bond. Procedures would be published as a "final rule in the Federal Register without resort to proposed rule-making procedures, as a matter of national security." There should be vigorous prosecution for false documents, false statements, illegal weapons, illegal entry, with backup plans should prosecution fail. Travel control would affect not only aliens "but citizens as well." Legal authority "need only be fleshed out with appropriate regulations, published as final rules in the Federal Register due to the exigencies of the situation, in order to become an effective provision of law." Given the large number of individuals involved, the plan "proposes to take advantage of the recently opened

Oakdale, Louisiana processing facility in order to house and isolate this population." The attorney general could "issue a policy directive . . . that certain classes of alien or nationalities be precluded or restricted from obtaining certain discretionary reliefs" (U.S. INS 1986, unpaginated). The policy covered not only illegal immigrants but also legal immigrants and nonimmigrants such as students. Several of these proposals are remarkably similar to what happened after September 11. For further information on Operation Boulder, the FBI files of civil rights attorney Abdeen Jabara are housed in the archives of the University of Michigan–Dearborn Center for Arab American Studies, which also has a copy of the INS proposal.

2. Amaney Jamal analyzed how the general population formed its attitudes, using data from the Detroit Area Study (Jamal 2007). She used a racialization model in that analysis.

3. Some observers were suspicious of the expressions of good will. Steve Salaita wrote that "while the goodwill of everyday Americans cannot be called into question," similar statements from leaders were suspect, especially if combined with "draconian legislation such as the USA Patriot Act" (Salaita 2005, 150–51). Salaita labeled such appeals to unity as Imperative Patriotism, an oppressive and intimidating call to yield up one's identity (for the related concept of disciplinary inclusion, see Shryock 2007; chapter 9, this volume).

4. The author is grateful to Ann Chih Lin (2004) for insights from her unpublished paper.

5. In-text differences are significant at the .05 level unless otherwise indicated.

6. By the time of the DAAS interviews in 2003, the FBI was also contacting citizens. Often they asked interviewees for their help if they learned of efforts to launder money or organize cells. These were typically responsible members of society—for example, students or businesspeople. Almost all perceived these contacts as threatening. In some cases, agents were polite. In others, they used intimidating techniques, as if they knew something about the person or could cause them harm if they did not cooperate. Some people felt a terrifying sense of déjà vu. As one person said to the author, "This is what they did in the old country, trying to get people to inform on each other."

7. There is an irony in this terminology. In civil liberties law, a suspect category emerges when a law causes special risk for a vulnerable group. Here a suspect category is subject to special restrictions. For a discussion of the issues involving charities, see Neil MacFarquhar, "Fears of Inquiry Dampen Giving by U.S. Muslims," *New York Times,* October 30, 2006, A1.

8. The Civil Rights Division of the Department of Justice defines profiling as "the invidious use of race or ethnicity as a criterion in conducting stops, searches and other law enforcement investigative procedures" (Swiney 2006, 7). Plaintiffs must show that the policy harmed them personally. Saying that a visit by the FBI was stressful would not cross the threshold of harm. Attorney General Ashcroft asserted in his memoir that his department did not profile but pursued high-risk individuals (2006).

9. There are also differences by ancestry. On the three items targeted at the public, Lebanese-Syrians average 28 percent supporting restrictions, Palestinian-Jordanians average 25.7, and Yemenis average 29.3. These are minimal differences, especially considering that the Iraqi average was 44.6. On the three restrictions targeted at Arab Americans, the three groups were also similar, their average support levels being 7.0 percent, 7.7 percent, and 3 percent. Again the Iraqis stand out at 22.3 percent. The Iraqi percentages are very low in an absolute sense but noticeably higher than the others. Palestinian-Jordanians were less likely to approve general surveillance, Arab American surveillance, and generalized stop and search.

10. Identity formation does not always follow academic models. In 2005, several students were asked whether they identified with the term Arab American. Two, both American-born, gave interesting answers. An Iraqi Chaldean said, "I do, but because of what is happening in my country, it is important for me to say I am an Iraqi." A Lebanese Maronite said, "Of course I am an Arab, but most Americans think Arab means Muslim so for the sake of my religion I have to say I am a Lebanese Christian." Neither of these would fit the Rudolph and Rudolph model.

11. The question had four responses: very proud, quite proud, not very proud, and not proud. With affirmation of patriotism a norm, proud was the default position, with very proud and two lower categories as deviations. The item was recoded into three categories: very proud (62 percent), proud (29 percent), and less than proud (6 percent).

12. Soon after September 11, the Institute of Social Research at the University of Michigan conducted a national survey (Traugott and Weir 2001). They found a strong linkage between having one's sense of security shaken and a willingness to approve civil liberties restrictions. Some of their questions were used in the DAAS.

13. Table 7.3 presents results for perceived coverage of Arab Americans and Chaldeans. The item on coverage of Muslims and Islam is fundamentally similar on all points. It is available from the author.

14. The odds ratio in the table reports the change in the dependent variable based upon change in the independent variable. For example, those who believe the

attacks of 9/11 reflect a conflict of values are 2.3 times more likely to approve restricting general rights. The comparison points show where changes occur. On surveillance none, education has a statistically significant impact at the highest level (level 5 versus level 1). On Arab rights, each age group (2 versus 1, 3 versus 1) has an impact. A number below 1.0 means the pattern reverses. Then the odds ratio is calculated by subtracting the number from 1.0. Finally, the reader should remember that a logistic analysis shows comparative impact (Christian more than Muslim, for example) but does not generalize to the whole group.

15. A third possibility was that they were personally insecure and were nervous during the interview, which did not prove to be the case (for a discussion of respondent fear, see chapter 8).

16. Given several high-profile terrorism cases dismissed by judges, there may be some validity in this assumption. Detroit was the focus of a major terrorism cell case that fell apart in the face of the evidence. In the end, the federal prosecutor was removed and himself put under investigation (see Ann Mullen, "Disorder in the Court: Federal Prosecutor Richard Convertino is Now the One Under Investigation," *Metro Times Detroit,* June 30, 2004; "Terror and Error: How a Justice Department Victory Went Poof," *Metro Times Detroit,* September 8, 2004).

17. Michael Suleiman independently reached similar conclusions through his own research, especially about trust being a subset of identity. He believes that "Arab Americans who are third or fourth generation (as well as some more recent arrivals fleeing persecution) strongly identify with the U.S. and internalize attitudes in ways indistinguishable from the general public. They come into public consciousness as Arabs during times of crisis, not by choice but because the media and the authorities so identify them. Hence the anguished cry by some: 'When if ever, do we become American?' " Religion is a factor in this, especially whether a religion or denomination is considered "American." Thus the Syrian Orthodox might hold different views from Maronites Catholics, or Christians from Muslims (personal communication, January 9, 2007).

18. Chapter 8 of this volume, on foreign policy, shows that for Arab Americans the concept of civil liberties needs to be expanded to include a wider range of issues than those in this chapter. Free expression and full participation are issues sometimes overlooked in legal-rights centered civil liberties research. To those whose roots and families are overseas, these rights are as important as the right to be free from legal harassment or an unfair security crackdown.

REFERENCES

Ajrouch, Kristine J. 2004. "Gender, Race and Symbolic Boundaries: Contested Spaces of Identity Among Arab-American Adolescents." *Sociological Perspectives* 47(4): 371–91.

Ashcroft, John. 2006. *Never Again: Securing America and Restoring Justice.* New York: Center Street Publishers.

Baker, Wayne, Sally Howell, Amaney Jamal, Ann Chih Lin, Andrew Shryock, Ronald Stockton, and Mark Tessler. 2004. "Preliminary Findings from The Detroit Arab American Study." Ann Arbor: University of Michigan Institute of Social Research and University of Michigan–Dearborn Center for Arab American Studies.

Bush, George W. 2003. *We Will Prevail: On War, Terrorism, and Freedom.* Forward by Peggy Noonan, introduction by Jay Nordlinger. New York: Continuum.

Council of American-Islamic Relations (CAIR). 2004. *Unpatriotic Acts: The Status of Muslim Civil Rights in the United States, 2004.* Washington, D.C.: CAIR.

Chong, Dennis. 1993. "How People Think, Feel, and Reason About Rights and Liberties." *American Journal of Political Science* 37(August): 867–99.

Davis, Darren W. 2006. *Negative Liberty. Public Opinion and the Terrorist Attacks on America.* New York: Russell Sage Foundation.

Davis, Darren W., and Brian D. Silver. 2004a. "Civil Liberties vs. Security in the Context of the Terrorist Attacks on America." *American Journal of Political Science* 48(1): 28–46.

———. 2004b. "One Nation Indivisible? Dimensions of Racial Reactions to the Terrorist Attacks on America." Presented to the Annual Meeting of the Midwest Political Science Association. Chicago (April 15–18).

Ellul, Jacques. 1969. *Propaganda: The Formation of Men's Attitudes,* introduction by Konrad Kellen. New York: Alfred A. Knopf.

Fischer, David Hackett. 1989. *Albion's Seed: Four British Folkways in America.* New York: Oxford University Press.

Fischman, Michael R. 1985. "Government Pressures Against Arabs in the United States." *Journal of Palestine Studies* 14(3): 87–100.

Hochschild, Jennifer L. 1986. "Dimensions of Liberal Self-Satisfaction: Civil Liberties, Liberal Theory, and Elite-Mass Differences." *Ethics* 96(January): 386–99.

Huddy, Leonie, Nadia Khatib, and Theresa Capelos. 2002. "Trends: Reaction to the Terrorist Attacks of September 11, 2001." *Public Opinion Quarterly* 66(3): 418–50.

Jamal, Amaney. 2007. "Mainstream America's Silence: The Racialization of Arab Americans." In *From Invisible Citizens to Visible Subjects,* edited by Amaney Jamal and Nadine Naber. Syracuse, N.Y.: Syracuse University Press.

Kettner, James H. 1978. *The Development of American Citizenship, 1680–1870.* Chapel Hill: University of North Carolina Press.

Kirk, Russell. 1953. *The Conservative Mind: From Burke to Eliot.* Chicago: Henry Regnery.

Lin, Ann Chih. 2004. "Civil Liberties and the Political Predisposition of Arab Americans." Presented to the Annual Meeting of the American Political Science Association. Chicago (September 2–5).

McCloskey, Herbert, and Alida Brill. 1983. *Dimensions of Tolerance: What Americans Believe About Civil Liberties.* New York: Russell Sage Foundation.

Mulligan, Kenneth. 2006. "Cognition, Affect, and the Dimensionality of Attitudes Toward Civil Liberties Issues Related to Terrorism." Department of Political Science Working Paper. Columbus: Ohio State University.

Nisbet, Eric C., and James Shanahan. 2006. "MSGR Special Report: Restrictions on Civil Liberties, Views of Islam & Muslim Americans." Media and Society Research Group. Ithaca, N.Y.: Cornell University.

O'Reilly, Kenneth. 1994. *Black Americans: The FBI Files,* edited by David Gallen. New York: Carroll and Gaff Publications.

Pew Research Center for the People & the Press (Pew). 2001. "Post-9/11 Attitudes: Religion More Prominent, Muslim-Americans More Accepted." Washington, D.C.: Pew Research Center. Available at: http://www.people-press.org/reports/pdf/144.pdf (accessed January 15, 2002).

———. 2003. "Religion and Politics: Contention and Consensus. Growing Numbers Say Islam Encourages Violence Among Followers." Washington, D.C.: Pew Research Center. Available at: http://www.people-press.org/reports/pdf/189.pdf (accessed September 6, 2003).

———. 2004. "Foreign Policy Attitudes Now Driven by 9/11 and Iraq." Washington, D.C.: Pew Research Center. Available at: http://www.people-press.org/reports/pdf/222.pdf (accessed October 30, 2004).

Rehnquist, William H. 1998. *All the Laws but One: Civil Liberties in Wartime.* New York: Vintage Books.

Rudolph, Lloyd, and Susanne Hoeber Rudolph. 1967. *The Modernity of Tradition. Political Development in India.* Chicago: University of Chicago Press.

Salaita, Steve. 2005. "Ethnic Identity and Imperative Patriotism: Arab Americans Before and After 9/11." *College Literature* 32(2): 146–68.

Shaheen, Jack G. 2001. *Reel Bad Arabs: How Hollywood Vilifies a People.* New York: Olive Branch Press.

Shryock, Andrew. 2007. "The Moral Analogies of Race: Arab American Identity, Color Politics, and the Limits of Racialized Politics." In *From Invisibility to Visibility: The Racialization of Arab Americans Before and After September 11,* edited by Nadine Naber and Amaney Jamal. Syracuse, N.Y.: Syracuse University Press.

Sniderman, Paul, Joseph F. Fletcher, Peter H. Russell, and Phillip E. Tetlock. 1996. *The Clash of Rights.* New Haven, Conn.: Yale University Press.

Stockton, Ronald R. 1994. "Ethnic Archetypes and the Arab Image," In *The Development of Arab American Identity,* edited by Ernest McCarus. Ann Arbor: University of Michigan Press.

Stouffer, Samuel A. 1966. *Communism, Conformity, and Civil Liberties.* Garden City, N.Y.: Doubleday.

Swiney, Chrystie Flournoy. 2006. "Racial Profiling of Arabs and Muslims in the US: Historical, Empirical, and Legal Analysis Applied to the War on Terrorism." *Muslim World Journal of Human Rights* 3(1): article 3. Available at: http://www. bepress.com/mwjhr/vol3/iss1/art3 (accessed January 11, 2007).

Tabrizi, Susan J. 2004. "At What Price? Security, Civil Liberties, and Public Opinion in the Age of Terrorism." In *American National Security and Civil Liberties in an Age of Terrorism,* edited by David B. Cohen and John W. Wells. New York: Palgrave Macmillan.

Traugott, Michael W., and David R. Weir. 2001. "Six Months Later: American Attitudes and Beliefs Changed by 9/11." *HAR (How America Responds).* Dearborn: University of Michigan, Institute of Social Research.

U.S. Immigration and Naturalization Service, Alien Border Control Committee (INS). 1986. "Alien Terrorists and Undesirables: A Contingency Plan." Mardigian Library Archives, University of Michigan–Dearborn.

Viscusi, W. Kip, and Richard Zeckhauser. 2003. "Sacrificing Civil Liberties to Reduce Terrorism Risks." Working Paper 03–1. Washington, D.C.: AEI–Brookings Joint Center on Regulatory Studies.

CHAPTER 8

Foreign Policy

Ronald R. Stockton

In 2003, as the U.S. army advanced into Iraq, protestors staged an antiwar rally in front of the Dearborn city hall. Hundreds of Arab American demonstrators held signs and cheered speakers. Just across the street was a second rally, also Arab American, where demonstrators announced with equal fervor their hatred of Saddam Hussein and their support for the invasion. Anyone who thinks there is a simple answer to how Arab Americans view world affairs should think about these contradictory demonstrations. They should also consider the words of a young Iraqi woman who was asked her opinion on the U.S. invasion of her homeland: "As an American I oppose the war, but as an Iraqi I support it."

Arab Americans often observe that "our experience exists on both sides of the hyphen. We are American but also Arab." Others state the case conversely: "We are not entirely American but neither are we entirely Arab." How these differences influence Arab American attitudes about foreign policy is the focus of this chapter. Scholars know a great deal about how the general public forms its opinions on foreign policy. What we do not know is whether Arab Americans arrive at their views in the same way. In this chapter we will see that Arab Americans cover the whole gamut of expression. Some support U.S. policies and some oppose; some are outspoken and some are reluctant to speak; some are confident and some think they are under siege for their views. We will also see that Arab American opinion formation is very similar to that of the general public in some respects, but quite different in others. Finally, we will see that, for Arab

Americans, the right to express foreign policy perspectives is in some ways a key aspect of citizenship, and not all Arab Americans feel they enjoy that right.

HOW AMERICANS VIEW FOREIGN POLICY

The foreign policy orientations of the American public are mostly cautious and supportive of international law and diplomacy, a tendency especially strong among informed leaders. Americans believe that they live in a threatening age and their country must play a major world role, but most "have a strong preference for multilateral policies" (Todorov and Mandisodza 2004, 343). Their internationalism has "a cooperative face and a militant face" (Wittkopf 1990, 25), and though militant internationalists emphasize "a conflictual world" of zero-sum violence and "the necessity of being prepared to use force," most Americans believe that "greater international cooperation rather than unilateral action will be necessary to deter and resist aggression" (Holsti 1996, 100, 142). Majorities of the public support the International Criminal Court, the Kyoto Treaty on global warming, the Ottawa (Land) Mine Treaty, the Nuclear Test Ban Treaty, antitorture policies, working through the UN to fight terrorism, and acceptance of unfavorable rulings by the World Trade Organization (Chicago Council 2004). All of these positions were inconsistent with those of the unilateralist administration of George W. Bush.

The Gulf War of 1990 to 1991 was a turning point in American foreign policy. John Mueller's study of public opinion during that war found that until combat began, large majorities of the public supported almost any alternative to war (1994). More than 70 percent favored sanctions and more than 65 percent preferred a long-term commitment of U.S. forces to Saudi Arabia rather than war (Mueller 1994, 225–26). Sixty-two percent said protecting oil supplies was not a reason to fight, and 91 percent said holding down oil prices was not (255, 250). Although there was exceptional hostility to Saddam Hussein, preventing him from getting nuclear weapons was the only issue that rallied a slim majority (54 percent) behind war (255). Regarding alternatives to war, "the public would have bought a reasonable, properly packaged settlement (including even the sort of negotiated compromise [George H. W.] Bush held to be totally unacceptable) as an alternative to the initiation of military action" (23).

As for the Israeli-Palestinian conflict, public support for Israel among Americans is overwhelming. The Anti-Defamation League found that when asked to choose between Israel and the Arabs, the percentages were 42 to 13, with 16 percent supporting both, 19 percent supporting neither (2005).

However, support is not unequivocal. On an evaluation thermometer (from 0 to 100, reflecting degrees of cool to warm feelings), Israel scored 53, similar to Mexico (54), the European Union (49), Korea (49), and France (47); but below the UK (70), Germany (58) and the UN (57); and above Muslim people (39) and Saudi Arabia (37). Moreover, 64 percent of the public and 89 percent of leaders want the United States to pursue even-handed policies regarding Israel and Palestine (Chicago Council 2004).

These attitudes follow religious and cultural lines. Regarding sympathy for Israel or Palestine, the Pew Research Center found that 55 percent of Evangelicals favored Israel, as did 39 percent of Catholics, 34 percent of Mainline Protestants, and 40 percent of African Americans and Hispanics (2002). A major factor shaping these positions is Christian Zionism, the belief that the creation of a Jewish state in 1948 was the fulfillment of biblical prophecy and is somehow linked to the return of Christ and the completion of God's plan for human history (Stockton 1987). When Americans are asked about this idea, 36 percent agree, 46 percent disagree, and 18 percent are unsure (Pew 2003). As with support for Israel, patterns follow religioethnic lines with 55 percent of Evangelicals agreeing, about 40 percent of blacks, Catholics, and Hispanics, and 34 percent of mainline Protestants. Not surprisingly, of those who see Israel as the fulfillment of prophecy, 57 percent favor the Israelis, 9 percent the Palestinians. Of those who do not believe Israel is the fulfillment of prophecy, 34 percent favor the Israelis, 18 percent the Palestinians. Because the vast majority of Americans have no familial or heritage link to the Middle East, these patterns clearly reflect cultural or ideological ways of thinking.

Moving from individual issues to integrated worldviews, decades of research have allowed scholars to identify three ways that the public structure their opinion: an elite-mass model, an ideological model, and an ethnic-nationalist community model. We will see that all three are operating within the Arab American community, but with variations.

The Elite-Mass Model

Early research on public opinion found little coherence in how people saw foreign policy issues. According to Gabriel Almond's classic study, views on domestic issues have a logical structure because they relate to the daily lives of citizens (1950; see also Converse 1964). Foreign policy matters are distant and confusing so that public opinion is incoherent, variable, or nonexistent. Although the educated elite have coherent views, the "orientation of most

Americans toward foreign policy is one of mood, and mood is essentially an unstable phenomenon" (Almond 1950, 54). Thus when a crisis occurs, attention comes without the benefit of an existing structure to integrate knowledge. Mass opinion swings wildly. Experiencing "the frustration of successive improvisations, none of which have been adapted to the complex character of the problem," the public can experience "withdrawal reactions" rooted in "hasty measures motivated by irritation and impatience" (58).

The Ideological Mode

Almond wrote in the cold war environment of the 1950s, when foreign policy bipartisanship "stopped at the water's edge." Party and ideology had little relationship to foreign policy issues. This tendency began to change during the Vietnam War. By the 1990s, researchers had identified two overarching foreign policy structures (Holsti 1996; Paige and Shapiro 1982). One was intervention versus isolation: should the United States be involved in the world? Most agreed that it should. The second issue was whether the United States should cooperate with other nation states or be unilateralist. Here, the public split. Most favored a cooperative approach but others were unilateral militarists. The patterns tended to follow partisan and ideological lines with Republicans and conservatives on the unilateralist side, Democrats and liberals on the cooperative side. Ole Holsti and James Rosenau labeled these dimensions militant internationalism and cooperative internationalism (1990).

The Ethnic Nationalist Community Model

Immigrants to the United States have had different experiences. One very common pattern was for individuals to leave their homelands to escape poverty or religious persecution. Such people looked to America as a land of freedom and opportunity. Examples would include the English Puritans and French Huguenots, who fled religious persecution; Swedes and Italians, whose lands were poor; the Scots-Irish of Northern Ireland, who left a place but not a nation; and the Dutch, who left a strong land for economic opportunity. Such experiences are associated with the powerful image of the Statue of Liberty, and the belief that immigrants willingly come to America to seek a new and better life. Groups who came to the United States on these terms absorbed a broad American identity and identified with their historic homeland primarily in terms of nostalgic ethnicity (Italians, Scots) or religious identity (Germans as Lutherans, English as Episcopalians). When many Americans think of early immigrants, it is these images and experiences that often come to mind.

There were, however, other experiences. Many people left against their will from places where oppression was heavy. As Matthew Jacobson showed in his study of Irish, Jewish, and Polish immigrants, "a lamentable absence from the Old World was," for Americans of these backgrounds, "among the most salient aspects of life in the New" (2002, 1). They continued to be gravely concerned about the welfare of those left behind, especially if their homeland was under occupation or their people in disarray or danger. Such immigrants functioned as overseas nationalist elements, raising money, mobilizing support, and trying to influence U.S. policy. Their American existence was charged with a sense of "pervasive nationalism" (Jacobson 2002, 3). Their novels, liturgies, newspapers, and holidays all reminded them of their obligation to a homeland and its liberation, or revival.[1] Such people saw their American identity as compatible with their nationalist identity. Being American served as a launching pad to argue as Americans for policies supportive of their homelands. American independence became a metaphor for supporting Polish independence, and American freedom segued into Jewish or Irish advocacy.[2] The American electoral system, which makes public officials responsive to local concerns, reinforced the pattern. In *The Last Hurrah,* a savvy, Boston-type mayoral candidate observed at the height of the cold war that, to him, the two most important foreign policy issues were "Trieste belongs to Italy" and "All Ireland must be Free" (O'Connor 1955, 255).

The importance of homeland nationalism among immigrants generates different hypotheses. If an ethnic group has a strong nationalist consciousness, such sentiments might permeate the group's political culture, and the group as a group would share common perspectives regardless of information available to individuals. Alternately, those most involved in ethnic community structures might be better informed, have more cohesive views, and constitute a core of community identity and leadership. This would be consistent with much existing research, which finds that those who are most involved in the life of the community are the best informed and the most adherent to group values (McCloskey 1964; McCloskey and Brill 1983).

HOW ARAB AMERICANS VIEW CONFLICT IN THE MIDDLE EAST

When we compare how Arab Americans and the general population view Middle East issues, there are striking similarities (table 8.1). Both were shaken by the events of September 11 and the war in Iraq. Both have doubts about the United Nations. Both are attentive to news about the war on terror and

Table 8.1 Attitudes on Middle East Related Issues

Scale/Item	General Public	Arab Americans
9/11 shook sense of safety		
Great deal	34%	33%
Not much	68	68
U.S.–Iraq War shook sense of safety		
Great deal	44	48
Not much	56	52
Confidence in UN		
Great deal or a lot	45	48
Not much	55	52
Support Palestinian state?		
Yes	33	70
Oppose	8	3
Don't know	59	27
U.S. involvement stabilizing Middle East		
Yes	51	33
No	45	58
No opinion	4	9
American media		
Very reliable	38	29
Somewhat reliable	56	47
Not reliable	6	19
Coverage of Israelis		
Biased in favor	26	72
Balanced	48	19
Biased against	25	3
Coverage of Palestinians		
Biased in favor	9	1
Balanced	46	27
Biased against	44	66
Coverage of Islam and Muslims		
Biased in favor	12	4
Balanced	47	46
Biased against	41	50

Table 8.1   (continued)

Scale/Item	General Public	Arab Americans
Follow war on terrorism		
Very closely or closely	77%	63%
Little or not much	23	37
Follow war in Iraq		
Very closely or closely	71	68
Little or not much	29	32

Source: Author's compilation.

the war in Iraq. The general public is more likely to see the U.S. media as balanced on Middle East issues than Arab Americans, who see it as biased in favor of Israel, but 44 percent feel that the media are anti-Palestinian—a noteworthy number.[3]

Two questions on the DAAS and DAS surveys addressed foreign policy issues. "In recent times, the United States has been deeply involved in the Middle East in various ways. On the whole, do you think that involvement is helping stabilize the region?" "Do you support or oppose the establishment of an independent Palestinian state on the West Bank and Gaza, or have you not thought much about it?" Even though in 2003 President Bush had just declared mission accomplished in Iraq, only 51 percent of the public and only 33 percent of Arab Americans believed the United States was a stabilizing force. Both groups favored the creation of a Palestinian state, the general public at a 4:1 ratio, Arab Americans at 23:1. However, a high percentage had no opinion—59 percent among the general public, 27 percent among Arab Americans.

Is America Stabilizing the Region?

At the time of the study, two places in the Arab world were in great distress, and the United States was intimately involved in both. The Palestinian territories were in the throes of the al-Aqsa Intifada (uprising) of 2000 to 2004 and the Israeli reaction to it. More than 4,000 people died in that violent confrontation, mostly civilians, 75 percent of them Palestinian. President Bush had offered vague endorsement for a Palestinian state, as did right-wing Israeli Prime Minister Ariel Sharon, but his reluctance to deal with the Palestinian Authority, his support for Israel, and his description of Sharon—then conducting a violent assault on the Palestinian Authority—as a "man of peace" generated skepticism.

The second place in distress was Iraq. Many Iraqis had suffered under Saddam Hussein and were happy to see him gone. In the run-up to the war, two local imams from the Detroit area, Iraqi by birth, met with President Bush and Deputy Secretary of Defense Wolfowitz, to offer their blessing. But most Arab Americans had doubts (for one perspective on these events, see Qazwini 2007, chapter 10). They feared that the war would destabilize the region or leave Israel free to crush the Palestinians. Some saw the invasion as an attack on Iraqi sovereignty. At the time of the interviews, the Iraqi resistance had not yet started and the domestic and sectarian violence had not become extreme. Hence, there was a broader range of opinion on this issue than on the Palestinian issue.

Looking at the data in light of our three models, we see a mixed result (table 8.2). In total, these patterns are interesting test cases for some of the major hypotheses in the public opinion literature. Almond's elite model, for one, does not work. Levels of education and information explain little, except whether individuals have an opinion, a matter we address separately. The partisan-ideological model works for those who are conservatives and Republicans but there is no meaningful distinction between moderates and liberals or Democrats and independents along these lines. In other words, the dominant position tended toward skepticism of American policy in the Middle East except among those who were conservative and Republican. It is no surprise that those who identified with the Bush administration believed it was pursuing correct policies. John Mueller has shown that partisan identity drives perceptions (1994). That finding holds true here as well.[4]

What of the nationalist community model? We found not a shared position but a mix of patterns based on the fact that Arab Americans are not a single community but a mosaic of communities. Three significant patterns emerged around ancestry, religion, and identity. Regarding ancestry, Iraqis were more likely to think that the U.S. role was stabilizing than non-Iraqis (47 percent to 30 percent). Many Iraqis in greater Detroit had fled Iraq and had chilling stories to tell. If the U.S. army could remove Saddam's regime, perhaps that was viewed as stabilizing in their eyes.[5] At 30 percent, Lebanese and Syrian support was lower and Palestinian and Jordanian the lowest at 22 percent. Yemenis were in the middle at 43 percent. Put differently, majorities in all groups had doubts about American policy, but some had more doubts than others.

Table 8.2   Source of Foreign Policy Attitudes

Scale/Item Independent Variables	U.S. Stabilizing p-est.	Policy Index p-est	Palestinian State p-est.	Clash of Civilizations p-est.	Conflict of Values p-est.
Education					
(1 < HS; 2 = HS; 3 = HS+; 4 = BA+)					
2 versus 1	0.739	0.611*	0.739	0.929	1.183
3 versus 1	0.854	0.513**	0.797	1.211	0.817
4 versus 1	0.717	0.628*	1.241	1.260	0.724
Political information					
(C37 + C38, 0 = none; 1 = one; 2 = two)					
1 versus 0	0.878	0.863	1.404	1.494	3.024****
2 versus 0	0.701	0.789	2.433***	1.172	2.800***
Conservative	1.140	1.221	1.303	0.751	0.921*
Republican	1.662	0.796	1.417*	1.156	2.076*
Christian Zionism	1.068	0.902	0.583	2.606***	1.662*
Community engagement					
(0 = none; 1 = medium; 2 = high)					
1 versus 0	0.895	0.729	0.933	0.781	1.019
2 versus 0	1.135	0.628	1.010	0.780	1.021
Identify as Arab American	1.328*	1.501**	1.197	1.356	1.189
Supporting Palestine Central	0.418*	0.481****	9.617****	1.118	0.993
Proud to be American					
(0 = not; 1 = proud; 2 = very proud)					
0 versus 1	2.876	1.224	1.136	0.840	2.015
0 versus 2	5.939***	1.985*	0.911	0.893	4.101*

(*Table continues on p. 236*).

Table 8.2 (continued)

Scale/Item Independent Variables	U.S. Stabilizing p-est.	Policy Index p-est	Palestinian State p-est.	Clash of Civilizations p-est.	Conflict of Values p-est.
Citizen	1.108	0.517*	0.947	1.782*	0.501*
Media hostile index (0 = low; 1 = medium; 2 = high)					
1 versus 0	0.492**	0.581*	1.049*	2.369**	1.132
2 versus 0	0.274****	0.570*	1.897***	1.984**	0.395**
Worry about future	0.660*	0.605*	1.292	1.613*	0.989
Male	0.950	1.190	0.815	0.945	0.993
Iraqi	1.500	0.768	0.591	0.657	2.139**
Palestinian-Jordanian	0.820	1.313	1.146	0.708	1.646
Enclave	0.561	0.884	0.374***	0.629	0.742
Muslim	0.813	2.085*	1.159	0.311***	0.458*

Source: Author's compilation.

Notes: Reporting logistic coefficients from regression of foreign policy issues on Education, Political information, Community engagement, Identity as an Arab American, Supporting Palestine central value, Proud to be American, Media hostile index, Worry about the future, and dummy variables (1 = yes, 0 = no) on conservative, Republican, Christian Zionist, Identify as Arab American, Palestine central to identity, Citizen, Male, Iraqi, Palestinian-Jordanian, Live in enclave, Muslim, Worry about the future (1 = yes on H8, responses 1 or 2). n = 788.

The Media hostility index contains two items (C36b and C36c) on whether the media are friendly, balanced, or hostile to Muslims and Islam and Arab Americans and Chaldeans. Respondents got one point for each perception of hostility.

Community engagement: total memberships on C16, 17, 18, 19, 20, 23. 0 = none; 1 = 1 or 2; 2 = 3 or more.

The Policy index gives one point each for thinking U.S. policy toward Israel or U.S. policy toward the Gulf might have been a cause of the September 11 attacks.

**** p < .0001, *** p < .001, ** p < .01, * p < .05.

The second pattern involved religious identity. Overall, Christians were more likely than Muslims to support the American role (42 percent to 29 percent). But this is not as simple as it seems. Religious groups are communities into which one is born, and communities share identities and interests. Consider the Iraqis: 50 percent of Christians supported the American role, as did 32 percent of Muslims. The Sunni and Shi'a tensions found elsewhere were not found here, the two groups being statistically identical in their assessment of the American role.[6] The Lebanese and Syrians showed 30 percent support overall, again divided by religion. Among Christians, 39 percent supported the American role, perhaps because the Bush administration was pressing Syria to withdraw its army from Lebanon (which it did in 2005). But the Shi'a saw Syria as a check on Israeli influence, and support fell to 26 percent.[7] Palestinian and Jordanians exhibited no religious differences, illustrating that certain aspects of their experience transcend religious identity.

The third factor involves national identification and what it means. Respondents who say they are proud to be American are significantly more confident in the American role than those who say they are not (39 percent to 8 percent), as are those who feel at home in America (41 percent to 11 percent). The question of the U.S. role in the Middle East measures not just an objective assessment of U.S. policy but a broader assessment of the U.S. role in world affairs and a sense of comfort with that role. Remember that 51 percent of the general population felt that the United States was stabilizing the region. Pride in being American and comfort in one's American life clearly increase evaluation of performance.

In the opposite direction, those who identified as Arab Americans were less supportive of the American role than those who chose a different identity label (32 percent to 48 percent). This difference may hinge on what it means to identify as Arab American. At one level, Arab is a bland descriptor of those who speak Arabic, come from the Arab world, or have ancestors from the region. Such definitions cover everyone in our study, and yet 30 percent did not identify as Arab American. Identity labels bear meaning and memory and are imbedded in history. As a means of self-identification, the word Arab is filled with political significance. As a pan-regional identity movement, Arabism was popularized by Gamal Abdel Nasser of Egypt in the 1950s and implied a challenge to Western power and outside control. Although not everyone today would have such a charged political identity, that individuals are choosing labels is significant, and these choices are reflected in how people evaluate American policy.

Interestingly, in spite of the fact that identifying with the term Arab and being proud to be an American pushed opinions in opposite directions, the terms were not incompatible. Those who identified as Arab American and those who did not were both more than 60 percent likely to be very proud of their American identity. Muslims were more likely to consider themselves Arab Americans, but many Christians insisted they were Arabs as emphatically as others insisted they were not. Putting these two items together into a matrix produces a double pattern. Among those who considered themselves Arab Americans, Christians and Muslims are not statistically different on whether the United States was stabilizing the region: both were close to the 32 percent average. Among those who said they were not Arab Americans, however, Christians were 56 percent confident in the American role, and Muslims 34 percent—a 22 point gap.

Palestine As an Issue

Two questions deal with the Palestinian situation, whether one supports a Palestinian state, and, in terms of "being an Arab or Chaldean . . . how much if at all, does [supporting Palestine] mean to you?" The results show across the board support for the Palestinians. Seventy percent support a Palestinian state with 3 percent opposed and 28 percent undecided. There is no identifiable group—religious, demographic, national, or ideological—that does not exhibit overwhelming support for a Palestinian state. The patterns are more mixed on the question of how important supporting Palestine is to one's identity, but even then there is a strong sense that this issue is central: 40 percent said a lot, 20 percent somewhat, 9 percent only a little, and 14 percent not at all. Seventeen percent did not answer. To the extent that there is an Arab American consensus on any political issue, Palestine is it. The Palestinian issue is a symbol of Arab identity that touches every individual in a personal and intimate way. When, in 1944, the Alexandria Protocol created the Arab League and declared that Palestine was an issue for the entire Arab world, it captured the way most Arabs feel (Alexandria Protocol 1944). Even those who do not like the Palestinian leadership believe that the fate of the Palestinians is linked to the dignity of all Arabs.

Given this high level of agreement, how does support for a Palestinian state vary within the Arab American population? Age and education matter. For those younger than twenty-five, 56 percent support a state, for those older than fifty-five, the level is 80 percent. By education, the least educated are 58 percent supportive, the most educated 80 percent. Yet in all age and education categories the number opposed is exceptionally low, ranging from 1 to 4 percent. But if 56 percent of the youngest category support a Palestinian state and 2 percent oppose, where are the others? They do not express an opinion. For the most educated, 18 percent have no opinion; for the least educated, 38 percent. For those older than fifty-five, 18 percent have no opinion; for those younger than twenty-five, 43 percent. In other words, deviations from the Arab American consensus are not in opposition but in lack of an expressed opinion. We explore this matter more fully later in the chapter but note here that this pattern is common in public opinion studies and is predicted by the Almond model. The young and the less educated are far less attentive to political issues than older and more educated respondents. Arabs fit the norm on this point.[8]

There was also a pattern determined by ancestry. Among 125 Palestinians and Jordanians, only one opposed Palestinian statehood. This group, at 11 percent, also had the lowest rate of nonresponses. The Lebanese and Syrians, whose history is intimately intertwined with that of the Palestinians, were close behind (75 percent support, 4 percent dissent, 21 percent no response), followed by Yemenis (66 percent support, 2 percent dissent, 32 percent no response). On the other end of the scale were Iraqis (60 percent support, 3 percent dissent, 38 percent no response). Iraqis have a long history of engagement with Palestinian issues and even as the least supportive group show overwhelming support versus dissent.

On the parallel issue of whether supporting Palestine is important to one's identity, there is no pattern by age, citizenship, gender, or whether one was born in the United States. Religion and ancestry are the only patterns. Muslims are more likely than Christians to consider Palestine important (64 percent to 57 percent). By ancestry, Palestinians-Jordanians are predictably the most likely to consider the issue central to their identity (87 percent), followed by Lebanese-Syrians (64 percent), Yemenis (51 percent), and Iraqis (45 percent).

To pull these different patterns together, we conducted a factor analysis of eight items.[9] We have seen three of the items already: support a Palestinian state, supporting Palestine is important, and believe the United States is stabilizing the region. Four additional items asked what might have caused the attacks of September 11. These items are discussed in the next section, but

Table 8.3   Factor Analysis of Eight Middle East Items

Item	Factor 1 Palestine Central	Factor 2 Culture Clash
U.S. Israeli policy cause of 9/11	0.723	0.328
U.S. Gulf policy cause of 9/11	0.701	0.348
Supporting Palestine important	0.649	−0.269
Supports Palestine state	0.640	0.271
U.S. stabilizing the region	−0.597	−0.161
Conflict of values cause of 9/11	−0.157	0.669
Clash of civilizations cause of 9/11	0.245	0.657
Christian Zionism	−0.150	0.535

Source: Author's compilation.
Notes: 48.46 percent of all variance is explained by these two factors.
Factor 1 explains 28.87 percent.
Factor 2 explains 19.59 percent.
This is a varimax rotation.

note that respondents were offered five explanations, of which they could choose any number, or even none. Four are included in this analysis. Two focus on U.S. policy in the Gulf and toward Israel. Two focus on ideology: a clash of civilizations (between Christianity and Judaism on one side and Islam on the other) and a conflict of values (that is, an attack on American values). The eighth item is Christian Zionism. Although the belief predisposes some Christians to be supportive of Israel and Jews, a politicized movement based on the teaching supports the right wing of the Israeli political system.[10] The question is as follows: "In 1948 Israel became an independent state. Some people believe that this event was the fulfillment of prophecy. Other people say that its existence has nothing to do with prophecy. In your opinion is Israel the fulfillment of prophecy?" Twelve percent of Arab Americans and 27 percent of the general public agreed.

Our analysis of these questions uncovered two distinctive ways of thinking (table 8.3). The first we call Palestine Central because supporting Palestine is a core element. It could, however, just as easily have been called American Policy Malfunction because of the prominence of American policy toward Israel and the Gulf as possible causes of the attacks of September 11. People who fall under these rubrics believe that there should be a Palestinian state and believe that supporting it is important. They resist the argument that conflict over values caused the September 11 attacks and do not believe the United States is stabilizing the region.

We call the second pattern Culture Conflict. Its key feature is the belief that the attacks of September 11 were provoked by a clash of civilization or a conflict of values. Christian Zionism is also present. Those who endorse this ideology do not reject the idea that U.S. policy played a role in the events of September 11, but controversial policies are not central to their understanding of the problem. Fundamental differences in cultural values and religious beliefs are.

The two most revealing orientations are Palestine as a central issue and the conflict of values. These two items appear on opposite sides and their signs reverse, meaning that people who embrace these orientations see things very differently. By contrast, four items—support a Palestinian state, U.S. policy toward Israel, and U.S. policy in the Gulf as possible causes of September 11, and the clash of civilizations—have different effects on how people think, but are not polarizing issues that drive opinion in opposite directions.

September 11 and the Clash of Civilizations

In 1990, Bernard Lewis wrote of a coming "clash of civilizations—the perhaps irrational but surely historic reaction of an ancient rival against our Judeo-Christian heritage, our secular present, and the world-wide expansion of both" (32). In 1993, Samuel Huntington wrote a controversial article that popularized the term. His thesis was that after the cold war "the fundamental source of conflict in this new world will not be primarily ideological or primarily economic. The great divisions among humankind and the dominating source of conflict will be cultural. Nation states will remain the most powerful actors in world affairs, but the principal conflicts of global politics will occur between nations and groups of different civilizations. The clash of civilizations will dominate global politics. The fault lines between civilizations will be the battle lines of the future" (Huntington 1993, 22).

Huntington emphasized two key civilizations, Western and Islamic. As he saw it, there was a political dimension to the struggle because the "West in effect is using international institutions, military power and economic resources to run the world in ways that will maintain Western predominance, protect Western interests and promote Western political and economic values" (1993, 40). Conflict occurs on two levels, between states and on the faultlines where civilizations meet and "struggle, often violently, over the control of territory and each other" (1993, 28). Clashes also occur when individuals from one civilization zone move to another. This would apply to Arab Americans. Any clash of civilizations would leave them on the horns of a dilemma. If they are patriotic Americans, they would feel strong pressure to support a confrontation with their ancestral homelands. If they align with their homelands, they would be seen by many as alien elements in a hostile country. Few would want to face this choice.

President Bush addressed these issues in his speech to Congress on September 23, 2001 (Bush 2003, 11–18). He portrayed Islam not as a civilization but as a system of religious beliefs. Those who attacked the United States practice "a fringe form of Islamic extremism . . . that perverts the peaceful teachings of Islam." Bush said the enemy was not Islam but "a radical network of terrorists" that he described as "evil." The president spoke of a struggle between those who were "civilized" and those who opposed civilization. As such, this is "civilization's fight. This is the fight of all who believe in progress and pluralism, tolerance and freedom." Responding to his own question, "Why do they hate us?" Bush said that we were attacked because of those things that make us good. "They hate what we see right here in this chamber—a democratically elected government. . . . They hate our freedoms—our freedom of religion, our freedom of speech, our freedom to vote and assembly and disagree with each other." In subsequent speeches he emphasized women's rights as a key point of conflict.

Bush warned of an ongoing threat. Al-Qaida had in place "thousands of these terrorists in more than 60 countries. . . . [They] hide in countries around the world to plot evil and destruction." But in addition to the domestic threat, the president was concerned about vigilante actions: "I ask you to uphold the values of America, and remember why so many have come here. We are in a fight for our principles, and our first responsibility is to live by them. No one should be singled out for unfair treatment or unkind words because of their ethnic background or religious faith."

On the other side, Osama bin Laden argued that there was a Jewish-Christian war against Islam, that Muslims in different places were being massacred with impunity, that the resources of the Islamic world were being pillaged by foreigners, and that corrupt Muslim regimes act against their own people. The attacks of September 11, "divided the whole world into two camps, the camp of the faithful and the camp of the infidels" (Lawrence 2005,

102). Bin Laden singled out two regions where the battle was fierce, Iraq and Palestine. He also noted the presence of American forces in Saudi Arabia: "To America, I say only a few words to it and its people. I swear by God, who has elevated the skies without pillars, neither America nor the people who live in it will dream of security before we live it in Palestine, and not before all the infidel armies leave the land of Muhammad, peace be upon him" (Lawrence 2005, 102).

Cultural and Political Lenses

We presented respondents with five possible explanations for the attacks of September 11. One emphasized the nature of the attackers, attributing the cause of the attacks to "the extremist beliefs of a few terrorists." Two explanations focused on American policies—"because the United States supports Israel" and "because of the U.S. intervention in the Persian Gulf." Two explanations were ideological. The clash of civilizations question said, "it's because of the conflict between Christianity and Judaism on one side and Islam on the other," whereas the conflict of values argument asserted that "it's because the United States believes in democracy, freedom, and equal rights for women." On the first three items, there was remarkable similarity between Arab Americans and the general public. Both populations agree that the attack was perpetrated by extremists (the general population at 77 percent, Arab Americans at 69 percent), that U.S. support for Israel was a factor (56 percent and 55 percent), and that U.S. policies in the Gulf were a factor (45 percent for both populations). Beyond these points, however, there is considerable divergence, with the general public far more likely to accept ideological explanations. Forty-five percent of the general population is drawn to a clash of civilizations explanation, 37 percent to a conflict of values. For Arab Americans, the figure is 22 percent in each case. A factor analysis of Arab American responses to these items (table not included) produced a three-factor solution, each representing a very different way of interpreting the 9/11 attacks. Factor I contained the two policy issues. Factor II included the two ideological questions. Factor III had only one item: that those who attacked on September 11 were extremists and terrorists.

Table 8.4 shows how specific items correlate. For both Arab Americans and the general population, the single highest correlation is between Gulf policy and Israel policy. Put simply, large numbers in both populations think Middle East policy is the best explanation for those attacks. This perspective runs contrary to Bush administration claims that U.S. policy had nothing to do with

Table 8.4   Possible Causes of 9/11 Attacks

Scale/Item	Gulf Policy	Clash of Civilizations	Conflict of Values	Extremists
Israel policy				
General population	.432	.391	.122	.199
Arab Americans	.622	.243	.032	.032
Gulf policy				
General population	—	.267	.100	.124
Arab Americans	—	.253	.029	.169
Clash of civilizations				
General population	—	—	.166	.233
Arab Americans	—	—	.264	.165
Conflict of values				
General population	—	—	—	.224
Arab Americans	—	—	—	.170

Source: Author's compilation.
Note: All correlations are significant at the .05 level except for the three that fall below .100.

the attacks. For the general population, a second high correlation involves the link between Israel policy and the clash of civilizations. This relationship is much stronger than among Arab Americans. One point on which Arab Americans stand out is the strong positive relationship between clash of civilizations and conflict of values—a way of thinking more consistent with administration statements. It reflects an important minority perspective within the Arab American community.

Earlier, we hypothesized that Arab Americans might have a community dynamic that would create more integrated views about foreign policy issues than would be found in the general public. This pattern does not appear to be the case if we assume that higher correlations reflect more integrated views. What we find instead is a double pattern: Arab Americans have more integrated views in terms of policy conflict, the general public more integrated views in terms of cultural conflict. A visual scan of the table shows six variable pairs on which the general public has higher correlations, three on which Arab Americans do. For the general public, all involve cultural explanations: conflict of values, clash of civilization, or extremist beliefs of terrorists. The two highest correlations for the general public involve Israel, one linking it to Gulf policy, one to the clash of civilizations. Because Israel is commonly portrayed in America media as a close ally that shares America's core democratic values, its place in popular American thought belongs as much to the cultural as to the policy realm. If this blurring is the case here, the evidence suggests that the general public tends to see Middle East conflict through a cultural lens, Arab Americans through a policy lens, with subgroups in each population that resemble the alternate pattern.

Ideological and Political Explanations of September 11

Given that the discourse around the clash of civilizations theory was muddled with inflammatory rhetoric, it is as important to show that something did not occur as it is to confirm that something did. As the data indicate (table 8.2), support among Arab Americans for the idea of a clash is not related to level of education or political information. Nor is it related to identity as an Arab American, pride in being an American, or being Iraqi or Palestinian-Jordanian. Likewise, it is not related to the complex of traditional values explored in chapters 5 and 6. A person's level of community engagement as measured by the number of group associations they belonged to also had no impact. Ordinarily institutional involvement would shape opinion but there are so many institutional groupings Arab Americans can join (religious, ancestry, business, advocacy) that the impact was not in a single direction.

Belief in a clash of civilization, instead, is driven mostly by a belief in Christian Zionism, being a citizen or a Christian, worry about the future, and a belief that the media are hostile. Belief in a conflict of values shares an association with being a Christian and believing in Christian Zionism but otherwise has a broader base. It is found among those Arab Americans who are more politically knowledgeable, Republican, Iraqi, and strongly proud of being American. The conflict of values is far more politically significant than the rather marginalized idea of a clash of civilizations. If there is a more mainstream American profile (see chapter 2, this volume) then the support base of a conflict of values approximates it.[11]

If we look closely at the two polar ways of thinking—cultural and political—and compare those Arab Americans who think in terms of a clash of civilizations with those who think in terms of policy conflict, there are dramatic differences. Those who saw the attacks as a reaction to American policy are more educated, more likely to identify as Arab American, more likely to support Palestine, and have greater pride in being American. Moreover, in those areas where the two orientations share characteristics, they move in opposite directions. Policy orientation is more associated with noncitizens and less associated with a perception of media hostility. Party identification is not significant, except for the belief that the attacks were on American values. Here, Arab American Republicans followed their leader. We will return to the cultural-political dichotomy in the concluding section.

Concealed Opinions?

When the research team presented its findings to a forum of community leaders, one of the first questions was whether there were views they had not tapped. It was a polite question that went to a core point. Many of the issues in this study are sensitive and complex, so it would not be surprising if some people were hesitant to offer an opinion. One thoughtful person put his fist on his stomach and said, "We have a saying: keep it in your gut. They will tell you what they think you want to hear."

Fortunately, there is research on patterns of nonresponse and concealed opinion. Adam Berinsky noted that answering questions has two kinds of costs (2001). Cognitive costs involve gathering enough information to form an opinion. Social costs involve the social interaction between the interviewer and the respondent. It is common to find that less-educated respondents feel insecure. Certain views may also be enough out of the mainstream that individuals hesitate to express them. In such a case, the dynamic of nonresponse is quite different. Such people would not only have opinions but would know what is acceptable—a sensibility that would produce a very different type of nonresponse.

What kind of issues produce nonresponses? Foreign policy issues are one. Studies of attitudes about the Korean and Vietnam wars showed that in the early months, when there was little public dissent, those who opposed the war tended to offer "don't know" responses. Later, when elite dissent emerged, citizens felt freer to express concerns. This was particularly true of black respondents, who had more doubts than whites but tended in the early stages of the wars to conceal their views (Berinsky 2001, 27).

How do these issues apply to Arab Americans, and what do they say about their role in American society? On three key topics (Iraq, Israel-Palestine, and September 11), patterns of elite discourse differ. On Iraq, there was exceptional dissent, including 230 members of Congress who voted against the war. Both

Michigan senators and seven Michigan representatives were in that group.[12] All were Democrats. In contrast, both parties and almost all national leaders were pro-Israeli, although most Arab community leaders openly disagreed. Regarding the attacks of September 11, the president insisted that U.S. policy was not the cause, and individuals were attacked for dissenting from that view.[13] It was safe to say bin Laden was a terrorist, but it was harder to say whether U.S. policy might have provoked the attacks. For Arab Americans, expressing dissent from a sensitive foreign policy position might be less a socially difficult response than a security difficult response. Having the interviewer think that you might not have an opinion could be less important than the possibility that a response might create a difficult situation for yourself or for your community. With a 73 percent interview success rate, this was not a population reluctant to express opinions, but with the FBI interviewing neighbors to ferret out sleeper cells, there were realistic concerns.

Berinsky found that the easiest questions involved "symbolic concerns relating to the ends of public policies long in the public's eye," and that issues of complexity produced more "don't know" responses (2001, 37, 85). For Arab Americans, a Palestinian state would be a long-desired goal symbolic of a shared identity. The role of the United States in the Gulf would be more complex, and the causes of the September 11 attacks would be the most difficult of all. We examined nonresponses to questions on whether the United States was stabilizing the region (9 percent nonresponse), support for a Palestinian state (27 percent nonresponse), and possible causes of the September 11 attacks (31 percent nonresponse). If nonresponses reflected lack of opinion, this should correlate with education, age, and attentiveness to the news. But if respondents had views they did not want to reveal, nonresponses might correlate with high information. If respondents were insecure, suspicious, or afraid, nonresponses should correlate with low levels of trust. The results of our analysis are presented in table 8.5.

The issue of a two-state solution to the Israeli-Palestinian conflict is complex, given the ambiguity of that term, yet several predictable patterns emerge. Younger people and women are less likely to have an opinion. The appearance of gender confirms a well-known pattern, that women have less political information than men (Burns, Schlozman, and Verba 2001; Stockton 2006). Interestingly, gender is not important in the general population.[14] Following this same logic, those who are less informed or less educated are also less likely to have opinions.

Table 8.5   Source of Concealed Opinions

Scale/Item Independent Variables	Support Palestine State p-est.	U.S. Stabilizing Middle East? p-est.	Causes of 9/11 p-est.
Age (1 = 18 to 25; 2 = 26 to 54; 3 = 55+)			
2 versus 1	0.291****	1.178	0.618
3 versus 1	0.129****	2.608	0.459*
Education (1 < HS; 2 = HS; 3 = HS+; 4 = BA+)			
1 versus 0	0.433*	0.719	0.494*
2 versus 0	0.697	0.942	0.411**
3 versus 0	0.489*	0.870	0.469*
4 versus 0	0.589	2.203	0.492
Male	0.686*	0.718	1.025
Information index (low, medium, high, see table 8.2)			
1 versus 0	0.539**	0.631	0.614*
2 versus 0	0.687	0.760	0.610
War news attentive index (0 = low; 1 = medium; 2 = high)			
1 versus 0	1.257	0.630	0.937
2 versus 0	0.825	0.424*	0.500*
Trust D.C. government	2.618***	1.771	1.449
Fair trial possible	1.579	0.795	1.688*
Trust legal system (C27, 1 = low; 2 = medium; 3 = high)	1.559	1.587	1.575
Group memberships			
1 versus 0	1.029	1.237	0.732
2 versus 0	0.674	1.733	0.489*
Muslim	0.630*	2.291*	2.177**
Proud to be American (2 = very; 1 = proud; 0 = not proud)	1.818	2.055	0.881
Nervous during interview? (4 = not; 3 = little; 2 = some; 1 = lot)			
2 versus 1	0.478	0.372*	0.349
3 versus 1	0.536	0.378*	0.217**
4 versus 1	0.511	0.266**	0.268*

Table 8.5   (continued)

Scale/Item Independent Variables	Support Palestine State p-est.	U.S. Stabilizing Middle East? p-est.	Causes of 9/11 p-est.
Worry about future (1 = low; 5 = high)			
2 versus 1	1.465	0.657	1.450
3 versus 1	1.798	1.788	2.601**
4 versus 1	2.671**	1.837	2.057*
5 versus 1	1.303	1.251	2.717*

Source: Author's compilation.

Notes: Reporting logistic coefficients from regression of absent opinion on Age, Education, Political information, Trust, Group memberships, Nervous, Worry about the future, Proud to be American. Dummy variables (1 = yes, 0 = no) are Male, Trust government in Washington, Fair trial is possible, Muslim.

War news index includes one point for each positive answer on H5 and H19.

Group memberships: includes activity on C16, 17, 18, 19, 20, 23. 0 = none; 1 = 1 or 2; 2 = 3 or more.

**** $p < .0001$, *** $p < .001$, ** $p < .01$, * $p < .05$.

Three issues of ill ease inhibit response: lacking trust in the government in Washington and worrying about the future are two. On the question of whether the United States was stabilizing the region, those described by the interviewers as being nervous were also less likely to respond. Trust reflects identification with the political system but can also mean "trust officials to pursue wise policies." In 2003, there was good reason why those who wished Palestinians well would doubt the Bush administration. Doubting government policy, or good will, requires a judgment, perhaps even a challenge. These are issues of political legitimacy, not issues related to level of information.

The final question involves possible reasons for the attacks of September 11. When we counted how many of the five options each respondent selected, we found that 31 percent did not select any. Given that those options cover the full range of explanations offered by commentators or officials, one wonders why, in the face of the most extensive and protracted media coverage of any event in American history, 31 percent of respondents could not offer a possible explanation. Another 19 percent accepted only one explanation of five, and of those, 69 percent said the attacks were by extremists. This is the easiest option in that the president and most major leaders endorsed it. Even those who felt that U.S. policy had contributed to the problem could agree that bin Laden was an extremist.

One possibility, presented here as a hypotheses because it cannot be proven with our existing data, is that some respondents believed in explanations not included in our list. A rich variety of theories circulated in Arab Detroit after the attacks, as they did elsewhere. Most of these fixated on the presumed involvement of the Israelis, the U.S. government, and other actors who were perceived to benefit from the 9/11 attacks. That these were widely dismissed as conspiracy theories stigmatized those who embraced them publicly. This effect was enhanced when the person endorsing such theories was Arab or Muslim. In such a case, a blank look may have been the most cautious answer.[15]

Whatever the explanation, the data converge with Berinsky's point that those who feel weak or exposed, especially minorities, may withhold dissent until powerful persons first express their thoughts. On the question of a Palestinian state or whether U.S. involvement was stabilizing the Middle East, there had been enough discussion that even an insignificant person could feel free to express an opinion. But there had been little debate over the events of September 11. Shock, fear, moral outrage, and affirmations of loyalty dominated public discourse. In several cases, individuals who questioned presidential explanations were publicly attacked. All this suggests that, for many Arab Americans, the conditions Berinsky outlined for free expression of dissent were absent. That the perpetrators of the attacks were not only Arabs but also Muslims, acting on what they proclaimed to be religious beliefs, created a very different dynamic among Muslim respondents. Age and gender are out of the picture but new elements emerge. Muslims knew they were at risk and were more than two times more likely to withhold opinions. Not surprisingly, being nervous during the interview persists as a factor. Three items appear for the first time. Those who believe that a person accused of terrorism could get a fair trial are more likely to express an opinion, as are those who are organizationally involved. Group involvement immerses individuals in discussion and enhances confidence (Stockton 2006). Those not involved should feel more isolated and worried about expressing controversial views. Here the level of institutional engagement works where it is most expected, on the questions about September 11. Education and political information are also important, with the less educated and less informed less likely to have an opinion. Being a Muslim is interesting because of the different patterns of response it yields.

Those who are Muslim are less likely to express an opinion on September 11 or the impact of the U.S. role in the region but are more likely to express an opinion on a Palestinian state.

Was our observer correct? Do Arabs keep it in their gut and tell you what you want to know? We would have to say yes and no. In fact, most people were quite open about their views and confident in expressing views that others would not accept. In most cases, the absence of an opinion is a product of poor information. However, although Arab Americans are in many ways confident, they are also vulnerable and exposed. Especially regarding September 11, community vulnerability deterred some individuals, especially Muslims, from uninhibited openness. It might also be that the person who expresses no opinion holds a view not included in the spectrum of possible responses. Given these things, we probably need to refine Berinsky's theories, which mostly grew out of nonresponse among African Americans. The data show that there are withheld opinions, but there are also absent opinions. Sometimes a person who says that they haven't thought about it is being cautious. Other times, they quite simply have not thought about it.

CONCLUSION

Not surprisingly, Arab Americans do not form their opinions in line with general patterns, but neither are they entirely different. To emphasize the similarities would deny the uniqueness of the group, just as emphasizing the differences would take the group out of history and out of the country, as if nothing in the American experience had an impact. As noted earlier, the Arab-American experience exists on both sides of the hyphen.

Arab Americans have two qualities that make them distinct. One is that they are an ethnic nationalist population charged with concern for their homelands. This quality is not rare in itself but their arrival in the United States is different from the experience of many other ethnic nationalist groups. Andrew Shryock and Ann Chih Lin note in chapter 2 how the influx of Arab immigrants has been "triggered, and has been periodically sustained, by complicated, often horrible, geopolitical events" in which U.S. policy played a disturbingly important role. The litany of details they provide is stunning. Other groups—Cubans, Jews, Lithuanians, Armenians, Irish—all found sympathy in the United States for their national causes. The same is not true with today's Arab Americans. If there is anger or passionate distress in this community, as individuals look back to their homelands and what has happened to them, it should not come as a surprise.

They are also unique in a second way. Arabs and Muslims are the only group in the country singled out today for systematic monitoring and even harassment. Not only do security forces have them under surveillance but private organizations and political interest groups attempt to reduce or marginalize their involvement in politics. Michael Suleiman called this a politics of exclusion (1999, 13). The stories are endless: persons appointed to advisory committees or staff positions or granted public service awards have their appointments and honors challenged and even cancelled (see chapter 3, this volume). Political candidates return donations from Arab Americans, both Christians and Muslims. Often the grounds are vague. Individuals are said to have made a loosely defined anti-Israeli or proterrorism statement or are linked to someone with such views. These rejections involve the very nature of citizenship. Citizenship is not just a passport and the right to vote. It includes the right to full political engagement, the right to assemble in organizations that disagree with public policy, the right to petition for redress of grievance through challenges to authority, and the right to participate in the political process. As Yvonne Haddad noted with regard to returned campaign donations, "many in the community feel disenfranchised, given the importance of donations in providing access to elected officials and determining American policies" (2004, 23; for a discussion on pre-September 11 incidents and patterns, see Abraham 1994). In this sense, there is a convergence of civil liberties issues and foreign policy expression, and many Arab Americans would see them as two dimensions of the same issue.

Let us look at this issue from a different perspective. On the causes of September 11 and whether the United States is stabilizing the Middle East, responses were related both to a sense of insecurity or threat and to levels of religious engagement. Regarding insecurity, resistance to the idea of a clash of civilizations is higher among those who worry about the future, report a bad experience after September 11, and perceive a media hostile to the community. The Media Hostility Index measures a sense of injustice, a belief that Arab Americans and issues important to them are portrayed in an unfriendly manner. Not surprisingly, such perceptions are linked to political views. The greater the sense of fear and injustice, the less confidence there is in the American role in the Middle East and the less sympathy for the idea of a clash.

On matters of religious engagement, we asked respondents how important it was to attend religious services. Those Arab and Chaldean Christians who thought it was important were significantly more likely to believe that the

United States was stabilizing the region than those who did not (44 percent to 34 percent). For Muslims, the impact was in the opposite direction: those who affirmed attending services were significantly less likely to have confidence in the American role (21 percent to 35 percent). This pattern was repeated in modified form when we asked whether individuals were religiously active. For Muslims, being involved at any level decreased confidence in the U.S. role (22 percent to 35 percent). For Christians, the level of involvement had no impact. For those who are active, Christians and Muslims are 23 percentage points apart, but for those not active, they are statistically identical (34 percent to 35 percent). Put differently, religious activity pushes Christians and Muslims in opposite directions, but the absence of religious activity leaves them open to converging perspectives, a tendency explored more in chapter 4.[16]

This pattern tells much about opinion structure, but the explanation lies less in religious ideology than in organizational dynamics. The congregation is a central institution that pulls people together, gives them a sense of social place, and helps shape their values (Stockton 2006). By their very nature, religious organizations emphasize group norms. The question of whether U.S. involvement is stabilizing the region can measure different things. Homeland self-interest or an assessment of policy effectiveness are two possibilities. The question also relates to comfort with U.S. power in the world. This brings us to the fact that it is easier for Christians to blend into American society than for Muslims. Chaldeans and Maronites, for example, are Roman Catholics with established identity groups in the United States. If Christians are developing a greater comfort level with their American lives, that may include a distinctive orientation to the American world role, an orientation less shared by Muslims. To borrow from Frederick Harris, Muslims are developing an oppositional culture and Christians, not entirely happy with American policies, are moving more toward a culture of comfort (1999).[17] As we saw in earlier chapters, Muslims are more likely to think of themselves as a threatened minority and Christians to consider themselves an immigrant community moving into the mainstream.

President Bush may have contributed to the problem. In his speech to the Islamic Mosque and Cultural Center after September 11, Bush drew a distinction between radical and mainstream Muslims. This qualification was beneficial at the time, protecting a vulnerable minority, but it contained a trap not immediately obvious. It compelled Muslims to claim the mantle of moderation. Put bluntly, they were presumed guilty unless they distanced themselves from Islamic militancy. Muslims could theoretically be accepted as individuals if they proved by words and expressions of patriotism to be moderate Muslims rather than radical. But even then there were limits. Leaders were repeatedly subjected to accusatory statements such as, "Why do you [or they] not renounce terrorism?" This question doubles as a nonfalsifiable accusation without an acceptable answer. The Council on American and Islamic Relations (CAIR), a high-profile Muslim group that organized a mass petition against terrorism titled "Not in the name of Islam" and put together a coalition of religious leaders to issue a fatwa (religious opinion) declaring attacks on civilians to be a violation of Islamic law, was still continually attacked for not renouncing terrorism. The technique was disturbingly reminiscent of the McCarthy-era query, "Are you now or have you ever been a Communist?" Such questions are designed to besmirch. They also imply that the person asking them has knowledge of misconduct and the moral authority to demand an answer. Any answer—an affirmation of innocence or a contemptuous refusal to respond—will be considered evidence of guilt or deceit.

But even when individuals are accepted, the community is still at risk. As Suleiman put it, "Arabs are doing fine as individuals, but not as a community. The whole community is suspect."[18] Suleiman's observation echoed what Sartre wrote about the French Jews. As Sartre described it, the French view of Jewish rights dating to the French Revolution had always been "everything for the Jew as an individual, nothing for the Jews as a community" (1944, 87). This put Jews into a dilemma of being accepted only if they were not Jews: "The perpetual obligation to prove that he is French puts the Jew in a situation of guilt. If on every occasion he does not do more than everybody else, much more than anybody else, he is guilty, he is a dirty Jew—and one might say, parodying the words of Beaumarchais: to judge by the qualities we demand of a Jew if he is to be assimilated as a 'true' Frenchman, how many Frenchmen would be found worthy of being Jews in their own country?" (Sartre 1944, 87). A similar predicament is pressing on Arabs in America today, especially Muslims.

It is not surprising that majority and minority religiocultural groups should react differently to cultural explanations of conflict. A majority group might be inclined to think in terms of cultural differences, a minority in terms of political differences that do not dwell on majority-minority distinctions. In the United States, many Arab Americans see the idea of a clash of civilizations as a threatening ideology that could compromise their position in American society. If the general public came to believe there was a fundamental clash of civilizations or conflict of values, that would be dangerous for Arab Americans, even for Christians. A sense of fear, insecurity, and perceived threat causes Arab Americans to react negatively to this rhetoric, which they see as coming from elements not friendly to their interests and welfare. In other words, questions about the U.S. role in the Middle East or the causes of September 11 are not entirely international issues but also have strong implications for domestic welfare and standing. The rhetoric around a clash or a conflict has more to do with mobilizing popular support for controversial foreign policies than with offering a detached, scholarly analysis of international conflict. It serves more to discredit those who question policies than anything else. In reality, though the idea of a clash of civilizations is often presented as a description of how they see us, it is more accurately a description of how we see them, and how *we* plan to treat those who resist our politics. For this reason, it is ultimately a domestic political debate over influence and status. As such, most Arab Americans, especially Muslims, are aware that they are being both targeted and marginalized by it.

This chapter illustrates the complexity of the Arab American population and the difficulty of making generalizations about it. For every pattern there is an exception. At the same time, however, the three models outlined at the beginning of the chapter all have some relevance. Almond's elite-mass model works in some cases: the educated and the elders are more likely to be informed than the less educated and the young. Arab Americans have shared perspectives but those are few, mostly having to do with the issue of Palestine. On other issues, Palestinians and Jordanians, Iraqis, Lebanese and Syrians, and Yemenis are different, as are Christians and Muslims. What really stands out more prominently, however, is the remarkable way in which foreign policy attitudes have a clear civil liberties dimension to them, and clear implications for their role as citizens. Arab American opinion about foreign policy issues is not only a function of historic ancestry but is also shaped by such factors as identity as an Arab American, level of religious engagement, pride in being an American, anxiety about the future, and a sense that a hostile media is bearing down on the community. Not surprisingly, all of these factors were also found to be important in our earlier discussion of civil liberties. The overlap of themes suggests that foreign policy issues are not simply an array of topics on which people can adopt and freely debate multiple points of view. For some Americans, particular issues of foreign policy become difficult tests of citizenship, and certain points of view cannot be fully or frankly debated. The post-9/11 crisis challenged American society in diverse ways; it challenged Arab

Americans by making their political views central to the way others view them both as members of American society and as potential threats to it.

NOTES

1. Robert Wiebe discussed nineteenth-century Norwegians, Irish, Germans, Jews and others (2001). David Fischer described four distinctive groups from Britain (1989). Gary Gerstle compared Arab Americans with nineteenth century Germans and Irish Catholics (2006).

2. De Tocqueville (1969, vol. I, part II, chap. 9) described in 1835 how ethnic mobilization worked even in newly independent America when he discussed a rally on behalf of Polish independence.

3. A study by Eric Alterman of seventy-one media pundits described sixty-one as reflexively pro-Israeli and most of the rest as strategically pro-Israeli, meaning they criticize Israel from a pro-Israeli perspective (commentary on MSNBC and Slate.com, March 28, 2002). A study of news coverage of the 2006 Israel-Lebanon war found that American newspaper editorials and political cartoonists "overwhelmingly supported" Israeli positions (ADL 2006). For example, thirty-one of thirty-three major newspapers advocated dismantling Hizbullah or displacing it from southern Lebanon. Only eight criticized Israel for prolonging the war. A previous survey (same source) found an "overwhelming majority" of newspapers critical of Yasser Arafat and his legacy.

4. All percentages are significant at the 0.5 level or less unless indicated. Partisan differences were significant at 0.8. By percentage, Democrats and independents were nearly identical at 29 percent and 31 percent. Republicans were at 48 percent. Liberals and moderates were identical at 32 percent, conservatives more supportive at 41 percent.

5. In 2004, one of my students asked permission to miss an examination. Her father, a young imam in 1980, had disappeared when the regime began a campaign against Shi'a clergy. A human rights organization had just uncovered a mass grave of imams and her family was going to Karbala for a memorial service. This student might well have seen the American invasion in its early months as a restoration of order.

6. The Chaldeans are an interesting case. In the 1980s, Michigan Chaldeans were friendly to Saddam Hussein because he had developed more open policies towards Christians. He even financed the expansion of a Chaldean church in

Detroit, much to the later embarrassment of the priest. Relations between Chaldeans and Saddam's regime cooled after the invasion of Kuwait in 1990.

7. A Zogby poll in Lebanon illustrated the pattern (Zogby International 2005). Regarding the assassination of former Prime Minister Rafik Hariri, Maronite, Shi'a, Druze, and Sunni had very different perspectives. Asked who was behind the assassination, 47 percent of Maronites mentioned Syria or a Lebanese-Syrian group, but only 9 percent of Shi'a did.

8. Regarding news consumption and information level, those who watch television news daily are more likely to support a Palestinian state than those who watch hardly at all (79 percent to 52 percent). Those who follow the war on terror closely are more likely to support a Palestinian state than those who do not follow it (78 percent to 46 percent). Those who could identify John Ashcroft as the (then) U.S. attorney general were more supportive (81 percent to 64 percent).

9. Factor analysis is a data reduction process that extracts patterns from a variety of variables using correlation techniques. The strength of an individual item on the factor is measured by how much it loads on that factor as represented by the figure reported. An item loads on a factor if its correlation with that factor is higher than its correlation on any other factor.

10. Ronald Stockton outlined the historical process that produced this ideology (1987). Robert Bellah explained the concept of covenant nationality and how it relates to Hebrew-centric thinking (1992). For examples of politicized Christian Zionist thinking, see Jerry Falwell (1980) and John Hagee (2007).

11. Of the 218 persons who accept the idea of a conflict of values, two groups are of particular interest, Iraqis and Christians. Only thirty-seven Muslims accept the idea. But because most Iraqis in the sample are Christian, and most Iraqi Christians are Chaldeans, how do these categories interact? Of 578 Christians, 181 (31 percent) accept the idea, 328 reject it, and 68 did not answer. Of 350 Iraqis, 120 (34 percent) accept it, 181 reject it, and 49 did not answer. Of those Iraqis who accept, 113 of 120 are Christian but 156 Christian Iraqis (63 percent) reject the idea and 41 did not answer. Regarding the 220 members of the Chaldean church (all but three are Iraqi), 76 (35 percent) accept the idea, 113 reject it, and 31 did not answer. Looked at yet another way, of the 181 Christians overall who supported the idea, 136 (75 percent) are from the Catholic tradition, which includes Chaldeans, Maronites, and Melkites; only 38 (21 percent) are from the Orthodox. The Catholic tradition has deep roots in American culture, so it is logical that they would be closer to the thinking of the general population.

12. The vote in the Senate was 52–47, in the House 250–183. The Michigan senators against were Levin and Stabenaw. The representatives were Bonior, Conyers, Dingell, Kildee, Kilpatrick, Levin, and Rivers.

13. Cautionary expression was not unique to those of Arab heritage. Late-night talk show hosts were stifled for months in their monologues. Cartoonist Art Spiegelman (2004), who wrote the graphic novel *In the Shadow of No Towers,* described his own experience: "At the end of 2002 there was a kind of fearfulness that went well beyond yellow or orange alerts. There was a shutdown, not just of irony, but of comedy and political conversation that could be seen in some ways as disloyal" (David Ansen, "Natural-Born Heroes," *Newsweek,* August 7, 2006, 50). The significant difference however, was the objectively greater exposure to retaliation by those of Arab-world ethnicity and a systematic monitoring of their community.

14. The pattern in the general population reflects more clearly the absence of opinion than withheld opinion. Level of formal education is gone but is replaced by level of media attention. As with Arab Americans, younger people are less likely to answer. Partisanship is not a factor, but identifying as a conservative does increase having an opinion on a two-state solution. Regarding the cause of the September 11 attacks—the most sensitive and difficult topic for Arab Americans—the only influences are age and degree of community engagement. Trusting the government in Washington, an issue important in Arab American opinion formation, affects only the item of a two-state solution where more trust is related to greater support for that outcome, the exact opposite of the Arab American pattern. Proud to be an American makes no difference; worry about the future makes no difference. Being black affects only one issue, the two-state solution, where many African Americans appear to be indifferent (65 percent versus 45 percent of non-blacks).

15. These suspicions were reinforced when the press reported the arrest on September 11 of four Israelis, illegally in the country on expired student visas, found with box cutters and large amounts of cash, taking photographs of the burning towers and behaving in a way that did not reflect the shock everyone else was feeling. *The New York Times* said they were "being glib in the face of tragedy" and "making light of the catastrophe" (Alison Cowan, "On the Inside Looking Out, Caught in a Net of Suspicion," October 8, 2001). The Israeli daily *Ha'aretz* was more blunt: They were "shouting in what was interpreted as cries of joy and mockery" (Yossi Melman, "Five Israelis Detained for 'Puzzling Behavior' After WTC Tragedy," September 17, 2001, available at: http://www.fpp.co.uk/online/01/09/WTC.html (accessed

September 17, 2001)). After months in detention and denials of wrongdoing, they were deported without charges. In May 2007, a national poll of Muslims asked, "Do you believe that groups of Arabs carried out the attacks against the United States on September 11, 2001, or don't you believe this?" (Pew 2007). Forty percent believed this, 28 percent did not, and the rest did not answer. Among the 24 percent of Muslims who were Arab Americans, agreement was linked to higher education, being older, and being less religious.

16. Jim Sidanius and his colleagues found a similar pattern at the American University of Beirut in late 2001 (2008, 12). With greater religious identification, sympathy for terrorism increased among Muslims but decreased among Christians. In other words, the more individuals identified with their religion, the more their attitudes diverged.

17. Frederick Harris discovered in African American churches an "oppositional disposition" that enabled individuals "to challenge their marginality through modes of action and thought that call for inclusion in the political system instead of exclusion from the polity" (Harris 1999, 40). This oppositional civic culture has a "dualistic orientation" to power, to "support civil society and oppose a system of domination with that society." This disposition promotes "inclusion within the polity rather than separation from existing political structure," incorporating "loyalty to the regime *and* opposition to aspects of that regime" (Harris 1999, 67; for how these ideas apply to Arab Americans, see Stockton 2006).

18. Suleiman was speaking at a conference of the Wilson Center for International Scholars on May 5, 2006. In his classic book on prejudice, Gordon Allport explained the logic of nonfalsifiable accusations (1958). Derrick Bell's comments on African American marginalization is strikingly similar (1992). He maintained that black leaders are called upon to condemn blacks who upset whites with their words or actions. If they do, they as individuals receive enhanced standing. If they do not, they are treated as if they themselves had committed the offense (Bell 1992, 109–26).

REFERENCES

Abraham, Nabeel. 1994. "Anti-Arab Racism and Violence in the United States." In *The Development of Arab American Identity,* edited by Ernest McCarus. Ann Arbor: University of Michigan Press.

Alexandria Protocol. 1944. MidEast Web. http://www.mideastweb.org/alexandria.htm.

Allport, Gordon W. 1958. *The Nature of Prejudice.* Garden City, N.Y.: Doubleday and Company.

Almond, Gabriel. 1950. *The American People and Foreign Policy.* New York: Harcourt Brace.

Anti-Defamation League (ADL). 2005. "American Attitudes Towards Israel and the Middle East." Press Release. Available at: http://www.adl.org/PresRele/IslME_62/4752_62 (accessed June 12, 2005).

———. 2006. "Political Cartoonists and U.S. Newspapers Support Israel and See Hezbollah as a Terrorist Group." Press Release. Available at: http://www.adl.org/PresRele/IslME_62/4883_62.htm.

Bell, Derrick. 1992. *Faces at the Bottom of the Well: The Permanence of Racism.* New York: Basic Books.

Bellah, Robert. 1992. *The Broken Covenant: American Civil Religion in a Time of Trial.* Chicago: University of Chicago Press.

Berinsky, Adam J. 2001. *Silent Voices: Public Opinion and Political Participation in America.* Princeton, N.J.: Princeton University Press.

Burns, Nancy, Kay Lehman Schlozman, and Sidney Verba. 2001. *The Private Roots of Public Action, Gender, Equality, and Political Participation.* Cambridge, Mass.: Harvard University Press.

Bush, George W. 2003. *We Will Prevail: On War, Terrorism, and Freedom,* forward by Peggy Noonan, introduction by Jay Nordlinger. New York: Continuum.

Chicago Council on Foreign Relations (Chicago Council). 2004. "American Public Opinion and Foreign Policy, Global Views." Chicago: Chicago Council on Global Affairs.

Converse, Phillip E. 1964. "The Nature of Belief Systems in Mass Publics." In *Ideology and Discontent,* edited by David E. Apter. London: Free Press of Glencoe.

de Tocqueville, Alexis. 1969. *Democracy in America,* edited by J. P. Mayer, translated by George Lawrence. New York: Harper Collins.

Falwell, Jerry. 1980. *Listen, America!* New York: Doubleday.

Fischer, David Hackett. 1989. *Albion's Seed: Four British Folkways in America.* New York: Oxford University Press.

Gerstle, Gary. 2006. "The Political Incorporation of Immigrant Groups: An Historical Perspective on the American Experience." In *American Arabs and Political Participation,* edited by Philippa Strum. Washington: Woodrow Wilson Wilson International Center for Scholars.

Haddad, Yvonne. 2004. *Not Quite American? The Shaping of Arab and Muslim Identity in the United States.* Waco, Tx.: Baylor University Press.

Hagee, John. 2007. *In Defense of Israel.* Lake Mary, Fl.: Strang Communications Co.

Harris, Frederick C. 1999. *Something Within: Religion in African-American Political Activism*. New York: Oxford University Press.

Holsti, Ole R. 1996. *Public Opinion and American Foreign Policy*. Ann Arbor: University of Michigan Press.

Holsti, Ole R., and James N. Rosenau. 1990. "The Structure of Foreign Policy Attitudes Among American Leaders." *Journal of Politics* 52(1): 94–125.

Huntington, Samuel. 1993. "Clash of Civilizations?" *Foreign Affairs* (summer): 22–49.

Jacobson, Matthew Frye. 2002. *Special Sorrows: The Diasporic Imagination of Irish, Polish, and Jewish Immigrants to the U.S.* Cambridge, Mass.: Harvard University Press.

Lawrence, Bruce, ed. 2005. *Messages to the World: The Statements of Osama bin Laden*. New York: Verso.

Lewis, Bernard. 1990. "The Roots of Muslim Rage." *The Atlantic* 266(September): 47–60.

McCloskey, Herbert. 1964. "Consensus and Ideology in the American Politics." *American Political Science Review* 58(June): 361–82.

McCloskey, Herbert, and Alida Brill. 1983. *Dimensions of Tolerance: What Americans Believe About Civil Liberties*. New York: Russell Sage Foundation.

Mueller, John. 1994. *Public Opinion and the Gulf War*. Chicago: University of Chicago Press.

O'Connor, Edwin. 1955. *The Last Hurrah*. Boston: Little, Brown and Company.

Paige, Benjamin I., and Robert Shapiro. 1982. "Change in Americans' Policy Preferences, 1935–1979." *The Public Opinion Quarterly* 46(1): 24–42.

Pew Research Center for the People & the Press (Pew). 2002. "Americans and Europeans Differ Widely on Foreign Policy Issues." Washington, D.C.: Pew Research Center. Available at: http://www.people-press.org/reports/pdf/153.pdf (accessed October 12, 2002).

———. 2003. "Religion and Politics: Contention and Consensus. Growing Numbers Say Islam Encourages Violence Among Followers." Washington, D.C.: Pew Research Center. Available at: http://www.people-press.org/reports/pdf/189.pdf (accessed September 6, 2003).

———. 2007. *Muslim Americans: Middle Class and Mostly Mainstream*. Washington, D.C.: Pew Research Center. Available at: http://www.pewresearch.org/pubs/483/muslim-americans (accessed May 29, 2007).

Qazwini, Imam Hassan. 2007. *American Crescent. A Muslim Cleric on the Power of His Faith, the Struggle Against Prejudice, and the Future of Islam in America*. New York: Random House.

Sartre, Jean-Paul. 1944. *Anti-Semite and Jew,* translated by George J. Becker. New York: Schocken Books.

Sidanius, Jim, P. J. Henry, Felicia Pratto, and Shana Levin. 2008. "Why Do They Hate Us So? The Clash of Civilizations or the Politics of Dominance?" working paper 187. New York: Russell Sage Foundation.

Spiegelman, Art. 2004. *In the Shadow of No Towers.* New York: Pantheon Books.

Stockton, Ronald R. 1987. "Christian Zionism: Prophecy and Public Opinion." *Middle East Journal* 41(2): 234–54.

———. 2006. "Arab American Political Participation: Findings From the Detroit Arab American Study." In *American Arabs and Political Participation,* edited by Philippa Strum. Washington: Woodrow Wilson Wilson International Center for Scholars.

Suleiman, Michael, ed. 1999. *Arabs in America: Building a New Future.* Philadelphia: Temple University Press.

Todorov, Alexander, and Anesu N. Mandisodza. 2004. "Public Opinion on Foreign Policy: The Multilateral Public That Perceives Itself as Unilateral." *Public Opinion Quarterly* 68(3): 323–48.

Wiebe, Robert H. 2001. *Who We Are: A History of Popular Nationalism.* Princeton, N.J.: Princeton University Press.

Wittkopf, Eugene R. 1990. *Faces of Internationalism: Public Opinion and Foreign Policy.* Durham, N.C.: Duke University Press.

Zogby International. 2005. "New Polling Shows Deep Fractures Among Lebanese." News release, May 7. Washington, D.C.: Zogby International. Available at: http://www.zogbyworldwide.com/news/Readnews1.cfm?ID=723 (accessed November 10, 2005).

CONCLUSION

CHAPTER 9

The Limits of Citizenship

Andrew Shryock and Ann Chih Lin

In previous chapters of this book, we have shown that Detroit's Arab and Chaldean communities are suspended precariously between two statuses: "not quite us" and "not quite them." This predicament is related to all the issues of citizenship and crisis we have explored, and it should now be clear that popular reaction to the 9/11 attacks cannot fully explain the ambiguities of belonging Arab Americans face. In 2003, when the Detroit Arab American Study (DAAS) was conducted, the vast majority of its respondents were already U.S. citizens, and they belonged to a community that, although predominately foreign-born, could trace its local roots back to the nineteenth century. Prejudice against Arabs has been commonplace in the United States for decades, yet by the mid-1990s many Detroit Arabs were part of the mainstream. Indeed, some—Jacques Nasser, CEO of Ford Motor Company, Steve Yokich, president of the United Auto Workers, and Spencer Abraham, U.S. senator for the State of Michigan—were members of national and global elites. The mood of distrust that surrounds all things Arab and Muslim in the United States today is not inevitable. It does, however, correspond to something deep and pervasive in the way Americans gauge the limits of citizenship.

In this final chapter, we argue that the marginalization of Detroit's Arab and Chaldean Americans is rooted in basic assumptions about nationality, about being American and being other. These assumptions belong to a space, as much an idea as a physical place, that is euphemistically labeled the mainstream. It is impossible to define this space precisely, but Americans of diverse ethnic, racial, religious, and class backgrounds nonetheless have a vivid sense—a sense often peculiar to members of their own group—of what does and what does not fit in the American mainstream. Arabs and Muslims are especially alert to the powers of the mainstream because they are often excluded from it. They see its promises and contradictions, as it were, from the outside. Although practical models of the mainstream serve well to mark and marginalize Arab difference in U.S. society, they also render some forms of Arab and Muslim difference acceptable. Reconfigured as evidence of diversity, Arab difference can be legitimating. As we saw in chapter 3, a generalized, institutional support for multiculturalism is essential to the success Detroit's Arab and Chaldean populations have had in building their own community institutions and creating durable links to the larger society. As blueprints for national inclusion and exclusion, the conceptions of belonging we will explore in this chapter can be thought of as ideological tools for delimiting and defining American-ness. They channel the relentless process of Americanization and ensure that individuals and communities who deviate from it will be perceived as alien and (at best) in need of cultural adjustment or (at worst) as threats to national security.

Before we can explore issues of national belonging, we need first to distinguish them from issues of legal citizenship. As we saw in chapters 2, 3, and 7, this status is related to national identity but does not always guarantee that acts of identification with the nation-state will be deemed authentic, or that these gestures will be reciprocated by fellow nationals or by agencies of the state.

LOCATING ARAB CITIZENSHIP

That nearly 80 percent of DAAS respondents are U.S. citizens, even though 75 percent are foreign-born and most have arrived since the 1980s, points to two obvious conclusions. First is that obtaining U.S. citizenship is important to Arabs and Chaldeans in Detroit, most of whom prefer it to permanent resident status. Second is that this commitment to U.S. citizenship has failed to protect Arabs and Chaldeans from widespread beliefs that they are not really Americans, that they do not really identify with or as Americans, and that their civil liberties can and should be infringed upon in the interests of public security (see chapter 7). Initial reactions to the DAAS findings gave ironic support to our contention that U.S. citizenship is not producing, for Arabs and Chaldeans, a publicly recognized sense of membership, or belonging, in America as Americans. When we presented DAAS results to colleagues and public audiences in Detroit, several of our interlocutors, Arab and non-Arab, doubted that U.S. citizenship rates were truly so high ("of course people are going to claim they're citizens, especially if they're not"); others, mostly Arab Americans, doubted that the community could be so foreign-born ("that can't be right; we've been living here since the 1800s"). It would seem that the misfit between a reality of pervasive citizenship and a reality of pervasive foreignness is troubling, even incredible, to Arabs, Americans, and Arab Americans alike.

The same disquiet characterizes scholarship on citizenship, an intellectual buzzword that, in recent years, has come to stand for both a problem and a solution. As a platform on which to debate the validity and availability of rights (human or civil, individual or communal), the concept of citizenship manages always to focus our attention on a simple fact of modern life. One can be a member of a nation-state, a legal citizen, without having access to the benefits (or the costs) of membership. Likewise, one can have access to the benefits (and the costs) of membership in a nation-state without being a legal citizen. There is a fateful slippage between the theory and practice of rights in all contemporary states, and there is hardly an identity category in existence—gender, race, ethnicity, class, religion, sexuality—that has not been shaped by a rich legacy of inequality. Indeed, these inequalities continue to multiply in tandem with international immigration, economic globalization, the evolution of new transnational and extraterritorial political bodies, and imperial policies that transcend the legal bounds of the nation-state.

In previous chapters, we have seen how thoroughly these global trends have affected the lives of Arabs and Chaldeans in greater Detroit. The arguments we have developed—whether they apply to values, identity formation, the 9/11 backlash, civil liberties, foreign policy, social capital, transnational ties, or religious practice—have centered on challenges, real and perceived, to the attainment of Arab American citizenship, not only as a legal status, but as a viable form of national belonging. What are these challenges? Where are they located? It is important to consider the location of Arab American citizenship, in space and time, since national belonging gives peculiar privilege to place and long-established ties to places. Arab and Muslim Americans are often seen as being attached to foreign countries—they have "homelands"—and their American identity is often described as a project of transformation (they are perpetually becoming American), a process that will perhaps be completed in the future but is still not finished.

This projection of Arab American identity into future time, and away toward other national spaces, is not simply a model imposed by outsiders; it also has wide currency among Arab Americans themselves. Many Arab immigrants do not want their children to act, talk, dress, or eat like *al-amrikan* (the Americans)—not to mention date and marry them—even as they prize their status as U.S. citizens and urge more relatives to immigrate to Detroit. At the same time, many Arab Americans who have lived in the United States for decades, or were born here, do not want their children to act, talk, dress, or eat like "boaters" (new immigrants, people from "back home," from "the old country"). Yet antiboater sentiment does not prevent American-borns from taking pride in their Arab heritage, doing diligent service on the boards of local mosques, churches, and Arab American community organizations, and defending "boaters"—who might, in fact, be their own relatives—from prejudice experienced at the hands of non-Arabs. In short, the incomplete overlap between citizenship and belonging is just as acutely discernible, and just as open to debate, within Arab American communities as it is between these communities and the mainstream. It would be more accurate, and more suggestive, to argue that a specific version of the American mainstream is located within the Arab American communities, where it functions as a kind of private, in-group assimilating engine. The keepers of the Arab American mainstream give positive connotations to the kinds of Arabness that are useful and acceptable in the United States; they stigmatize, mute, and select against forms of Arabness that are identified, in larger Arab-American contexts, as "backward" or "embarrassing." This Americanizing process is contested, and the rules often change, but if something akin to it were not happening, terms like "boater" would not make sense; they would not be conceivable.

BEYOND THE LIMITS

What is noteworthy about this process, in which people turn mere citizenship into a practical, Arabized sense of American identity, is that a version of it is taking place in nearly all new U.S. immigrant populations, "remaking the American mainstream" in diverse forms that, nonetheless, share common points of reference (Alba and Nee 2005). As we argued in chapter 2, Arab Americans are unusual in that many non-Arabs think this process is not possible for them, that Arab and Muslim Americans do not (and perhaps should not) contribute to the remaking of the American mainstream. DAAS respondents were keenly aware of these attitudes. Forty percent said Arab Americans are not respected by members of society at large; 42 percent of Muslims said their religion is not respected; 50 percent of the sample believed U.S. media is biased against them; and 58 percent of Muslims worry about the future of their families in the United States. To make matters more complex, 86 percent of DAAS respondents claimed they feel at home in the United States, and 91 percent said they were proud to be American. Among those with U.S. citizenship, the figure rose to 94 percent.

The latter, more positive findings raise questions in the minds of Arabs and non-Arabs alike, many of whom wonder if the people we interviewed meant what they said. "They *had* to say that," is a common refrain. "What did you expect them to say?" This response is not always ill considered, nor does it flow from a predictable bias. We encounter this reaction among progressive activists who are strong supporters of Arab and Muslim American communities; we encounter it among observers who entertain serious doubts about Arab Americans and their loyalties. This collusion across the political spectrum shows the extent to which Arabs are simply not allowed, by friend or foe, to be ordinary Americans (much less patriotic ones) no matter what they might "really" feel. Feelings and authentic loyalties, the emotive content of national identity, are dangerous terrain on which to discuss the nature of Arab American citizenship, yet discussion of Arab and Muslim identity in the United States is repeatedly pushed onto this terrain. Why does this happen, and what does it say about citizenship and belonging?

To answer these questions, we cannot restate the obvious. If we argue that Arabs and Muslims are demonized because they are associated, in the popular mind, with political enemies of the United States; or, if we argue that Arabs and Muslims are subject to racist, discriminatory treatment in the United States because they are portrayed, in popular discourse, as inferior, violent, anti-American, and backward, then we are unable to explain the acts of recognition and public support—the service awards, financial donations, political appointments, and event sponsorships described in chapter 3—that link Detroit's Arab and Muslim communities to the city's mainstream political, economic, and educational institutions. In other words, assigning enemy status can explain why the Federal Bureau of Investigation would build a new, $65-million office in Detroit (David Shepardson, "Local FBI's No. 1 Job: Terror War," *Detroit News,* October 23, 2005), from which it will conduct massive counterterrorism investigations; but can "enemy status" status adequately explain why Ford, GM, Daimler-Chrysler, Comerica Bank, the U.S.

Congress, and other mainstream interests would contribute nearly $16 million to the construction of the Arab American National Museum in Dearborn (*Arab American Affairs* 2003)? Can "enemy status" explain why the combined operating budgets of Detroit's premier Arab American organizations—ACCESS and ACC—now stand at roughly $30 million per year, most of which is provided by private foundations and federal and state government agencies? Clearly, some Arab Americans are considered friends, and the extensive friendship networks laid out in chapter 3 are essential to any nuanced understanding of the terms on which Arabs participate in (and are denied access to) the political and economic life of greater Detroit.

To make sense of inclusion and exclusion, both of which are essential to the disciplinary function of citizenship, we must again take up the challenge of "the limit figure" (Agamben 1998), the person or collectivity that does not belong to a group yet is located within it, that is part of a society yet is associated with external things. In Detroit, Arabs and Muslims are limit figures of this type; the boundary anxieties they provoke and experience are structured by three factors that underlie popular assumptions about citizenship: likeness (what Benedict Anderson [1991] called the "anonymous communion" of fellow nationals; the unum of e pluribus unum); conviction (willingness to commit oneself to the national project; to believe and have confidence in it); and solidarity (affinity for fellow nationals and shared national projects; a feeling that causes people, in conflict situations, to favor their own nation over rivals). These factors amplify and complement each other. Together, they constitute allegiance, and when one factor is in doubt, the other two are rendered suspect as well. As a result, public discussions of Arab and Muslim American citizenship revolve around a fairly limited range of concerns. "Are they like us?" "Do they believe in America?" "Are they with us, or against us?"

The cultural mainstream, for Arab and Muslim Americans, is an idea and a place whose limits are (inordinately) defined by how other people answer these questions. The evidence presented in chapters 6 and 9—and in a growing body of polling and survey data (see Traugott et al. 2002; Pew 2003; Pew Global Attitudes Project 2006; Farley et al. 2006)—suggests that many Americans believe Arabs and Muslims are not like "us," do not believe in America, and are perhaps not really "with us." Because most Arab and Muslim Americans agree that they are indeed perceived this way, we can use this field of perceptions as our common context of evaluation, our testing ground of Arab

American citizenship and belonging. The DAAS findings allow us to treat these perceptions as empirical claims. Not only can we determine whether the claims are accurate, we can also rephrase them in language that is suppler and, we think, truer to the complexities of citizenship in practice.

Are They Like Us?

As we saw in chapter 2, Arab Americans are like and unlike non-Arabs in countless ways, but differences also stand out and are used by Arabs and non-Arabs alike to attribute distinctiveness to Arab Americans. The DAAS was not designed to examine all forms of difference; it has nothing to say, for instance, about dress, foodways, holiday celebrations, dance, art, music, and other forms of cultural expression important to Arabs and Arab Americans. Still, the DAAS findings equip us to explore systematically—in ways that have not been possible before—several key dimensions along which Arab Americans are thought to be (and think themselves to be) different from the larger society in Detroit. These areas of distinctiveness, and the often dramatic degrees of difference they suggest, are captured in the following variables:

- Language—DAAS respondents are far more likely to speak a language other than English at home (86 percent) than the general population (12 percent).
- Enclave—DAAS respondents are far more likely to live in Dearborn and Dearborn Heights (29 percent) than the general population (4 percent). The association of Arab Americans with Dearborn is pronounced, locally and nationally, and this concentration is often referred to as "the enclave," a word that carries strong connotations of cultural distinctiveness and separation.
- Other identification—DAAS respondents are far more likely to identify as other (31 percent) in response to racial identity questions than the general population (3 percent).
- Foreign birth—DAAS respondents are far more likely to be born outside the United States (75 percent) than the general population (10 percent).
- Noncitizenship—DAAS respondents are far more likely not to be U.S. citizens (21 percent) than the general population (5 percent).
- Transnational ties—DAAS respondents are far more likely to communicate with family and friends living abroad (41 percent) than the general population (12 percent).

- Family size—DAAS respondents have larger households (4.0 members on average) than the general population (2.7 on average).
- Moral conservatism—DAAS respondents are far more likely to believe gambling (75 percent), drinking (58 percent), premarital sex (68 percent), and homosexuality (79 percent) are never acceptable than do members of the general population, who believe these practices are never acceptable at rates of 23 percent, 19 percent, 26 percent, and 39 percent respectively.

These contrasts figure prominently in both popular and scholarly discussions of Arab American identity. In the two most inclusive studies to date, these issues belong to a sturdy matrix in which Arab American identity is analyzed and expressed (Suleiman 1999; Abraham and Shryock 2000). We should note, however, that these zones of difference appear frequently in discussions of other American immigrant and ethnic populations. Studies of Latinos (Davila 2001; Sanchez 1993; Gutierrez 1995; Valle and Torres 2000), Asian Americans (Ong 2003; Okihiro 1994; Chan 1991), today's second-generation immigrants (Portes and Rumbaut 2001), and American immigration in historical perspective (King 2002) all return consistently to matters of language, ethnoracial identification, concentration and dispersal of enclave populations, citizenship status, transnational ties, family size, moral values, and time spent in the United States. These topics dominate immigration studies because they correspond to widely held—yet contextual and evolving—notions of normative modernity and mainstream Americanness; in short, they are markers of cultural citizenship.

On brute statistical grounds, it would be easy and accurate to conclude that Arab Americans are a highly distinctive population in Greater Detroit. To argue that Arab Americans are "not like us," however, is to add a moral coloring to the data that obscures important points. First, the areas of contrast on display here consist of numerical averages that do not capture variation in time or space. DAAS respondents might be highly unlike the general population in greater Detroit, but many American settings (certain Asian and Latino immigrant communities, for instance) would resemble the DAAS sample. There are other settings (among, say, fundamentalist Christians) that would resemble the moral conservatism of the DAAS sample. American urban culture is filled with enclaves of diverse kinds, one for almost every new wave of immigration since the founding of the republic. In this sense, Arab Detroit is comparable to many other Americas, minoritized and localized, which are considered distinctive, even unusual, without necessarily being considered an enemy camp. In fact, it is just as easy and accurate to conclude that the presence of culturally distinctive immigrant and ethnoracial populations is a commonplace of American society and history.

What the DAAS findings reveal, with precision, is the taken-for-granted backdrop against which Arab Americans become visible as a minoritized population. The mainstream, as it appears to Arabs and Chaldeans in Detroit, is dominated by native-born, English-speaking, U.S. citizens who live in small households, whose friends and family reside mostly in the United States, who are on familiar terms with their state-certified racial identities (and do not feel compelled to check other), and are tolerant of a wide range of habits and pastimes considered immoral in the Arab world. Though unattractive and threatening in some ways, this vision of the American mainstream is also appealing to Arabs and Chaldeans. As we argued in chapter 2, the mainstream is a zone of privilege, and the ability to live in it comfortably, benefiting from the institutions and opportunities found there, is proof that certain aspects of American citizenship have been attained. In chapters 2, 5, and 6, we saw that many Arab Americans have already entered the cultural mainstream, and they have recognizable features, such as higher incomes and levels of education, greater English fluency, and less active transnational ties; they also tend to be U.S. citizens, American-born, and more likely to identify as white.

In chapter 6, Baker, Jamal, and Tessler found that higher levels of cultural membership correspond to higher levels of social capital, and that both qualities increase as Arab Americans spend more time in Detroit. The highest levels of social capital are associated with American-born Arabs, who, not surprisingly, have the lowest measures of cultural distinctiveness. These patterns are consistent with straight-line models of assimilation that are now decidedly out of fashion. They also account for the heavy emphasis Arab American advocacy groups place on high incomes, college degrees, and deep historical presence in the United States when celebrating the accomplishments of the Arab American community. The in-group assimilation engine, mentioned earlier in this chapter, runs best on "model minority" fuel of exactly this sort. In sum, cultural distinctiveness has predictable contours among Detroit's Arab and Chaldean populations, and many of these patterns confirm long-standing American folk models of immigrant adaptation, upward mobility, and entry into the mainstream over time. If we conclude that DAAS respondents, as a statistical aggregate, are not like "us," then we must also conclude that many

Arabs and Chaldeans are more like "us" than others, that "we" are becoming (and have become) more like each other over time, and that Arab differences are structurally analogous to those found among many other immigrant and ethnic groups, who must likewise come to terms with their peculiar location in American society.

Do They Believe in America?

Our consideration of likeness and difference has skirted an issue important to many Americans: namely, are Arabs different in ways that make them less likely to identify with America and its values? Do Arabs believe in America, and can Americans trust them? These questions are often confused and rarely kind. What does it mean to believe in a nation-state? Because abstract principles such as life, liberty, equality, democracy, and the pursuit of happiness have never been exclusively American values, we think a more practical way of assessing this question is to focus on confidence in key institutions of American society. Specifically, do Arab Americans have confidence in their public schools, the U.S. legal system, the police, and the federal government? How do their levels of confidence compare to those prevalent in the larger society?

Figure 9.1 juxtaposes confidence levels for the DAAS and the general population. Whatever confidence actually measures—satisfaction, trust, approval, a sense of ownership, faith in the system, respect—it would appear that Arabs and Chaldeans, across the board, have more of this quality than members of the general population do. Moreover, as table 9.1 indicates, DAAS respondents who have lived in the United States longer, who read English well, and thus have had more opportunity to observe American institutions at work, are likely to have lower confidence levels (or, to be more precise, to have confidence levels more congruent with those of the general population). By contrast, Yemenis, who are among the most culturally distinctive of Detroit's Arab populations, are newest to the United States, score lowest on measures of social capital, and actually have the highest levels of confidence in American institutions.

Table 9.1 also shows that Arabs in Detroit have more confidence in local institutions—public schools and local police—than in the legal system and the federal government. Confidence in the latter two institutions seems to track experiences: having a bad experience after 9/11 reduces, by about 25 percent, the proportion of those expressing confidence in the legal system or the federal government. Confidence in local institutions is also depressed by having

Figure 9.1   Confidence in Public Institutions

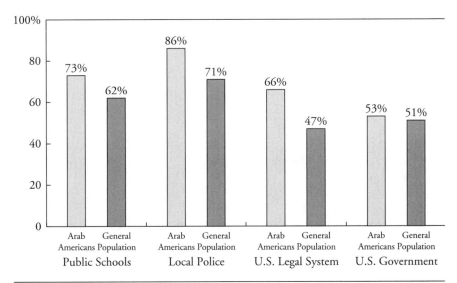

Source: Authors' compilation.

a bad post-9/11 experience, but only by about 10 percent. In general, Arab Americans in Detroit are likely to believe in U.S. institutions most readily when they are new to the country, a pattern that is not surprising, given that immigration to the United States is a momentous undertaking that exacts great costs from individuals and families. Would large numbers of Lebanese, Iraqis, Yemenis, and Palestinians come to Detroit if they were convinced that life there would be miserable?

A more interesting pattern is the tendency for Arab Americans who fit the profile for low social capital, as discussed in chapter 6, to have more confidence in American institutions. This finding suggests that higher levels of cultural distinctiveness among Arabs and Chaldeans in Detroit do not lessen confidence in American institutions, they increase it, and that the accumulation of social capital over time reflects not an absolute loss in confidence in American society, but more realistic assessments of how, and to what extent, key local and national institutions actually work. Both conclusions are inconsistent with the idea that Arab Americans are uniquely disaffected from the larger society and have trouble supporting American institutions. The Arab Americans who are furthest from the cultural mainstream, have the greatest

Table 9.1   Confidence in Public Institutions

Scale/Item	Public Schools	Local Police	Legal System	Federal Government
Country of origin-ancestry				
Iraq	68%	85%	67%	59%
Yemen	82	87	71	70
Palestine-Jordan	73	87	66	49
Lebanon-Syria	75	87	65	46
Time in United States				
Born in U.S., one or two parents born in U.S.	75	82	59	45
Born in U.S., parents born abroad	71	79	50	38
Arrived before 1969	74	90	70	51
Arrived 1970 to 1979	70	87	63	45
Arrived 1980 to 1989	72	86	69	52
Arrived 1990 to 1995	77	91	78	69
Arrived 1996 or later	73	84	73	66
Religion				
Christian	70	86	67	54
Muslim	78	85	66	53
Household income				
Under $20,000	75	87	77	70
$20,000 to $49,000	75	84	60	49
$50,000 to $99,999	72	87	66	50
$100,000+	74	85	60	44
Education				
Below high school	78	88	70	62
High school	67	79	58	42
Some college	73	84	59	46
BA	76	87	71	44
BA+	73	86	67	53
Race				
Arab-other	70	84	64	48
White	74	87	68	55
Arab American				
Describes me	75	86	67	50
Does not describe me	68	85	65	59
Bad experience after 9/11				
No	77	88	74	60
Yes	65	79	49	37

Source: Authors' compilation.

reason to feel disenfranchised, and display the lowest levels of social capital are those who believe most firmly in their public schools, local police, legal system, and even the federal government.

Are They with Us, or Against Us?

The inevitability of political disagreement is built into the structures of U.S. governance, and expressing minority opinion is a right of citizenship. What, then, do people mean when they suggest that Arab Americans are "not with us," that they might harbor anti-American feelings? Why are Arabs and Muslims so often seen as people whose affinities and actions fall outside the legitimate range of political disagreement? For many people, the gut response to this question is "because they flew airplanes into the World Trade Center." Given the false universal at the heart of this claim—who are "they," exactly?— it is vital to stress, yet again, that Arab and Muslim Americans have been firmly associated, in the public mind, with anti-American and anti-Israeli political movements since the 1960s, and the ease with which even highly educated, media savvy Americans lump Arabs and Muslims into an undifferentiated enemy class—a class that contains even U.S. regional allies—is the product of decades of negative imagery and political interpretation. The 9/11 attacks, in short, were immediately intelligible to most Americans within a robust, pre-existing discourse of Arab and Muslim threat.

Many Arab American scholars and community leaders argue that the political beliefs common among Arabs and Muslims—most notably, support for Palestinian statehood, criticism of Israel, and opposition to U.S. interventions in Arab and Muslim countries—are different enough from attitudes common in the American political mainstream, and critical enough of current U.S. policy, that these beliefs generate and are used to justify practices of anti-Arab exclusion (Jabara 2006; Naber 2006; Samhan 2006). The experience of political exclusion, according to this argument, engenders a strong, oppositional sensibility among Arab Americans that leads them to doubt the commitment of U.S. society to its own ideals. This critical stance is often portrayed, in American popular media, as both a cause and an effect of Arab and Muslim difference (more evidence that "they are not like us"). It is also thought to diminish belief in the United States as a national project and to weaken solidarity with conationals (see Abdo 2006).

The DAAS findings, however, suggest that this model of political alienation is much too simple. In chapter 8, we saw that measures of pride in American identity and feeling at home in the United States are generally high among Arab

Americans, and we have just seen that confidence in American institutions is likewise quite strong. These patterns coexist with political beliefs that are at odds with mainstream opinion. In 2003, Arab Americans were more likely than non-Arabs to believe that U.S. intervention in the Middle East was destabilizing the region. They were far more likely to support Palestinian statehood and less likely to believe that the 9/11 attacks were caused by cultural or religious differences between the West and the Arab and Muslim worlds. Although this political posture is widely shared in Arab Detroit, there are systematic variations within it. Most discernibly, being Iraqi and being Christian make a person more likely to support U.S. policy in the Middle East, less likely to say Palestine is central to their identity, and less likely to identify as Arab American. As Ronald Stockton argues in chapters 7 and 8, these views belong to a significant, politically influential minority in Arab Detroit. Disproportionately Chaldean, people who hold these views are oppositional to an Arab American political sensibility that is itself oppositional—a fact that, in Greater Detroit, produces mixed patterns of support for and criticism of the U.S. invasion of Iraq and, more generally, the war on terror.

Equally revealing of Arab Detroit's political complexity is that the people who express the strongest support for Palestine and the most critical positions on U.S. intervention in the Middle East are often those who have high levels of confidence in U.S. institutions, high levels of social capital, and low levels of cultural distinctiveness. Arab Americans with higher incomes and more education are more likely to be pro-Palestinian, for instance, and Palestinian Americans themselves, who in Detroit are largely a Christian, suburban population with low cultural distinctiveness and high social capital, are most closely identified with the political profile many Americans associate with consistent rejection of U.S. foreign policy. Similarly, Yemenis, who in Detroit have long been associated with labor activism and organized protest against U.S. policy in the Middle East, are associated in the DAAS findings with the highest levels of confidence in American institutions. The combination of factors that, according to media pundits and social scientists alike, is producing riots and radicalization among Muslims in Europe—that is, poverty, segregation, alienation, and oppositional politics—is not consistently materializing in Arab Detroit. Instead, political opposition is sometimes linked to affluence and integration; poverty is linked to confidence in institutions; residence in Arab-majority enclaves seems not to increase or diminish levels of social capital; and, as we saw in chapters 2 and 3, the most influential and politically integrated Arab American organizations are located in the Arab Muslim enclave of Dearborn, where oppositional politics and confidence in American institutions are fully on display (in pro-Hizbullah demonstrations on the steps of City Hall, in avid support for predominately Arab American high school athletic teams, and in the prevalence of "I love Dearborn Police" bumper stickers).

In the face of these variations—whose logic and history have been amply explored in previous scholarship on Arab Detroit (for example, Stockton 2006; Terry 1999; Shryock and Abraham 2000; Abraham and Abraham 1983)—what stands out are the much more uniform and predictable political opinions of the larger society. Although Arab Americans and non-Arabs are both likely to believe that U.S. support for Israel and U.S. involvement in the Arab Gulf were underlying causes of the 9/11 attacks, members of the general population are, as we saw in chapter 8, much more likely to believe the 9/11 attacks were the product of differences in cultural values and religious beliefs, and these assumptions in turn are closely correlated with the idea that U.S. support for Israel caused the 9/11 attacks. The latter position predisposes those who embrace it to see Arabs and Muslims not only as opponents of Israel, but also as a threat to American values, even though Arab Americans vary among themselves in the degree to which they support Palestine, U.S. intervention in Iraq, and even Arab American identity as a political label for their personal status and communal affiliations.

More problematic still is the tendency for Americans to confuse Arab American opposition to U.S. foreign policy with opposition to U.S. national identity and social institutions. Arab American support for the latter is very strong. Even on the issue of moral values, where Arab Americans are much more conservative than the general public, we saw in chapter 5 that the Arabs who live in the Middle East are closer in their moral attitudes and beliefs to Americans than they are to Europeans, and Arab Americans and other Americans are closer to each other in their value orientations than either group is to the historically Protestant countries of Europe. At both a practical and ideological level, it is difficult for Detroit's Arab Americans to be "against us" when their oppositional politics only accentuate the extent to which they embrace American society, its public institutions, and its dominant ideals. As we saw in Chapter 3, this embrace is not always warm or reciprocal, but it is nearly unavoidable, and it engenders a political style in which oppositional and integrationist trends are equally developed.

ARAB/AMERICAN AS ENEMY/FRIEND

What does all this tell us? In short, Arabs and Chaldeans are a highly distinctive population (the United States is a pluralist society filled with such populations), but the negative valuations placed on their difference, and the idea that their difference is exceptional and possibly enduring, are not consistent with the DAAS evidence. Arab American distinctiveness does not dampen confidence in American society; if anything, it increases it. Despite the ill will directed toward them, Arab Americans have a very positive view of key U.S. institutions. Many Arab Americans have oppositional political sensibilities, but these seem unrelated to confidence and are related to patterns of distinctiveness in multiple, often contradictory, ways.

The implicit message that pervades discussion of Arab American citizenship (you are not like us, you do not believe in us, you are not with us) is hard to substantiate, both on its face and at deeper levels of interpretation. The more tenable conclusion to be drawn from the popularity of this Othering message, and one consistent with DAAS and DAS findings, is that Americans generally do not believe in Arabs, that "we" are against "them," and that most Americans consider themselves and their society different from the Arab and Muslim worlds in ways that make identification and interaction across this divide undesirable, even dangerous. As polls conducted in the Arab world show, these attitudes are mirrored in the Middle East, where the reputation of the United States and the American people has steadily declined in recent years (Pew Global Attitudes Project 2006; Zogby 2002; Zogby International 2006). This mutual disaffection is consistent with an enemy-friend model (see Schmitt 1996) in which the terms Arab and American are posed in a hostile relationship to each other. The principal challenge of Arab American citizenship, now and in the foreseeable future, is the need to continually take apart and reconfigure this enemy-friend relationship within the United States even as it flourishes abroad.

As we saw in chapter 4, the enemy-friend model weighs most heavily on Arab Muslims, who feel more vulnerable, more disrespected, and less optimistic about their future in America than Arab Christians do. This discrepancy is troubling in its own right, but its peculiar relationship to the Americanization process makes it even more unsettling. As levels of education, income, and time spent living in the United States increase among Arab Muslims, so does their sense of estrangement from the larger society. Socioeconomic integration, it would seem, goes hand in hand with a heightened sense of political and cultural marginalization. Rather than conclude that this trend represents a malfunction in Arab Muslim citizenship, Sally Howell and Amaney Jamal suggest that Arab Muslims are constructing, for themselves, a national identity that realistically expresses the alienation—the unrealized desire to be accepted as Americans by Americans—that pervades their everyday encounters with the larger society.

CONCLUSION: CITIZENSHIP, AGAINST THE ODDS

The DAAS was conducted in the aftermath of a terrorist attack that exacerbated anti-Arab, anti-Muslim sentiment, prompted the U.S. invasion of Afghanistan, provided pretext for the invasion of Iraq, and led to the creation of massive new federal bureaucracies dedicated, in large part, to the surveillance and selective policing of Arabs and Muslims in the United States and around the world. For many of Detroit's Arabs, it was a low point in a long history of political and personal crises. The DAAS findings provide vivid and comprehensive evidence of exactly how alienating this climate can be. Since 2003, the communities studied here have faced additional crises: the intensification of violence in Iraq, further dispossession and bloodshed in Gaza and the West Bank, a devastating Israeli invasion of Lebanon in 2006, and the continued scrutiny, suspicion, and tactical harassment of Arab and Muslim Americans by the law enforcement arms of their own government. In short, the case for pessimism is strong, and the DAAS findings support it.

The case for pessimism is also partial, and there are good reasons to argue that beneath the politics of crisis—and as part of this politics—another historical process is unfolding. The DAAS tells us much about this process, its consequences, and its potential futures. Readers who have studied our chapters carefully will have noticed several patterns that connect our arguments:

- Immigration from the Arab countries to Detroit has increased radically since the 1970s, and Detroit's Arab and Chaldean populations continue to grow even in the post-9/11 era. Thus Arab Detroit is large, has been large for decades, and is still getting larger.
- Arab and Muslim immigrants are generally adapting well to life in Detroit; the longer they live in the United States, the more likely they are to live in middle-class suburbs, among non-Arabs, and to have values and lifestyles that resemble those of the general population; those born in the United States tend to have higher levels of education and income.
- Transnational ties, strong among the newly arrived and Arabic speaking, tend to grow weaker over time, but identification with and as Arab Americans has

grown stronger over time, suggesting that homeland attachments are evolving into ethnic identities that are American in configuration.

- DAAS respondents in large numbers identify proudly as Americans, have become American citizens, and express high levels of confidence in the key institutions of American society.
- DAAS respondents in large numbers express their anxieties about personal and community safety, about being disrespected for reasons of ethnicity or religion, about media bias against them, about unfair outcomes in the courts, and about U.S. foreign policies that adversely affect Arabs and Muslims. They believe their community organizations should vocally address these concerns, and that the larger society should be responsive.
- The Arab and Muslim communities of Detroit are highly institutionalized; their principal organizations are effective, politically prominent, and receive generous support from benefactors in the public and private sector.
- Greater Detroit has a large, prominent enclave that serves as a focus of identity display and immigrant absorption, but it also has large, dispersed populations that are well integrated into the general population. Both sectors are thriving.

The DAAS captures a unique point in time, and its findings must be interpreted in the context of local and global histories. The patterns we isolate here will not necessarily continue into the future; there is little doubt, however, that they are firmly established in Greater Detroit today. They make the city's Arab communities exceptional when compared to Arab Americans nationwide, but they are what local Arab Americans (and their allies and opponents) have come to expect, and they explain why new Arab and Chaldean immigrants continue to choose greater Detroit as a place to settle. According to U.S. Census data, the Arab population of Michigan has risen from 116,331 in 2000 to 153,843 in 2005, a 32 percent increase (American Community Survey 2005). In the months following the 9/11 attacks, when fears of deportation and internment camps gripped the Arab community, few people would have predicted this expansion. Yet it is happening, and it suggests that analyses that dwell on the bleak, on patterns of exclusion and estrangement, are missing something important about conditions in greater Detroit.

One of the most interesting facts about the seven patterns mentioned is that the 9/11 crisis did not fundamentally alter any of them. Instead, it reinforced or intensified them. This outcome supports the claim, made throughout this book, that Arab American identity is a highly adaptive response to crisis, and that the 9/11 attacks were a horrific instance of exactly the kind of crisis situation Arab Americans have confronted many times in the past, when the United States and its allies have come into conflict with regimes, movements, and nation-states understood to be Arab or Muslim. These conflicts, since the 1960s, have actually increased immigration to the United States from the Arab world; they have intensified American, Arab, and Arab American identifications in Detroit; they have prompted the founding and funding of community organizations; and they have caused Arab Americans to reassess and reconfigure their transnational ties. This historical trend is highly peculiar for the degree to which it combines, first, a generalized experience of discipline—of being watched, chastised, doubted, and asked to prove the loyalties of individuals and entire communities—and, second, a simultaneous experience of inclusion—of being allowed in, incorporated, recognized, supported, and rewarded for participation in the American system.

If we can say anything distinctive about Arab American citizenship in Detroit, it is that this mode of belonging tightly interweaves experiences of inclusion and stigmatizing discipline. This tight combination, we would argue, is both a challenge to Arab Americans and, as a spur to organization and activism, essential to the Arab community's success in greater Detroit. This insight might also help us explain why Arab and Muslim communities in other American cities have not fared as well as those in Detroit. Because they lack one or several of the seven trends we discuss, they are easily pushed toward and overcome by forces of inclusion or stigmatizing discipline, eventually proving incapable of combining the two in a useful, animating balance. Some communities are too dispersed; some are too geographically concentrated; some are very new and do not have viable links to older immigrant communities; some are confined largely to the working or the professional classes, without crosscutting institutions; some eschew American politics in preference for homeland politics. Scholars and organizers at work in Los Angeles, Chicago, New York, Houston, Boston, and other American cities will perhaps recognize these patterns. A detailed understanding of how they develop, the constraints and advantages they confer, awaits future comparative research. The DAAS provides a solid foundation on which to build this work. It also enables us to understand how Arab Americans are securing and asserting their citizenship, against incredible odds, through creative, vigorous engagement with the crises that shape their world.

REFERENCES

Abdo, Geneive. 2006. *Mecca and Main Street: Muslim Life in America after 9/11*. New York: Oxford University Press.

Abraham, Nabeel, and Andrew Shryock, eds. 2000. *Arab Detroit: From Margin to Mainstream*. Detroit, Mich.: Wayne State University Press.

Abraham, Sameer, and Nabeel Abraham, eds. 1983. *Arabs in the New World: Studies on Arab-American Communities*. Detroit, Mich.: Wayne State University Center for Urban Studies.

Agamben, Giorgio. 1998. *Homo Sacer: Sovereign Power and Bare Life*. Palo Alto: Stanford University Press.

Alba, Richard, and Victor Nee. 2005. *Remaking the American Mainstream: Assimilation and Contemporary Immigration*. Cambridge, Mass.: Harvard University Press.

American Community Survey. 2005. "Data Profile Highlight, Dearborn, Michigan." Washington: U.S. Bureau of the Census.

Anderson, Benedict. 1991. *Imagined Communities: Reflections on the Origin and Spread of Nationalism*, rev. ed. London: Verso Books.

Arab American Affairs. 2003. "The First Arab American National Museum Celebrates Groundbreaking." *Arab American Affairs* 31(209). http://www.arab-american-affairs.net/editorials/museum.htm.

Chan, Sucheng. 1991. *Asian Americans: An Interpretive History*. New York: Twayne Publishers.

Davila, Arlene. 2001. *Latinos, Inc.: The Making and Marketing of a People*. Berkeley: University of California Press.

Farley, Reynolds, Maria Krysan, and Mick Couper. 2006. "Attitudes about Arab-Americans: Detroiters' Views." Paper presented at the Sixty-First Annual Conference of the American Association for Public Opinion Research. Montreal, Canada (May 16–18).

Gutierrez, David. 1995. *Walls and Mirrors: Mexican Americans, Mexican Immigrants, and the Politics of Ethnicity*. Berkeley: University of California Press.

Jabara, Abdeen. 2006. "Electing Arab Americans to Congress: An Activist Reflects on Problems and Prospects." In *American Arabs and Political Participation*, edited by Philippa Strum. Washington: Woodrow Wilson International Center for Scholars.

King, Desmond. 2002. *Making Americans: Immigration, Race, and the Origins of the Diverse Democracy*. Cambridge, Mass.: Harvard University Press.

Naber, Nadine. 2006. "The Rules of Forced Engagement." *Cultural Dynamics* 18(3): 235–67.

Okihiro, Gary. 1994. *Margins and Mainstreams: Asians in American History and Culture.* Seattle: University of Washington Press.

Ong, Aihwa. 2003. *Buddha is Hiding: Refugees, Citizenship, the New America.* Berkeley: University of California Press.

Portes, Alejandro, and Ruben Rumbaut. 2001. *Legacies: The Story of the Immigrant Second Generation.* Berkeley: University of California Press and the Russell Sage Foundation.

Pew Global Attitudes Project. 2006. *The Great Divide: How Westerners and Muslims View Each Other.* Washington, D.C.: Pew Research Center.

Pew Research Center for the People & the Press (Pew). 2003. "Religion and Politics: Contention and Consensus. Growing Numbers Say Islam Encourages Violence Among Followers." Washington, D.C.: Pew Research Center. Available at: http://people-press.org/reports/pdf/189.pdf.

Samhan, Helen. 2006. "Losing the Battle: How Political Activism Guarantees Ethnic Integration (in Spite of Defeats Along the Way)." In *American Arabs and Political Participation,* edited by Philippa Strum. Washington: Woodrow Wilson International Center for Scholars.

Sanchez, George. 1993. *Becoming Mexican American: Ethnicity, Culture and Identity in Chicano Los Angeles, 1900–1945.* New York: Oxford University Press.

Schmitt, Carl. 1996. *The Concept of the Political.* Chicago: University of Chicago Press.

Shryock, Andrew, and Nabeel Abraham. 2000. "On Margins and Mainstreams." In *Arab Detroit: From Margin to Mainstream,* edited by Nabeel Abraham and Andrew Shryock. Detroit, Mich.: Wayne State University Press.

Stockton, Ronald. 2006. "Arab American Political Participation: Findings from the Detroit Arab American Study." *In Arab Americans and Political Participation,* edited by Philippa Strum. Washington: Woodrow Wilson International Center for Scholars.

Suleiman, Michael, ed. 1999. *Arabs in America: Building a New Future.* Philadelphia: Temple University Press.

Terry, Janice. 1999. "Community and Political Activism among Arab Americans in Detroit." In *Arabs in America: Building a New Future,* edited by Michael Suleiman. Philadelphia: Temple University Press.

Traugott, Michael W., Robert M. Groves, and Courtney Kennedy. 2002. "How Americans Responded: Public Opinion After 9/11/01." Paper presented at the Fifty-Seventh Annual AAPOR Conference. St. Pete Beach, Fla. (May 17).

Valle, Victor, and Rodolfo Torres. 2000. *Latino Metropolis.* Minneapolis: University of Minnesota Press.

Zogby International. 2006. "Annual Arab Public Opinion Survey." Conducted by the University of Maryland and Zobgy International. Shibley Telhami, Principal Investigator. http://www.bsos.umd.edu/SADAT/2006%20Arab%20Public%20 Opinion%20Survey.ppt (accessed January 15, 2007).

Zogby, James J. 2002. *What Arabs Think: Values, Beliefs, and Concerns.* Washington, D.C.: Zogby International.

INDEX

Boldface numbers refer to figures and tables.

AAPOR. *See* American Association for
    Public Opinion Research
Abbas-Chami, Rena, 77, 97*n*17
Abraham, Nabeel, 35, 103
Abraham, Sameer, 35
Abraham, Spencer, 129*n*14, 265
ACC. *See* Arab American and Chaldean
    Council
ACCESS. *See* Arab Community Center
    for Economic and Social Services
ACLU of Michigan, 96*n*14–15
ADC. *See* American-Arab Anti-
    Discrimination Committee
Agamben, Giorgio, 64–65
Ahmed, Ismael, 75, 129*n*14
Alba, Richard, 152
Aleinikoff, Alexander, 8
Alexandria Protocol, 238
Alien and Sedition Acts of 1798, 193
Ali-Haimoud, Farouk, 84
Allport, Gordon, 259*n*18
Almarabh, Nabil, 84
Almond, Gabriel, 229–30, 234, 255

Alterman, Eric, 256*n*3
Amen, Ronald, 76–77, 82
American-Arab Anti-Discrimination
    Committee (ADC), 58, 77, 87–88,
    90, 128*n*4
American Arab Chamber of Commerce,
    5, 58, 88
American Association for Public
    Opinion Research (AAPOR), 19–20
American exceptionalism, 70, 157
Americanization. *See* integration/
    adaptation/incorporation
American mainstream: within Arab
    American communities, specific ver-
    sion of, 268; Arab difference and
    national belonging in, 265–66; Arab
    exclusion and inclusion, making sense
    of, 268–71; confidence in public insti-
    tutions, **275–76**; the enemy/friend
    model of Arab Americans and,
    280–81; political beliefs of Arab
    Americans, 277–79; values, Arab
    American values *vs.*, 135–37, 158–59;

American mainstream (*cont.*)
vision of as backdrop for Arab American identity, 273. *See also* citizenship; identity; integration/adaptation/incorporation; national identity

American Moslem Society, 108, 127

Anderson, Benedict, 10

Anti-Defamation League, 228

Arab American and Chaldean Council (ACC), 74, 87, 270

Arab American Center for Civil and Human Rights, 88

Arab American National Museum, 58, 88–89, 270

Arab American News, 58

Arab American Political Action Committee (AAPAC), 95*n*11

Arab Americans: the American mainstream and (*see* American mainstream); as an ethnic label, willingness to accept, 52–55, 111, 118–19; backlash against following 9/11 (*see* backlash following 9/11); civil liberties, positions regarding, 194–95, 201–16 (*see also* civil liberties); communities of in Detroit (*see* Arab Detroit; community); confidence in public institutions, **275–76**; the enemy/friend model of, 280–81; foreign-born in the United States, 39; foreign policy and world affairs, opinions regarding (*see* foreign policy); identity as (*see* identity); as immigrants (*see* Arab immigrants); integration into the larger society (*see* integration/adaptation/incorporation); as "limit figures," 270; Muslim and Christian, differences between (*see* Muslim/Christian Arabs); public service among, 74–75; social capital of (*see* social capital); U.S. citizenship as highly prized among, 45, 266 (*see also* citizenship); in the U.S. population, 27*n*3; values of (*see* values); the war on terrorism and (*see* backlash following 9/11; war on terrorism)

Arab Community Center for Economic and Social Services (ACCESS), 58, 72, 74, 87–89, 270

Arab Detroit: as an ethnic community, 37; Arab public servants in, 74–75; backlash following 9/11 in (*see* backlash following 9/11); citizenship and crisis in, 36–37, 64–65; concentration of Arabs in, 73; contradictions of, 63–65; data on, sources of, 16–20; economic demographics in, 73–74; educational achievement in, 45–47, **50–51**, 73–74; English fluency and multilingualism in, 45–46, **50–51**; ethnic identification in, 52–55; as exceptional, 25–26, 70–76; global and local attention attracted by, 35–36; identity formation in, 37–39 (*see also* identity); immigration to (*see* Arab immigrants); income in, 47, **50–51,** 73–74; lobbying organizations in, 74; patterns of the historical process unfolding in, 281–83; political complexity of, 277–79; political incorporation of Arab Americans in, 92–93; population of, 36; portrait of, 4–6; racial identification in, 54, 56–57; religion and incorporation into political society in, 103–7 (*see also* integration/adaptation/incorporation; religion); as representative or exceptional of Arab

America, tensions between, 69–71; Syrian Colony in, 40; the war on terror in, community reactions to, 87–92; the war on terrorism in, federal law enforcement and, 83–87. *See also* Dearborn

Arab immigrants: "boaters" as derogatory term for, 213, 268; compatibility of Islam and American culture for, 112; country of origin, 40, **41**; Dearborn as an enclave of, 73 (*see also* Dearborn); economic and educational demographics of, 73–74; gender of, 44; generation and decade of arrival in the United States, **42**; incorporation into the larger society (*see* integration/adaptation/incorporation); lobbying organizations representing, 74; religious affiliation of, 43–44; time in the United States, 40–43; U.S. foreign policy and, 61–63, 251; values of, 143, **147–49** (*see also* values)

Arab International Festival (Dearborn), 58, 88, 128*n*4, 135

Arabism, 237

Arab League, 238

Arab nationalism, in Detroit, 111–12

Arafat, Yasser, 256*n*3

Asbahi, Mazen, 127

Ashcroft, John, 82, 84, 222*n*8, 257*n*8

assimilation. *See* integration/adaptation/incorporation

backlash following 9/11: in Arab Detroit, 13, 16, 69–71, 92–94; civil liberties and (*see* civil liberties); community reactions to federal law enforcement efforts, 87–92; federal law enforcement efforts, 82–87; participation in ethnic associations and, **81**; place of birth and, **79**; public opinion and the ideological, 195–96; religion and, **80**; security of Arab Americans, 76–82, 195; values of Arab Americans, impact on, 153–54

Baker, Wayne, 22–23, 273

Bakri, Youssef, 96*n*13

Bauböck, Ranier, 8

Bell, Derrick, 259*n*18

Bell, John, 85, 90

Bellah, Robert, 257*n*10

Berinsky, Adam, 246–47, 250

Berry, Michael, 75

bin Laden, Osama, 242–43

Blair, Tony, 216

Bonior, David, 258*n*12

Bouchard, Mike, 129*n*14

Brady, Henry, 104

BRIDGES. *See* Building Respect in Diverse Groups to Enhance Sensitivity

Brill, Alida, 199–200

Britain, reaction to London bombings, 216–17

Building Respect in Diverse Groups to Enhance Sensitivity (BRIDGES), 90–93

Bush, George H. W., 228

Bush, George W.: American Muslims, actions regarding, 82, 195, 234, 253; convictions of terrorism suspects, claims regarding, 85; mission accomplished in Iraq, declaration of, 233; Palestinian state, skepticism regarding endorsement of, 233–34; on the terrorist threat, 242; "with us or against us" challenge issued by, 70

Carens, Joseph, 11

causes of 9/11 attacks: the clash of civilizations, 241–43, 245 (*see also* clash of civilizations); concealed opinions regarding, 249–51; possible explanations, comparison of general public and Arab American opinions regarding, 243–45; two patterns of opinion regarding, 240–41

Central Intelligence Agency (CIA), 88

Chaldeans: Arab American label, willingness to accept, 53; Arabness, relationship to, 59–60; Assyrian identity, embrace of, 128*n*4; description of, inclusion in study and, 27*n*5; ethnonationalism of in Arab Detroit, 111; first church established in Detroit by, 108; political participation by, 121; Saddam Hussein, relations with, 256–57*n*6

Chebanni, Ahmed, 89

Chong, Dennis, 200

Christian Zionism, 229, 240, 245, 257*n*10

citizenship: of Arab Americans, crisis and, 12–16, 36–37, 64–65; concept of in contemporary political discourse, 7; cultural, 11; definitions of, 7–8; the Detroit Arab American Study as an experiment in, 26; disciplinary inclusion, 16; dual, 8; the enemy/friend model of Arab Americans and, 280–81; legal, 45, 149–50; "limit figure" and, 270; limits of, the American mainstream and, 265–66 (*see also* American mainstream); limits of for Arab Americans, 266–68; multicultur-

alism theme of, 9–12; political crisis and, 4; restrictions on civil liberties, as factor in opinions regarding, 202–4 (*see also* civil liberties); rights theme of, 7–9; social capital and, 169–70; two zones of Arab American, 57–60. *See also* identity; integration/adaptation/incorporation; national identity

civic participation. *See* political participation

civil liberties: Arab American perspectives on, 201–16; Arab American responses to restricting, accounting for the range of, 217–20; Arab American support for restricting, factors linked to, 210–16; But Not Us model of restrictions on, 200–201; citizenship status and restrictions on, 202–4; erosion of as post-9/11 concern, 82; expansive conception of, transnational considerations and, 223*n*18; fear and restrictions on, 208–10; federal law enforcement post-9/11, trampling by, 82–87; foreign policy expression and, convergence of issues regarding, 252, 255; history of and pride regarding American, 193–94; identity as "American" or "Arab American" and positions regarding, 205–7; liberal model of restrictions on, 199–200, 214, 217–19; perspectives on, **199**; post-9/11 attitudes regarding, 194–95; religion and national origin in positions on restricting, **205**; religion and restrictions on, 204–5; restrictions on, comparison of general public and Arab American attitudes regarding, 198–99;

restrictions on, public opinion regarding, 197–98; traits associated with accepting restrictions on, **211–12**. *See also* discrimination; rights

clash of civilizations: the argument regarding, 241–43; belief in as alternative to geopolitical explanations of conflict, 112–13; as a cause of 9/11 attacks, 241, 245; dilemma posed for Arab Americans by rhetoric of, 254–55; religion and acceptance of the idea of, 257n11

Cohen, Donald, 170

community: of Arab Americans in Detroit (*see* Arab Detroit); aspirations and desires of the Arab American, 60–62; conception of, 60; ethnic, language used to describe, 37; reactions to discrimination in the war on terrorism, 87–92

Convertino, Richard, 84–85

Conyers, John, 127, 258n12

Corallo, Mark, 83–84

Council on American-Islamic Relations (CAIR), 87, 254

Creed, Gerald, 60

crisis: Arab American identity as highly adaptive to, 283; citizenship for Arab Americans and, 12–16, 36–37, 64–65

cultural citizenship, 11, 136, 166

cultural values. *See* values

DAAS. *See* Detroit Arab American Study

Dabaja, Kenwah, 91–92

DAS. *See* Detroit Area Study

data, sources of, 16–20

Davis, Darren, 208

Dearborn: as an Arab enclave, 73, 111, 152–53; Arab American National Museum, 58, 88–89, 270; Arab International Festival, 58, 88, 128n4, 135; as capital of Arab America, 58; as epicenter of threats to avenge 9/11, 77; political positions on display in, wide variety of, 279; war on terror, as backdrop for coverage of, 69. *See also* Arab Detroit

detainees in the war on terrorism, 83

Detroit: American born and U.S. citizenship, percentage of among the general population, 45; Arab American communities in (*see* Arab Detroit); family income in metropolitan, **48**; politics of inclusion in, 16; public opinion regarding Arab Americans in, 12; racial identification among the general population in, 57

Detroit Arab American Study (DAAS): as an experiment in citizenship, 26; Arab American identity in its public forms, suited to the analysis of, 38; data, as source of, 16–20, 25–26

Detroit Area Study (DAS), 16–20, 25

DeVos, Dick, 95n11

Dingell, John, 127, 258n12

disciplinary inclusion, 16

discrimination: community reactions to federal law enforcement post-9/11, 87–92; federal law enforcement post-9/11 as, 82–87; profiling by law enforcement officials and the media, 82, 86, 90, 201, 221–22n8; religion

discrimination (*cont.*)
and attitudes about, 120, **121–22**;
rights, definition of, 7; security, acceptance of by Arab Americans to gain,
79–80. *See also* civil liberties; rights
diversity. *See* multiculturalism

education: in Arab Detroit, levels of,
45–46, **50–51,** 73–74, 110–11; by
place of birth in Arab Detroit, **47**;
social capital and, 179; values, impact
on, 155
Elder, Azzam, 75
Elder, Charlene Makled, 75
Ellul, Jacques, 196
Elmardoudi, Abdel-Ilah, 84
Engler, John, 95*n*10
ethnic associations: grassroots support
for, 93–94; participation in and
empowerment, 80–81
ethnicity. *See* race/ethnicity

factor analysis, 257*n*9
Falwell, Jerry, 257*n*10
Farrakhan, Louis, 194
Federal Bureau of Investigation (FBI):
Arabic translators hired by, 96*n*17;
award to Hamad, proposal and denial
of, 93; BRIDGES, participation in,
90–92; Detroit mosques, targeting of,
113; hunt for terrorists by, 83–87,
203, 221*n*6; new office in Detroit,
building of, 269; recruitment ads in
Arab American publications, 88
Federation of the Islamic Associations of
the United States and Canada, 109
Feldstein, Lewis, 170
Ficano, Robert, 76, 89

Fischer, David, 256*n*1
Fogel, Robert William, 139
Foley, Michael, 104
Ford, Henry, 5
foreign policy: American public opinion
regarding issues of, 228–29; Arab
American opinions regarding,
227–28, 251–56; Arab immigration
and Arab American identity shaped
by, 61–63, 251; causes of 9/11 attacks
(*see* causes of 9/11 attacks); civil liberties issues and, convergence of, 252,
255; concealed opinions, sources of,
248–49; concealed opinions of Arab
Americans, 246–50; explanations of
public opinion regarding, 229–31;
Middle East issues, comparison of
general public and Arab American
opinions regarding, 231–33; Middle
East items, factor analysis of, **240**;
Palestinian state, Arab American support for a, 238–40; source of attitudes
regarding, **235–36**; stabilizing the
Middle East, opinions regarding
American contribution to, 233–38;
war on terrorism (*see* war on terrorism)
freedom. *See* civil liberties; rights
Fuligni, Andrew, 104

Garvey, Marcus, 194
gender: of Arab immigrants, 44; concealed opinions and, 247; religious
commitment and church/mosque
attendance by, 113–15; values,
impact on, 156
Gerstle, Gary, 256*n*1
Gilbertson, Greta, 167

globalization, national sovereignty and, 8
Global Linguistic Solutions, 97*n*17
global social capital, 180–84. *See also* social capital
Granholm, Jennifer, 87, 126–27
Guibord, Greg, 78
Guido, Mike, 78
Gulf Cooperation Council, 89
Gulf War of 1990-1991, 228

Haddad, Yvonne, 252
Hagan, Jacqueline, 170–71
Hagee, John, 257*n*10
Hamad, Imad, 78, 90, 92–93, 97*n*21
Hamadeh, Imad, 96*n*13
Hammar, Tomas, 8
Hannan, Ahmed, 84
Hansen, John, 104
Hariri, Rafik, 257*n*7
Harris, Frederick, 253, 259*n*17
Heisler, Martin, 8–9
Hitti, Philip, 103, 107, 126
Hizbullah, 95–96*n*13, 95*n*11
Hochschild, Jennifer, 217
Hoge, Dean, 104
Holsti, Ole, 230
Homeland Security, U.S. Department of, 3, 96–97*n*17
Howell, Sally, 21–22, 281
Human Rights Watch, 78
Huntington, Samuel, 10, 241
Hussein, Saddam, 228, 234, 256–57*n*6

Ibish, Hussein, 83
identity: American, function and characteristics of, 207; Arab American label, percent accepting by country of origin and religion, **53**; Arabism as a pan-regional identity movement, 237; of Chaldeans, 111; civil liberties restrictions and perceptions of, 205–7 (*see also* civil liberties); community aspirations and Arab American, 60–61; contradictions of Arab American, 63–65; crisis and Arab American, 283 (*see also* crisis); demands placed on Arab American, 13–16; ethnoracial as backdrop for, 49–57 (*see also* race/ethnicity); foreign policy and Arab American, 61–63, 237–38; immigration of Arab Americans as backdrop for, 39–44; incorporation of Arab Americans into the larger society as backdrop for, 44–49, **50–51**; mainstream American (*see* American mainstream); national (*see* national identity); Palestine as issue for Arab American, 238–39; religious and ethnic, 117–19; socioeconomic integration and crisis in Arab American, 36–37; two zones of Arab American, 57–60; uncommon denominators within Arab American, 47–49. *See also* citizenship
immigration: of Arabs to metropolitan Detroit, 5–6, 36 (*see also* Arab immigrants); the ethnic nationalist community model of public opinion following from, 230–31; integration into the receiving society (*see* integration/adaptation/incorporation); Muslim to Michigan, timing of, 108; national sovereignty and, 8; social capital and, 170–72; U.S. foreign policy and, 61–63

Immigration and Naturalization Service (INS), 83, 194, 220–21*n*1

Imperative Patriotism, 221*n*3

inclusion, politics of, 16

income: in Arab Detroit, 47, **50–51,** 73–74, 110–11; of families in metropolitan Detroit, **48**; social capital and, 179; values, impact on, 155

Inglehart, Ronald, 141

INS. *See* Immigration and Naturalization Service

integration/adaptation/incorporation: assimilation, traditional model of, 9–10, 166, 273; education, 45–46, **47**; English fluency, 45; income, 47, **48**; legal citizenship, 45; measures of, 44; political, 92–93 (*see also* political participation); religion and, 103–7; routes to by Muslim and Christian Arabs, 107–13; uncommon denominators influencing, 47–49

Investigation PENTTBOM, 83

Iraq, invasion of: Arab American opinions regarding, 234, 237; Arab American political participation and, 126

Islamic Center of America, 108, 127

Islamic Mosque and Cultural Center, 195

Israel: Christian Zionism and Arab American support for, 240; U.S. policy towards as a cause of 9/11 attacks, 244–45; U.S. support for, 61–62

Israeli-Palestinian conflict: American foreign policy addressing, Arab American opinions regarding, 233–34; American public opinion regarding, 228–29; media bias regarding, 233, 256*n*3

Jabara, Abdeen, 221*n*1

Jacobson, David, 10–11

Jacobson, Matthew Frye, 231

Jamal, Amaney, 21–23, 221*n*2, 273, 281

Japanese internment, 193–94, 203

Jawad, Ali, 127

Justice Department, U.S.: BRIDGES, support for, 92; profiling, definition of, 221–22*n*8; the war on terrorism, 83–84 (*see also* war on terrorism)

Kayal, Philip, 109

Khatib, Maysoun, 78

Kildee, Dale, 258*n*12

Kilpatrick, Carolyn Cheeks, 258*n*12

Kim, Wan, 91

King, Martin Luther, 194

Klusmeyer, Douglas, 8

Koubriti, Karim, 84

Kymlicka, Will, 10–11

language: English fluency in Arab Detroit, 45, **50–51**; global social capital and, 182, 184; second language spoken at home in Arab Detroit, **46**; values and, relationship of, 151

League of Arab States, 89

Levin, Carl, 127, 258*n*12

Levin, Sander, 258*n*12

Levitt, Peggy, 104, 106

Lewis, Bernard, 241

Life for Relief and Development (LIFE), 91

Lin, Ann Chih, 20–21, 25, 124, 251

Lincoln, Abraham, 193

Lipset, Seymour Martin, 70

local social capital, 172–80. *See also* social capital

Logan, John, 152

mainstream, American. *See* American mainstream

Makled, Hassan, 75

Malcolm X, 194

Maroun, Manuel, 75

Marshall, Thomas, 7–8

Mattson, Ingrid, 105

McAlister, Melani, 62

McCain, John, 127

McCloskey, Herbert, 199–200

media, the: bias on Middle East issues, perceptions of, 233, 256*n*3; depictions of Arabs and Muslims in, 195–96; distrust of by Arab Americans, 215; trust in and fears about restricting civil liberties, 208–9

media consumption by Arab Americans, 181–82, 184

Michigan: Arab concentration in, 17; Arab Detroit (*see* Arab Detroit); Arab migration to, 5–6; Dearborn (*see* Dearborn); Detroit (*see* Detroit); homeland security as growth industry in, 86–87; the president's post-9/11 challenge targeted at, 70

Michigan Civil Rights Commission, 87

migration. *See* immigration

Moore, Laurence, 108

Mueller, John, 228, 234

Mulligan, Kenneth, 200–201

multiculturalism: desires of the Arab American community and, 61; diversity, differing views of, 10–11; social capital and, 170; as a theme of citizenship, 9–12; treatment of Arab Americans as contradicting values of, 15. *See also* values

Murphy, Stephen, 86, 90

Muslim/Christian Arabs: Arab and religious identity among, 117–19; discrimination, attitudes about, 120, **121–22**; distinction in identity and incorporation between, 104–7, 125–28; ethnic and sectarian divisions within, political incorporation and, 120–25; foreign policy positions and perception of position in America, relationship of, 252–54; incorporation of, differing routes to, 107–13; political participation of, 116–17, **117–18,** 125–27; religious commitment and church or mosque attendance, 113–16; restrictions on civil liberties, positions regarding, 204–5, 217–19; shared values of, 151–52

Nasser, Gamal Abdel, 237

Nasser, Jacques, 265

Nasser, Karim, 96*n*13

national identity: among immigrants, foreign policy concerns and, 231; confidence in public institutions, **275–76**; deep diversity and, 11; mainstream American (*see* American mainstream). *See also* citizenship; identity; integration/adaptation/ incorporation

national sovereignty, impact of globalization and immigration on, 8

9/11 attacks: Arab Americans, impact on, 12–13; backlash against Arab Americans following (*see* backlash following 9/11; civil liberties); causes of (*see* causes of 9/11 attacks); Muslims as focus of stereotyping and suspicion following, 112–13; normalization of changes following, intervention in, 3–4; patriotic expressions following, 195; president's challenge following, 70

Norris, Pippa, 141

Obama, Barack, 127, 128*n*1

Ong, Aihwa, 13

Operation Boulder, 194

Palestine: Arab American attitudes regarding, 238–40; Israeli-Palestinian conflict (*see* Israeli-Palestinian conflict)

PATRIOT Act. *See* USA PATRIOT Act

Pipes, Daniel, 106, 196

political incorporation. *See* integration/adaptation/incorporation

political participation: of Arab Americans compared to the general population, 172, **175–76**; religion and, 104–5, 116–17, **117–18,** 120–27; returned campaign donations from Arab Americans, 252; social capital and, 169

Poncy, Chip, 96*n*13

Portes, Alejandro, 104, 171

Powell, Colin, 89

profiling, 82, 86, 90, 201, 221–22*n*8

public opinion: Arab Americans, regarding, 12; civil liberties, on restricting (*see* civil liberties); the elite-mass model of, 229–30, 234, 239, 255; the ethnic nationalist community model of, 230–31, 234; on foreign policy and world affairs (*see* foreign policy); held by and about Arab Americans, relationship of, 251–56; the ideological backlash following 9/11, 195–96; the partisan-ideological model of, 230, 234; sources of Arab American (*See* Detroit Arab American Study; Detroit Area Study)

Putnam, Robert, 170

race/ethnicity: Arab American identity and, complications of, 14–15, 52; ethnic identification in Arab Detroit, 52–54, **54–55,** 118–19; homeland nationalism of ethnic groups, 231; identity based on, American political life and, 49, 52; identity based on, religion and, 118–19; profiling based on, 82, 86, 90, 201, 221–22*n*8; racial identification in Arab Detroit, 54, 56–57; trust related to, 173–74

Rahal, Nemr Ali, 95*n*13

religion: American public opinion regarding the Israeli-Palestinian conflict shaped by, 229; Arab American identity and, complications of, 15; in Arab Detroit, 72, 109–10; of Arab immigrants, 43–44; backlash following 9/11 and, **80**; conflict of values/clash of civilizations and, accepting the idea of, 257*n*11; cultural values and, 141–42; demographics of among immigrants in Detroit compared to their home countries, 6; discrimination and, attitudes about, 120, **121–22**; foreign policy attitudes and, 237–38, 252–53; identity based on, 117–19; incorporation into American society and, 103–7, 125–28; Muslim and Christian Arabs in Detroit, distinction between (*see* Muslim/Christian Arabs); piety (religious commitment) and church/mosque attendance, implications of, 113–25; political participation and, 104–5, 116–17, **117–18,** 120–27; restrictions on civil liberties, as factor in opinions regarding, 204–5; routes to incorporation and, 107–13; social capital and, 179; values and, relationship of, 151–52

rights: citizenship and, 267; definition of political, 7; definition of social, 8; politics of, 200; as a theme of citizenship, 7–9. *See also* civil liberties; discrimination

Rivers, Lynn, 258*n*12

Roberts, Daniel, 91

Robertson, Pat, 196

Rokeach, Milton, 137

Rosaldo, Renato, 11

Rosenau, James, 230

Rosenstone, Steven, 104

Rudolph, Lloyd, 205

Rudolph, Suzanne Hoeber, 205

Rumbaut, Rubén, 104

Said, Edward, 62, 64

Salaita, Steve, 221*n*3

Sartre, Jean-Paul, 254

Schenk, Theodore, 96*n*13

Schlesinger, Arthur A., Jr., 10

Scholzman, Kay, 104

security, civil liberties and. *See* civil liberties

September 11 attacks. *See* 9/11 attacks

Shaheen, Jack, 195–96

Sharon, Ariel, 233

Shryock, Andrew, 20–21, 25, 103, 124, 251

Siblani, Osama, 89

Sidanius, Jim, 259*n*16

Silver, Brian, 208

Silvestrini, Blanca, 11

Sniderman, Paul, 199–200

social capital: benefits of, 167, 169–70; bonding and bridging, 165–66, 185–86; civic participation and informal networks, **175–76**; dimensions of local, comparison of, **168**; frequent contact outside the United States, **181**; global, Arab Americans compared to the general population regarding, 180–84; inequalities in, 171–72, 182; local, Arab Americans compared to the general population regarding, 172–80; local and global, assessment of, 166–67; local and global compared, 184–85; socializing, average number of days per year for, **173**; sociodemographics, summary of main effects of, **184**; trust, faith-based engagement, and associational involvement/participation, **177–78**; trust, levels of generalized and racial, **174**

Social Capital Benchmark Survey, 166, 186*n*1

social distance, 27*n*2

Solomos, John, 8
Soros Foundation, 92
Soysal, Yasemin, 8, 11
Spiegelman, Art, 258*n*13
Stabenow, Debbie, 126–27, 258*n*12
State Department, U.S., Foreign
  Terrorist Organizations (FTO) list,
  96*n*13
Stockton, Ronald, 23–25, 129*n*13,
  257*n*10, 278
Stouffer, Samuel, 200
Suleiman, Michael, 223*n*17, 252, 254
Swor, Bill, 78, 84–85

Taylor, Charles, 11
Tessler, Mark, 23, 273
Tocqueville, Alexis de, 256*n*2
transnational migration. *See* immigration
transnational networks, social capital
  and, 167, 180–81
Treasury, U.S. Department of, 97*n*19

United Nations Development Programme, Human Development
  Index, 141–42
U.S.-Arab Economic Forum, 89
USA PATRIOT Act: civil liberties and,
  3; governmental authority to spy on
  U.S. citizens, expansion of, 12–13;
  legal challenge to, 96*n*15; swift pas-
  sage of, 70

values: the American context, interpreting in, 156–58; American exceptionalism, 70, 157; of Arab Americans,
  immigrant status and, 143; of Arab

Americans *vs.* mainstream American
  society, 135–37, 158–59; conflict of
  between "civilizations" (*see* clash of
  civilizations); cross-cultural study of,
  instrument for, 137–38; cultural
  membership as source of variation in,
  149–53; definition of, 137; dimensions of, 136–39; economic development and, 140–42; experiences after
  9/11 as source of variation in,
  153–54; global map of cultural,
  139–43; justifiability of abortion and
  importance of God, comparisons on,
  160; sociodemographic factors as
  source of variation in, 155–56; statistical results for Arab Americans and
  the general public, **144–46**; statistical results for immigrant Arab
  Americans, **147–49**; variations in,
  143–49
Verba, Sidney, 104
Viscusi, Kip, 201

Waldinger, Roger, 167
Warner, Stephen, 104
war on terrorism: Arab American assistance in, 89–90, 93, 96–97*n*17;
  Arab Americans as potential threats
  and assets in, 82–83; Arab and
  Muslim Americans, impact on,
  12–13; backlash following 9/11, as
  part of (*see* backlash following 9/11);
  civil liberties and (*see* civil liberties);
  community reactions to in Arab
  Detroit, 87–92; distinction between
  Muslim and Christian Arabs, inten-

sification of, 107; the federal law enforcement agenda, 82–87; financial initiatives, significance of, 97n19; Orientalist assumptions as ideological prop for, 62
Wiebe, Robert, 256n1
Winn, Craig, 196
Wittner, Judith, 104

Wolfowitz, Paul, 234
World Values Surveys, 137–38

Yokich, Steve, 265

Zeckhauser, Richard, 201
Zhang, Wenquan, 152
Zogby, James, 59, 75